Happy Golden Birthday,
Julia!

From a member of Jamba juice smoothies
To preparation for Italian gelati ... Enjoy!

We love you so much. Always and forever,

Mommy and Daddy

August 19, 2000

# ROME

*A Guide
to the
Eternal
City*

**BARNES
&NOBLE**
BOOKS
NEW YORK

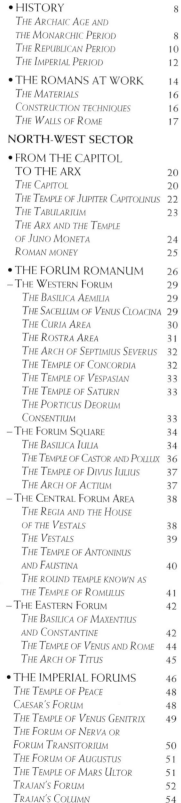

**Texts**
Sofia Pescarin

**Editorial coordination**
Fabio Bourbon

**Graphic Design**
Patrizia Balocco Lovisetti

**Drawings**
Monica Falcone
Roberta Vigone

**Translation**
A.B.A., Milan

# CONTENTS

- PREFACE  7

- HISTORY  8
  *The Archaic Age and the Monarchic Period*  8
  *The Republican Period*  10
  *The Imperial Period*  12

- THE ROMANS AT WORK  14
  *The Materials*  16
  *Construction techniques*  16
  *The Walls of Rome*  17

## NORTH-WEST SECTOR

- FROM THE CAPITOL TO THE ARX  20
  *The Capitol*  20
  *The Temple of Jupiter Capitolinus*  22
  *The Tabularium*  23
  *The Arx and the Temple of Juno Moneta*  24
  *Roman money*  25

- THE FORUM ROMANUM  26
  – THE WESTERN FORUM  29
  *The Basilica Aemilia*  29
  *The Sacellum of Venus Cloacina*  29
  *The Curia Area*  30
  *The Rostra Area*  31
  *The Arch of Septimius Severus*  32
  *The Temple of Concordia*  32
  *The Temple of Vespasian*  33
  *The Temple of Saturn*  33
  *The Porticus Deorum Consentium*  33
  – THE FORUM SQUARE  34
  *The Basilica Iulia*  34
  *The Temple of Castor and Pollux*  36
  *The Temple of Divus Iulius*  37
  *The Arch of Actium*  37
  – THE CENTRAL FORUM AREA  38
  *The Regia and the House of the Vestals*  38
  *The Vestals*  39
  *The Temple of Antoninus and Faustina*  40
  *The round temple known as the Temple of Romulus*  41
  – THE EASTERN FORUM  42
  *The Basilica of Maxentius and Constantine*  42
  *The Temple of Venus and Rome*  44
  *The Arch of Titus*  45

- THE IMPERIAL FORUMS  46
  *The Temple of Peace*  48
  *Caesar's Forum*  48
  *The Temple of Venus Genitrix*  49
  *The Forum of Nerva or Forum Transitorium*  50
  *The Forum of Augustus*  51
  *The Temple of Mars Ultor*  51
  *Trajan's Forum*  52
  *Trajan's Column*  54

*The Trajan Markets*  56

- THE CAMPUS MARTIUS  58
  – THE SOUTHERN CAMPUS MARTIUS  59
  *The Porticus Octaviae*  59
  *The Theater of Marcellus*  60
  *The Temples of Apollo Sosianus and Bellona*  61
  – THE CENTRAL CAMPUS MARTIUS  62
  *Largo Argentina Sacred Area*  62
  *The Theater of Balbus*  63
  *The Theater and Portico of Pompey*  63
  *Agrippa's Baths*  64
  *The Pantheon*  64
  *The Saepta*  66
  *The Temple of Matidia*  66
  *The Temple of Hadrian*  66
  *Nero's Baths*  67
  *The Odeon of Domitian*  67
  – THE NORTHERN CAMPUS MARTIUS  68
  *The Column of Marcus Aurelius*  68
  *The Column of Antoninus Pius*
  *The Horologium and the Obelisk on Piazza Montecitorio*  70
  *The Ara Pacis*  71
  *The Mausoleum of Augustus*  72

- THE FORUM BOARIUM AND THE HOLITORIUM  74
  *The Circular Temple of Hercules Victor*  75
  *Sant'Omobono Sacred Area*  76
  *San Nicola in Carcere and the Three Temples in the Holitorium*  76
  *The Arch of the Argentari*  77
  *The Four-Faced Arch of Janus*  77
  *The Isola Tiberina*  78
  *The Vatican Area*
  *The Ager Vaticanus*  79

- HADRIAN'S MAUSOLEUM  80

## SOUTH-WEST SECTOR

- THE PALATINE HILL  82
  – THE WESTERN PALATINE HILL  84
  *The Temple of Magna Mater*  84
  *The House of Livia and Augustus*  85
  *The Temple of Apollo*  86
  *The Domus Tiberiana*  87
  – THE EASTERN PALATINE HILL  87
  *Domitian's Palace*
  *The Domus Flavia and Domus Augustana*  88
  *Isis Hall*  92
  *The House of the Griffins*  93
  *The Severian Complex*  94
  *Painting in Rome*  96

- THE CIRCUS MAXIMUS  98
  *The Mithraeum*  99

- THE AVENTINE HILL  100

- THE TESTACCIO  101
- THE PYRAMID OF CAIUS CESTIUS  102
- TRASTEVERE  103
- THE JANICULUM  103

## SOUTH-EAST SECTOR

- THE CAELIAN HILL  104
  *The Temple of Divus Claudius and the Clivus Scauri*  106
  *The Arch of Dolabella*  106
  *The Military Hospital Area*  106
  *The Lateran*  107

- THE PORTA MAGGIORE AREA  108
  *The Tomb of the Baker Eurysaces*  108
  *The Underground Basilica of Porta Maggiore*  109
  *The Sessorium*  109

- THE LESSER AVENTINE  110

- CARACALLA'S BATHS  110
  *A day at the baths*  114

- THE VIA APPIA  116
  *The Tomb of the Scipii*  117
  *The Colombarium of Pomponius Hylas*  119
  *The Arch of Drusus*  119
  *The Circus of Maxentius*  120
  *The Tomb of Caecilia Metella*  122

## NORTH-EAST SECTOR

- COLISEUM VALLEY  124

- THE COLISEUM  126
  *Ludus Magnus*  130
  *Games and Spectacles*  132

- THE ARCH OF CONSTANTINE  134
  *The Meta Sudans*  137
  *The Statue of Nero*  137

- THE ESQUILINE AND OPPIAN HILLS  138
  *The Domus Aurea*  139

- TITUS AND TRAJAN BATHS  140
  *The Arch of Gallienus*  142
  *The Basilica of Junius Bassus*  142
  *The Trophies of Marius*  142
  *The Temple of Minerva Medica*  143
  *The Hypogeum of the Aurelii*  143

- THE QUIRINAL AND THE VIMINAL  144
  *The Castra Praetoria*  145
  *The Diocletian Baths*  146

- HADRIAN'S VILLA  148

- OSTIA  156

- GLOSSARY, BIBLIOGRAPHY PHOTOGRAPHIC CREDITS  166

1 The Arch of Septimius Severus, built in 203 AD in memory of the emperor's victories against the Parthians, stands on the western side of the Roman Forum, where the ancient Via Sacra began its ascent toward the Capitol.

2-3 Rome experienced enormous urban development during the imperial era. One example is the Palatine Hill, in the foreground. Over the centuries, the luxurious dwellings of nearly all Roman emperors were built here, beginning with Augustus.

4 top The detail shown here is from one of the Constantinian medallions and depicts Apollo as the Sun emerging from the sea. The relief can also be observed in its original position on the east end of the short side of Constantine's Arch.

4-5 The heart of ancient Rome, especially during the republican era, was certainly the Roman Forum. Even today, millions of visitors come to admire the archaeological remains of this area, which are still being studied.

© 1999 White Star S.r.l.
Via Candido Sassone, 22-24
13100 Vercelli, Italy.

This edition published by Barnes & Noble, Inc., by arrangement with White Star S.r.l.
2000 Barnes & Noble Books

ISBN 0-7607-2021-5
M10987654321
Printed in Italy by Grafedit.

6-7 and 6 bottom  The Coliseum, an imposing structure that is still in excellent condition, is one of the most significant monuments in ancient Rome, striking the imagination of not only visitors, but the capital's residents as well. The name itself is of popular rather than historical origin, and comes from Nero's Colossus, which stood a short distance away at the foot of the Velia, where the remains of the Temple of Venus and Rome are now found (photograph bottom).

# PREFACE

Writing a guide to Rome is a difficult but stimulating enterprise, given the considerable developments in the state of the art. Because new excavations and discoveries have changed the history and archaeology we have always known, and because an increasingly vast public has become interested in Roman culture, I was spurred to offer a guide that is not only a new tool for popularization, providing a complete picture, but also an examination of the current state of archaeology.

The peculiarities of the city of Rome, with its three thousand years of practically uninterrupted occupation, creating perhaps the largest example of a stratified site in the world, force the traveler to move through monuments in a manner that is rarely chronological or typological. For this reason, I decided to follow two different directions in presenting the work: the historical introduction, which explains the development of the city horizontally, with detailed references to the monuments in order of their appearance; and the guide itself, which provides an accurate description of the sites within the city, divided into four sectors.

The point of view presented is intended to offer a different, in some ways "upside down" approach. The goal is to use the monuments of Rome to recount its history and that of the famous and unknown people that inhabited it. This procedure is possible and becomes particularly clear precisely because this is not just any city, but Rome. In *Urbs* (as Rome was known to its inhabitants), the city *par excellence*, every temple, every basilica, every arch, street, portico or aqueduct, was potentially a political act,

intimately bound to the person who built it. Buildings, like people, were celebrated in coins, listed in public calendars, and subject to satire and poetry, praise and invective from generations of historians and poets.

The guide is thus designed as a tool for a contemporary reader to orient him or her self in ancient Rome, and acts as a compass, with points of reference (maps, reconstructions and chronological tables) that offer a continuous explanation of the traveler's position in time and space at any given moment, whether the voyage is real or virtual. This helps the reader to make an ongoing comparison between the urban structure of ancient Rome and that of the modern city, between everyday, visible Rome and the invisible city of the ancients.

Another innovation is the use of settings that use in-depth charts, designs and reconstructions, to lead the reader/visitor to consider the city as more than just a group of monuments to analyze coldly and separately, but essentially to contemplate it in its human dimension. Context is thus considered as a fundamental element in the descriptions; too often we forget to provide those explanations that are vital to understanding the inhabitants, their lives and what they built. Finally, the reader is allowed to orient himself within the setting of ancient Rome, using information on Rome's archaeological parks and sites, museums of the Roman world, and even Rome on the Internet.

Thus, this guide should not be considered yet another manual for the specialist, but a tool for orientation and knowledge that is both detailed and scientific — in brief, the record of a trip through archaeology.

# History

*The tradition and ancient legends of Rome, which have been passed down to us through some of its greatest writers, have given us a precious document that we can use to at least partially reconstruct the history of Rome. Archaeology has sometimes confirmed, sometimes modified, but always added to the pages of the history that we can read today.*

*8 center  The story of Romulus and Remus is told by this bas-relief on the back of the Ara Casali, from about 200 AD, on display at the Pio Clemente Museum.*

*8-9  Even today, the she-wolf is the symbol of Rome. It must originally have been the totem animal of primitive Rome, even before it became part of an almost cult-like tradition. In the legend, the she-wolf suckled Romulus and Remus, the sons of Rhea Silvia and Mars, who were abandoned on the banks of the Tiber by order of Amulius.*

## THE ARCHAIC AGE AND THE MONARCHIC PERIOD

Scholars usually separate the history of Rome into three main periods, based on the type of government established: the Monarchic Period, the Republican Period, and the Imperial Period. Rome's origins may be traced back to the 8th century BC, a date supported not only by ancient tradition, but also by excavations. In reality, there are traces of well-defined communities on the surrounding hilltops that even predate the 8th century. These were small settlements of farmers and shepherds who lived in simple straw-roofed huts of the kind found in excavations on the Palatine. The especially favorable position of one of these hills, the Palatine, allowed it to dominate the others. The Palatine was located not only near the most precious, vital resource, the Tiber, but was also the only place where it was easy to ford the river, at Tiber Island. Controlling this area clearly meant being in a position of superiority against anyone coming from the south who was attemping to reach the Etruscan cities to the north, for example. Salt also traveled along this road (in fact Via Salaria, comes from "sale", salt); the salt trade was of primary importance in ancient times. The market that arose near the river

became an extremely important gathering place and trading center; the port on the Tiber grew so much that it shaped city life. Perhaps its geographical position did not affect only the commercial and political development of Rome, but also the mentality of its inhabitants, who over time maintained a sort of tension between being open to the outside world and being devoted to the ancient traditions of the ancestors. According to legend, the monarchic period began with the mythical founding of Rome by Romulus in 753 BC. The historian Titus Livius, in his *Ab Urbe Condita Libri*, accurately recounts not only the principal historical events, but also reports the legends that the Romans customarily handed down, primarily in oral tradition.

According to these tales, Rome's origins can be traced back to Aeneas, who after the destruction of Troy, approached the coasts of Latium and founded a city after marrying the daughter of the Latin king. His son Ascanius then created Alba Longa in the Albani Mountains. When the

last king, Proclus died leaving the reign to his two sons, such a rivalry arose between the two that one of them, Amulius, who had originally been excluded from the government, usurped the throne and killed his brother, then forbade the brother's daughter, Rhea Silvia, from marrying and had her consecrated as a priestess. But the young woman nevertheless gave birth to twins, Romulus and Remus, sons of the god Mars, who were saved from Amulius' wrath by a she-wolf and a kind-hearted shepherd. When they grew into manhood, they decided to found a city at the place where they had been exposed to die. A disagreement arose, however, on the choice of hill, the Palatine or the Aventine. The omens gave Romulus the victory, and thus it was up to him to identify the borders of the new city on the Palatine, by plowing a furrow with a yolk of oxen.

Modern historians have noted that the name Romulus is nothing more than an eponymous hero from whom the Romans traced their origins. Historical and archaeological investigations have also proved that Rome initially went through a long period (753 to 506 BC) under a monarchic regime, although it was not an absolute monarchy. In reality, there must have been many more than the 7 legendary kings, who include Romulus, Numa Pompilius, Tullus Hostilius, Ancus Marcius, Tarquinius Priscus, Servius Tullus and Tarquinius Superbus. Most of the events recounted about these figures mask real events, such as the wars against the Sabines conducted by Romulus and the later unification with these people, who had settled on the Quirinal; the foundation of Ostia at the mouth of the Tiber; the construction of architectural works like

the Mamertine Prison by Ancus Marcius, the Cloaca Maxima, the Forum, the Circus Maximus and the Temple of Jupiter on the Capitoline. Under the reign of the last kings, represented by an Etruscan dynasty that occupied the throne between the 7th and 6th centuries BC, Rome was transformed into a large city. It was an urban center with a wealth of monuments, open to new influences, primarily through trade, from the Punic East, Asia Minor and Greece. These new contacts soon caused Roman civilization to turn outwards, to conquer first neighboring populations and then those from the Mediterranean basin, at the same time absorbing their customs, artistic and architectural influences, philosophical and literary theories, and military tactics. When the last king of Rome, Tarquinius Superbus, was driven out in 509 BC, a new political form was established in Rome, the Republic.

The theory of the Republic was based essentially on the balance of power between two consuls elected annually by the people, and the senators, lifetime representatives of the patrician aristocracy, who essentially controlled the destiny of the state. Throughout the Republican period, Rome was the setting for a number of extremely significant events. Some of the first conflicts included the struggle for political parity between the patricians and the plebeians, with the latter increasingly numerous for reasons that included profound changes caused by the wars of conquest.

Between the 5th and 3rd centuries BC, Rome conquered almost the entire Italian peninsula. There were conflicts first with the Latins at Lake Regillus (494)–according to legend, the battle turned in the Romans' favor due to the appearance of the Dioscuri, to whom a temple was later dedicated in the Forum. Following were the conquests of the Volsci, the Equi and the Etruscans. The latter, who had settled in the Tiber valley, were certainly their most formidable adversaries.

Rome's expansion was abruptly halted due to the invasion of the Gauls, who swept in from their territories across the Alps to sack Rome. They laid siege to the few brave fighters holed up in the Capitol, who had climbed up to the last bulwarks to defend their land. Again according to tradition, their enemies would have succeeded in taking the hill if honking geese, sacred to Juno, had not sounded the alarm (perhaps this is the reason the temple on the Capitoline was called Juno Moneta, or she who warns). When the Gaulish period was over, Rome once again began its wars of conquest against Campania, central Italy (the Samnites) and southern Italy (Taranto).

As the 3rd century dawned, mighty Carthage became aware of the danger that Rome might soon pose, especially in the area of trade, if it extended its grasp to the Mediterranean. Conflict was inevitable, and was long (264 – 146 BC) and eventful. In the end, Rome succeeded in defeating this formidable enemy and also conquering Sardinia, Corsica, Cisalpine Gaul, Illyria, Greece, Syria, Macedonia and part of Asia Minor.

There had been a change in basic motivations that led to a policy which became more offensive than defensive, with the threefold goal of reducing any type of threat of harm to Rome, achieving victories that would quickly and plentifully satisfy an army that now consisted of professional soldiers, and finally, obtaining enormous wealth. Contact with not only the cities of Magna Graecia, but especially with Hellenistic civilization, provided a significant impetus to the arts, philosophy, and the sciences, until it changed the austere and simple Roman customs

*10 top  The bronze head of this person (probably from the 3rd century BC), who may be the famous Brutus, founder of the republic, belonged to a statue that unfortunately has been lost.  His expression is quite intense and seems to emanate the characteristic gravity and diligence that were expected of Roman patricians.*

*10 bottom  This marble frieze from the Temple of Juno shows the Capitoline geese who, according to tradition, saved Rome from the Gauls when residents were alerted by their cackling.*

and permeated everyday life. It then became the fashion to study Greek, read Homer, and go to lectures by rhetoricians or grammarians who had opened their own schools in Rome, and bring in Greek artists to create fine sculptures or paintings. While Roman architecture had initially taken some structural elements from the Etruscans, such as the arch and the vault, the Greek world was now the source of decorative modules, such as the Doric, Ionic and Corinthian orders. And these were not the only consequences. In addition to the political order, even the economic structure underwent a profound change, the greatest consequence of which was the gradual disappearance of small properties and the rise of large estates. The latter, owned by the wealthy or nouveau rich, was put to pasture or cultivated by slaves, who provided free labor. Peasants could do nothing but move to the city in hopes of finding a job, but actually only swelled the ranks of the unemployed, desperate plebeians, many of whose

only hope of survival was to become the client of a rich Roman willing to give them shelter and food for the day (the so-called *sportula*). The situation most certainly required clear agrarian reform like that designed by the Gracchus brothers (133-121 BC), but aroused the discontent and opposition of the dominant oligarchy. This struggle continued later as well and erupted in civil wars, first in the bloody battles between Marius and Silla, and then between Pompey and Caesar. Julius Caesar broke the power of the oligarchy, becoming a dictator whose power was based on popular consensus, thus opening the way for the Augustan imperial period. He was so appreciated and loved that he became a model and point of reference for all emperors to follow. In addition to extending the borders of the Empire to Gaul, Germany and Britain, he initiated a detailed system of reform in all fields, and also began a radical

renewal of construction. He restored the Republican Forum area, rebuilding the Senate headquarters and Curia, and behind this built a new Forum with a temple dedicated to Venus Genetrix. He built numerous edifices on the Field of Mars and wanted to reclaim and expand this area and even dreamed of diverting the course of the Tiber.

*11 Emerging victorious from his battle with Pompey, Caesar quickly ascended to power. Although Rome permanently left the Republican age when this charismatic man became dictator, Caesar nevertheless ensured the support of a large portion of the populace through his reforms, victorious wars, and attitude, which focused more on moderation and clemency than on vengeance. He became an almost divine model for emperors in the centuries to follow.*

Julius Caesar was murdered on March 15 in 44 BC, the Ides of March, through a senseless conspiracy. Thus, it was up to his nephew Octavianus to take over the reins of government and control of the state. After defeating Antony and Cleopatra at Actium (31 BC), Octavianus was received in Rome as *princeps*, and took the name of Augustus.

The imprint this emperor left is so profound, not only in the administrative, political and military system, but also the urban system, that it spelled a true turning point in the history of Rome. On one hand, he began a program of reconstruction and restoration of many edifices and monuments, and on the other built magnificent architectural works like the Forum of Augustus, with the Temple of Mars Ultor (i.e., avenger of Caesar), his Mausoleum, the Ara Pacis, the

Pantheon and the Baths of Agrippa.

When Augustus died, his adopted son Tiberius came to the throne, within a system of succession by heredity maintained by all emperors in the Julian-Claudian dynasty (Tiberius 14-37; Caligula 37-41; Claudius 41-54; Nero 54-68), and after a brief period of anarchy, continued in the Flavian dynasty (Vaspasian 69-79; Titus 79-81; and Domitian 81-96).

The construction policy initiated by Augustus was essentially continued by later emperors in richer and more eclectic forms, many of which were based on Hellenistic inspiration. Suffice it to consider Nero's construction of the great Domus Aurea, after the disastrous fire of 64 AD, in which much of Rome burned; the Flavian Amphitheater (now known as the Coliseum); the Arch of Titus built in memory of the Judaic war

conducted by this emperor; the Trajan Forum complex; the Temple of Venus and Rome and Hadrian's villa in Tivoli, and the Aurelian Column, depicting the victories over the Quadi and Marcomanni.

Upon Domitian's death, the Senate elected Nerva, from the Antonine dynasty, thus beginning a new system of succession based on adoption (Nerva 96-98; Trajan 98-117; Hadrian 117-138; Antonius Pius 138-161; Marcus Aurelius 161-180; and Commodus 180-192 AD). This solution temporarily averted the problem represented by the appointment of new emperors, a problem that would return later and become ever more pressing, enough to undermine the stability of the Empire itself. Its cause lay in the increasing awareness by high-ranking military forces like the Praetorians of their significance in the political arena. With growing pressure from the barbarians on its borders, the army became increasingly indispensable for the survival of the empire. At first, simple solutions were used, such as allowing certain groups of barbarians to settle within the borders. Sometimes they were recruited in the army as feudarati and were paid a sort of salary, which actually was a form of tribute.

In the Severian era, (Septimius Severus, 193-211; Caracalla, 211-217; Macrinus, 217-218, Elagabalus, 218-222; and Severus Alexander, 222-235) it was still possible to control this situation, due in part to the strong, military, absolutist personalities of the emperors, who conducted and concluded successful border campaigns and focused less and less attention on the capital. From the mid-3rd century, however, the situation began to deteriorate. There was a succession of emperors who were elected and eliminated through the whims of a military that now had practically lost sight of the vastness and unity of the Roman Empire, and thus created great imbalance.

It was not until Diocletian (284-305) and then Constantine (312-337) that truly significant figures emerged. They introduced reforms (suffice it to consider the tetrarchic system of succession) that at least temporarily restored unity and grandeur to the Roman world. Even the architectural works left by these emperors are extremely significant, such as, for

example, the great Basilica of Maxentius (completed by Constantine), St. Peter's Basilica, and the Arch of Constantine. The first signals of a fragmenting empire were Constantine's transfer of the capital to Constantinople, the new Rome, as he wanted it to be called.

With the beginning of the 5th century, the situation came to a head. The Huns appeared on the western scene for the first time, and following hard on the heels of other barbarian peoples (such as the Visigoths of Alaric), drove them deep into Italy, while true Roman barbarian realms formed on the borders. The Roman world at that time, now divided into the West and East empires, permanently lost its unity, and while the eastern-Greek portion survived for another thousand years, the arrival of Odoacer spelled the end of the West Roman Empire.

*12 and 13 When Nerva adopted Trajan, a valorous general from the provinces, he initiated a new form of succession to imperial power that was no longer based on heredity. This decision also assured the emperor the support of the military, which was playing an increasingly significant role in the political life of Rome.*
*One of the greatest military successes of the*

*new emperor, Trajan, who made enormous efforts to expand and consolidate central power, was his military campaigns against the Dacians, depicted in the long, spiral-shaped frieze on his honorary column. The numerous scenes that follow uninterrupted provide a wealth of information on episodes in the wars, arms, ships, clothing, tactics, and assault techniques.*

# CHRONOLOGICAL TABLE

- *FOUNDATION*
753 BC    Traditional date for the founding of Rome
- *THE MONARCHY*
753 BC    Romulus
715    Numa Pompilius
673    Tullus Hostilius
642    Ancus Marcius
616    Tarquinius Priscus
578    Servius Tullius
535    Tarquinius Superbus
- *THE REPUBLIC*
509 BC    Foundation of the Republic
451    Laws of the Twelve Tables
421    The plebeians gain equal rights
396    Defeat of Veius
272    Fall of Tarantum (Taranto)
270    Beginning of expansion into the Mediterranean
202    End of the Second Punic War
146    Sack of Corinth. Destruction of Carthage
90/88    Social war
88/82    Civil war between Marius and Silla
49/45    Civil war between Pompey and Caesar
48 BC    Octavian
48/44    Dictatorship of Caesar
44/31    Civil war
- *THE EMPIRE*

| | |
|---|---|
| 31 BC | Caesar Octavian Augustus |
| 14 AD | Tiberius |
| 37 | Caligula |
| 41 | Claudius |
| 54 | Nero |
| 68-9 | Galba, Otho, Vitellius |
| 69 | Vespasian |
| 79 | Titus |
| 81 | Domitian |
| 96 | Nerva |
| 98 | Trajan |
| 117 | Hadrian |
| 138 | Antoninus Pius |
| 161 | Marcus Aurelius |
| 180 | Commodus |
| 193 | Septimius Severus |
| 211 | Caracalla |
| 218 | Elagabalus |
| 222 | Alexander Severus |
| 235 | Maximinian |
| 238 | Gordian I, II, III |
| 244 | Philip the Arab |
| 249 AD | Decius |
| 251 | Trebonianus Gallus |
| 253-60 | Valerian |
| 253-67 | Gallienus |
| 268 | Claudius Gothicus |
| 270 | Aurelianus |
| 276 | Probus |
| 284 | Diocletian - Maximinian |
| 305 | Maximinian - Constantius |
| 306 | Maxentius - Severus |
| 309/10 | Galerius |
| 312 | Constantine |
| 337 | Constantine II - Constans I - Constantius II |
| 364 | Valentinian I |
| 375 | Gratianus |
| 383 | Valentinian II |
| 395 | Honorius |
| 423 | Valentinian III |
| 475 | Romulus Augustolus |
| 476 | Odoacer |
| 493 | Theodoric |

# THE ROMANS AT WORK

## THE MATERIALS

The Romans distinguished themselves from other ancient peoples by their construction skills, and left a legacy that to some extent survives to this day. The *De Architectura* by Vitruvius, a writer who lived during the era of Caesar and Augustus, provides a precious, exhaustive source of information on the architecture, engineering and general culture of ancient Rome.

The development of construction techniques in any civilization is closely related to the quality and quantity of material available in the area. Thus, during an older period when trade is not yet fully developed, it is natural for construction to be intimately connected to this factor, which of course also controls development. It is also true that the choice of construction materials is highly dependent on the type of building, its size and location, economic resources, and, last but not least, current tastes. Vitruvius indicates the qualities that had to be sought and pursued by architects in the form of three golden rules: *firmitas*, or solidity of the structures; *utilitas*, or functionality, which was based on how space was organized; and *venustas*, an elegant aesthetic appearance.

Because of the geo-morphological characteristics common throughout Lazio, the materials used beginning in the 7th century BC are quite similar. Using materials naturally available, rather simple structures were built, such as huts of reeds and clay with straw roofs. Later, rock such as tufa was used that was available and easy to quarry from the hills of the city.

Quarrymen worked in the quarries and

resistant blocks. With the end of the second century BC, travertine began to be used. This was considerably superior to other rocks due to its solidity and durability. Augustus then began experimenting with marble. He increased the quarries in Luni, in Etruria, which produced an excellent white marble that was shipped to Rome by sea as far as Ostia, and then sent up the Tiber.

used a simple tool to cut the rock horizontally and vertically to the required size, thus obtaining blocks that were sometimes finished on site. Some of the various rocks that Vitruvius mentions, such as tufa, had to be quarried in the summer and were then exposed to the air for two years before being used, to eliminate humidity and lead to the use of the most

Imported marble was used for the decorative parts of monuments such as columns, friezes, trabeations, floors and sculptures. It is said that, before dying, the emperor told his friends that he had inherited a city of bricks and had left one of marble.

Of course, many parts of buildings were still made of wood, including ceilings, trabeations and partitions. But overall, at least until concrete was introduced, the most commonly used material for walls was green brick. This was a clay brick that was allowed to dry slowly, covered, for about two years. Its great limitation was that it could not support more than one floor.

We can essentially divide materials into two categories: those more appropriately used for construction, and those used for decoration. Among the first, we should certainly note the category of tufas: Campidoglio, Fidene, and Grotta Oscura tufa, *lapis gabinus*, and Monteverde tufa. Some of the most commonly used tufas in the 7th century BC included *capellaccio*, a grayish, rather brittle tufa that was easy to

work, but was also resistant, and came from the area around Rome. From the second century BC, peperino and travertine were widely used in construction. They came from quarries that are still in use today, the first in Marino and the second in Tivoli. Marble is a material that was commonly used in architecture, in both interior and exterior decoration. Some of the best known marble includes that from the quarries of Luni, Pentelic marble, cipolin, pavonazzetto, verde antico, granite and porphyry.

# CONSTRUCTION TECHNIQUES

From above:
(1) *opus quadratum*, one of the oldest techniques, was used from ancient times and was characterized by rows of regular, rectangular-shaped rocks aligned with each other;
(2) *opus incertum*, a technique that characterized outer faces of *opus caementicium*, with irregularly placed tufa blocks inserted into the nucleus in wedge fashion;
(3) *opus quasi reticulatum*, where the ashlars are placed in more regular fashion; in the first century BC the technique developed into (4) *opus reticulatum*, with placement becoming completely regular.
(5) *opus vittatum*, a type of outer face introduced in the first century, consisting of curtains of horizontally aligned bricks.

The most common masonry system until the end of the Republican period was so-called *opus quadratum*. It involved simply placing rectangular blocks one beside the other (all laid upright or on edge, or else alternatively upright and on edge). The blocks were then fixed by connecting them with wooden or metal cramps. While this technique had the advantage of being quite solid and resistant, it had severe limitations when covering large areas, which had to be done in wood using a truss or simple overhang.

One of the problems that drove Roman engineers to develop more complex technological solutions was covering and elevating buildings (Rome's overcrowding in fact required a quite intensive use of space). The introduction of *opus caementicium*, which was commonly used by the Romans starting in the third century BC and continues to this day, allowed them to

such as the so-called *opus incertum*, using small blocks of tufa placed irregularly on the two faces; *opus quasi reticulatum*, with a more regular placement of the blocks; *opus reticulatum*, where the outside face had a regular, pleasing appearance due to the orderly placement of four-sided, cone-shaped blocks inserted deeply into the center; *opus mixtum*, which made it possible to build walls more economically, as it alternated reticulate bands with bands of brick; and *opus latericium* or *testaceum*, which was initially (first century BC) reserved for especially damp areas. This latter technique was a

build colossal, complex structures like aqueducts, theaters, thermal baths, etc. Roofing for the buildings could be cast directly, creating impressive vaults (such as with the Pantheon). The first building constructed in concrete was the *Porticus Aemilia*, which was located in the new business district at the foot of the Aventine. Concrete work consisted of a very solid, durable mixture formed of fragments of tufa, stone, terra-cotta or gravel mixed with grout. To strengthen and protect the structure, two faces were added so that the concrete would remain on the inside and weld with the masonry, constituting various types of composite "works." Once the stage of simple *opus quadratum* had passed, other types of masonry were soon introduced,

success and ended up replacing all others starting from the reign of Antoninus Pius and Marcus Aurelius. Fired bricks, unlike primitive green bricks, were furnace-baked in a square shape and then broken into triangular forms that were inserted into the center like a wedge, with the edge broken and the face refinished. Domitian began the custom of inserting a band of whole bricks (known as "two-footed" bricks) at determined distances. These rows crossed the wall of masonry completely and leveled the masonry layers. A further development in the late antique epoch of green brick work was the so-called *opus vittatum*, which was characterized by alternating layers of green bricks and rectangular tufa blocks,

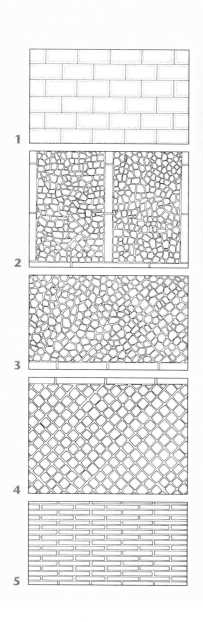

often re-used.

Brick factories were quite active in Rome and also produced materials for special facilities like thermal baths and aqueducts. They also sold roof tiles and pan tiles for roofs, and green bricks for outdoor flooring, with the typical on edge, herringbone or spiked (*opus spicatum*) arrangement.

The flooring problem led them to adopt various techniques, depending on need: For example, streets could be paved with cobblestones or large sheets of rock set into layers of sand and pebbles for durability. Swimming pools, or areas used to hold water, were covered with a mixture of concrete and green brick, known as *opus signinum*, that made the walls impermeable.

One could say that the vitality of Roman building techniques lay in the ability to find ever new solutions to problems, taking old techniques and adapting them to their needs until they created new solutions. Even today, we can get an idea of the magnificence of Roman structures if we observe the traces that Roman architects have left throughout the empire, in the form of imposing edifices, aqueducts, thermal baths, fortifications, villas and temples.

### The Servian Walls

According to tradition, Tarquinius Priscus built a circuit of walls 11 km long, in the first half of the 6th century BC. The walls were completed by Servius Tullius in *opus quadratum*, using outcrop. In the early 4th century, after part of Rome was occupied by the Gauls, it was reconstructed, in part reusing the old blocks of outcrop, and in part adding new blocks of Grotta Oscura tufa. The walls were over 10 meters high and about 4 meters thick. Some points, which were especially exposed, had to be reinforced using an embankment and ditch behind the walls. The longest section still in existence today is next to the Termini train station. Another section is along Viale Aventino, on Piazza Albania, where the walls formed a recess, probably to protect a gate. In reality, even at the end of the first century BC, the city had expanded so far that the walls included only a small part of it, leaving the rest mostly undefended.

### Aurelian Walls

A circuit of almost 19 km, enclosing about 1372 hectares, was rapidly built between 271 and 275 AD when a need was perceived for more effective protection against the barbarians, who had easily been able to push to Rome. The speed with which the walls were built is also evidence that many already existing structures were used and included, such as the *Castra Praetoria* wall.

The walls were in green brick with a concrete center. They were 3.5 meters thick

and about 6 meters high. Square towers were inserted every 30 meters (100 Roman feet), and had an upper chamber for the sentries. The most important gates consisted of a roofed, arched double entry surrounded by two semicircular towers. Thirty years later, Maxentius restored the walls in *opus listatum*, adding a parapet. Later, in 401 AD, Honorius repaired them, doubling the height and replacing the parapet walk with a covered tunnel, above which was the new walk with merlons. He also added the Mausoleum of Hadrian to the fortification, as an outpost castle on the right bank of the Tiber. The walls, restored numerous times, survived to protect the city until 1870.

The best-preserved portions are the so-called Tortian Wall, the stretch from Porta San Giovanni to Porta Ardeatina, from Porta Ostiense to the Tiber, and Porta San Pancrazio on the Janiculum.

*16 left Known as the Temple of Fortuna Virile, the Temple of Portunus, shown in the photo, was built in the Cattle Market at the ancient Tiberian gate and dedicated to the god who protected sailors and ports. The edifice is Ionic, made of tufa and travertine covered with stucco.*

*16-17 A circuit of brick walls surrounds Caracalla's Baths. Opus testaceum, the construction technique that used rows of fired bricks as an outer face for opus caementicium, began to be used as early as the 1st century AD, and quickly became the most frequent and common construction system. In the photograph, we can see the windows with depressed arches, with bricks tilted in a fan-shaped pattern, a technique commonly used to obtain ample lighting without making the buildings too tall.*

*17 left Ostia has numerous masonry structures in opus reticulatum with brick fascia and arches. These were the faces of tufa or fired brick rectangles, chiseled to obtain a pyramid form that could be inserted into the nucleus like a wedge. Often, rows of bricks alternated with tesserae, to level the floors and even out the internal concrete mix. Opus reticulatum, which was introduced in the Augustan era, was widely used during the first and second centuries. AD.*

*17 right Porta San Sebastiano, with its two tall towers, is one of the most characteristic gates within the Aurelian Walls still visible today. Its present appearance is due to remodeling by Honorius around 401 AD.*
*The bricks that were most frequently used in Roman architecture were bessales (19 x 19 cm), sesquipedales (44 x 44 cm), and especially bipedales (59.60 x 59.60 cm).*

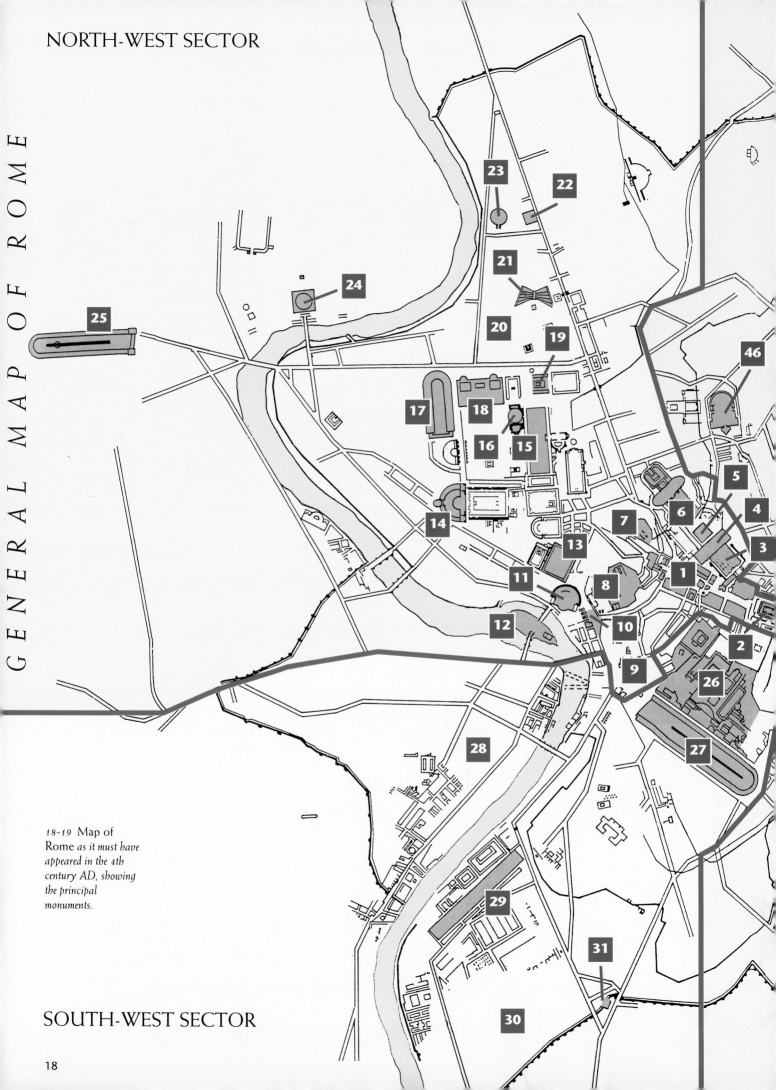

GENERAL MAP OF ROME

18-19 Map of
Rome *as it must have
appeared in the 4th
century AD, showing
the principal
monuments.*

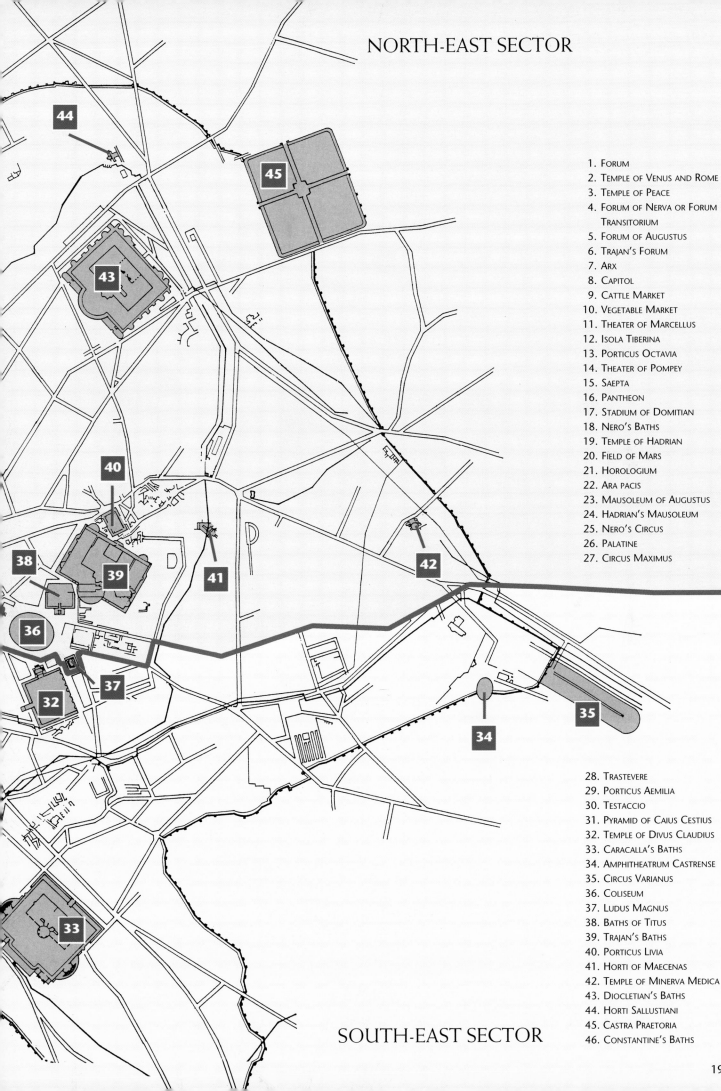

1. FORUM
2. TEMPLE OF VENUS AND ROME
3. TEMPLE OF PEACE
4. FORUM OF NERVA OR FORUM TRANSITORIUM
5. FORUM OF AUGUSTUS
6. TRAJAN'S FORUM
7. ARX
8. CAPITOL
9. CATTLE MARKET
10. VEGETABLE MARKET
11. THEATER OF MARCELLUS
12. ISOLA TIBERINA
13. PORTICUS OCTAVIA
14. THEATER OF POMPEY
15. SAEPTA
16. PANTHEON
17. STADIUM OF DOMITIAN
18. NERO'S BATHS
19. TEMPLE OF HADRIAN
20. FIELD OF MARS
21. HOROLOGIUM
22. ARA PACIS
23. MAUSOLEUM OF AUGUSTUS
24. HADRIAN'S MAUSOLEUM
25. NERO'S CIRCUS
26. PALATINE
27. CIRCUS MAXIMUS

28. TRASTEVERE
29. PORTICUS AEMILIA
30. TESTACCIO
31. PYRAMID OF CAIUS CESTIUS
32. TEMPLE OF DIVUS CLAUDIUS
33. CARACALLA'S BATHS
34. AMPHITHEATRUM CASTRENSE
35. CIRCUS VARIANUS
36. COLISEUM
37. LUDUS MAGNUS
38. BATHS OF TITUS
39. TRAJAN'S BATHS
40. PORTICUS LIVIA
41. HORTI OF MAECENAS
42. TEMPLE OF MINERVA MEDICA
43. DIOCLETIAN'S BATHS
44. HORTI SALLUSTIANI
45. CASTRA PRAETORIA
46. CONSTANTINE'S BATHS

# FROM THE CAPITOL TO THE ARX

20 center Hypothetical reconstruction of the Capitoline Hill. *As time passed, numerous buildings were constructed on the* Capitolium (1), *remains have been found* of the great Temple of Jupiter Capitolinus (2), *with the* Temple of Ops *and the* Temple of Fides *to the right, and to the left the* Gens Iulia *altar – the* Ara Pietatis *– built by the Senate during Livia's illness, in* 22 AD. *In the first century BC, the* Tabularium (3), *the state archive, was built at the foot of the hill. In the background was the* Arx *with the* Temple of Juno Moneta (5) *and the* Auguraculum.

THE CAPITOL

20 left General map of the Capitol. *The Capitoline Hill had a tall peak to the north,* Arx, *where omens were read from the flight of birds, and where the* Temple of Juno Moneta *was located, a lower promontory to the south, the* Capitolium, *where* the Palazzo dei Conservatori *stands today, which from ancient times was used exclusively for religious purposes; and a col, the* Asylum, *which connected the two peaks, where Romulus was said to have gathered fugitives from neighboring communities.*

1. CAPITOLIUM
2. TEMPLE OF JUPITER OPTIMUS MAXIMUS
3. TABULARIUM
4. ALTAR
5. TEMPLE OF JUNO MONETA

Until the 16th and 17th centuries, when the government building was built here, the Capitoline Hill continued to retain something of its original appearance, although the central role it had once played had changed entirely. It is thus of fundamental importance to treat the Capitoline Hill as a true mirror of Roman history, culture and mentality.

The small hill, a perfect fortress due to the steep rocky walls and the position from which it dominated Tiber Island and the Tiber ford, had a slightly higher peak to the north, known as *Arx*, and a lower promontory to the south, the true

*21 top left An archaic cinerary urn in the form of a primitive hut. The dwellings of early Iron Age inhabitants must have looked like this. This is also confirmed by archaeological discoveries, which have revealed ancient traces of huts on the tufaceous surfaces of the hill. The huts had an oval design, with one or two poles supporting the roof, a hearth in the center and a small portico before the entrance.*

*21 center Surviving fragments of the statue of Constantine are preserved in the courtyard of the Palazzo dei Conservatori. For example, we can see the head, which is 2.6 meters tall. With its rigid, compact lines and the enormous,*

*wide-open eyes looking upwards, the face reveals his magnificence and the ideals of a monarch and master with divine enlightenment.*

*21 top right Equestrian statue of Marcus Aurelius, Capitoline Museums. The statue, a replica of which has now been restored and placed in the center of the Piazza del Campidoglio, was probably built in 166 AD, when the emperor was granted the title of Pater Patriae. It must originally have been located in the villa of his mother Domitia Lucilla, near the Lateran. It was moved here in the 16th century through the initiative of Michelangelo, and was mistakenly believed to be a portrait of the emperor Constantine.*

called *Centum Gradus* and the *Scalae Gemoniae*, where bodies of executed prisoners from the nearby *Carcer* were thrown), only the *Clivus Capitolinus* was a carriage road. This was a route that ascended from the *Forum Romanum* up to the Arch of Septimius Severus, a natural continuation of the Via Sacra.

Tradition holds that at the time of Romulus, the Sabines succeeded in conquering the Capitoline Hill due to the betrayal of a Roman woman, Tarpeia, who was supposedly killed by the invaders themselves, crushed under their shields. In reality, the legend seems to be a figment of the collective imagination, based on the existence of a statue standing on a pile of arms, representing the patron goddess of the hill, which was originally known as *mons tarpeius.*

One of the most important episodes in the history of Rome was the 6th century BC construction of the great *Temple of Jupiter Capitolinus* by the first Etruscan king, Tarquinius Priscus. It encompassed two pre-existing sanctuaries, *Terminus* and *Iuventas*, which could not be moved. In a votive deposit, discovered under the present-day *Protomoteca*, ancient objects from the 7th century BC were found. One of these included a bucchero clay cup with an Etruscan inscription that further confirms the importance of the Etruscan presence in Rome.

After the city was occupied by the Gauls in 390 BC, it became necessary to reinforce the hill through a large terracing work that also acted as a fortification. There were numerous fires (in 83 BC, 69 BC and 80 AD) that destroyed Capitoline buildings, which had to be rebuilt again and again. In actuality, this area, especially the square facing the Temple of Jupiter, the so-called *Capitoline Area*, was full of buildings. It was crowded with edifices, statues and monuments like porticoes, shrines, victory memorials and fountains, which periodically had to be

removed. The remains of an altar have been found that may be the *Ara Pietatis* or *gens Iulia altar*, built by the Senate in 22 AD on occasion of the illness of Augustus' wife Livia. It was probably similar to the *Ara Pacis* in size and chronology. Farther south in this area, there was also a *Temple of Ops* and a *Temple of Fides*. Two bilingual inscriptions were also found here (in Greek and Latin), dedicated to the people of Asia Minor. It is believed that these dedications may belong to the *Temple of Fides*, the deity who watched over negotiations and diplomatic relations.

As proof of the political and religious importance of the place, the Capitoline Hill was also the site of some of the government's most important official ceremonies. It was from here that generals departed for the provinces, and it was here that their triumphs culminated with a sacrifice. Government hearings (comitia) were also held here during the Republic, along with consul investitures.

LATEST INFORMATION. A replica of the equestrian statue of Marcus Aurelius has been returned to the center of the recently restructured present-day square, after restoration work revived its bright color and the bronze patina of the surface. The original, conserved in the Capitoline Museums, was built in honor of the emperor in 166 BC, after he was granted the title of *Pater Patriae*. Originally located in the villa of Marcus Aurelius' mother, Domitia Lucilla, and mistakenly believed to portray Constantine, Michelangelo had it transported here in the 16th century, and may have designed the pedestal.

*Capitolium*, where the Palazzo dei Conservatori is located today. Between the two high points was a depression, the *Asylum*, a place where, according to legend, Romulus created a sort of safe zone, a meeting place for fugitives from neighboring communities. Tradition holds that there was an ancient settlement on the Capitoline Hill, and this appears to be borne out by the discovery of Bronze Age pottery (14th-13th centuries BC) from the St. Omobono Sacred Area at the foot of the hill. Among the various access routes that climbed up to *Arx* (the so-

# THE TEMPLE OF JUPITER CAPITOLINUS

In the 6th century BC, north of the *Capitolium*, Tarquinius Priscus and later Tarquinius Superbus erected the most important religious center of the Roman state, the temple of the Capitoline Triad (Jupiter Optimus Maximus, Juno Regina and Minerva). Its construction had a strong political connotation; in fact, it was built as a replacement for the *sanctuary of Mons Albanus* with the goal of moving the center of the Latin League to Rome, creating a focal point for all the

subjects of Lazio. Within the temple were the *Sibylline books*, which were consulted by a board of priests in case of a serious crisis. This went on until at least 83 BC, when Augustus transferred the reconstituted collection to the Temple of Apollo on the Palatine Hill.

This is the largest archaic Tuscan temple known (53 x 63 meters). Built on colossal foundations of outcrop in *opus quadratum*, its construction was known as *peripteral sine postico* (i.e., it had a colonnade on three sides, while the back wall was blind). It had a deep pronaos preceded by a flight of steps and three cells (cellae) devoted to the deities. The one on the right was dedicated to Minerva and the one on

the left to Juno, while the central cella was attributed to Jupiter. A gigantic *chryselephantine statue* of the deity was placed here in 65 BC, the work of the famous *Apollonius*, who is also known for the so-called *Belvedere Torso*. We can get an idea of its graceful appearance from the replicas that were made of it for the temples of Jupiter in the colonies and in the Roman municipalities (for example, the Jupiter of Otricoli in the Vatican Museums). The temple was decorated with painted terra-cotta sculptures; one of the largest was the *quadriga*, or chariot drawn by four horses, which acted as an acroter and was perched on the roof. Nothing remains of it today except the name of the artist, passed down to us by Pliny the Elder (*N.H. XXXV*, 157). In fact, the workshop of Vulca, who also created the Apollo of

Portonaccio, was in charge of the temple's decorative work. The *quadriga* was replaced with another bronze one in 296 BC. The temple was destroyed numerous times and was rebuilt in marble in the first century AD, probably utilizing the columns of the temple of Zeus Olympus in Athens (*N.H. XXXVI*, 45).

Only a few traces of the foundation wall remain visible in the back portion, in the garden of the Palazzo dei Conservatori.

LATEST INFORMATION. A statue depicting the Capitoline Triad has recently been discovered in a sumptuous villa in Guidonia: while not the original from the Capitoline Hill, it is the first direct archaeological evidence of a late copy or imitation, and was probably made by the villa's owner for private worship.

22 *This relief shows Marcus Aurelius in a toga, head covered, as he makes a sacrifice on a portable altar before the Temple of Jupiter Capitolinus and a portico with sculpted scenes of a wild boar hunt. Due to the ritual characteristics, it is probably a sacrifice celebrated after a*

*victory. The relief was probably part of the same monument from which panels were taken for the attic on the Arch of Constantine.*

22-23 *The group of sculptures representing the Capitoline Triad comes from a sumptuous villa in Guidonia; it provides the first direct archaeological testimony of the*

*original work portraying the three deities, although this is a reproduction or late imitation that the villa's owner had probably commissioned.*

## THE TABULARIUM

The *Tabularium* was the building where state records (*tabulae publicae*) were kept. The name of the building and its builder have been passed down to us through a medieval transcription of a now-lost epigraph: *"Quintus Lutatius Catulus,..., consul, by decree of the Senate, contracted the work for the substructure and public archives and performed the inspection"* (*CIL*, VI, 1314). We thus know that Lutatius Catulus, who was in charge of rebuilding the Capitol in 83 BC,

erected both the substructure and the *Tabularium*. There were, in fact, two distinct structures. The first, the *substructio*, was a sort of foundation on which the second was built, and had the purpose of leveling the area while at the same time establishing an architectural background for the Forum. It consisted of a wall carved into the tuff that supported an embankment made in *opus quadratum*. On the first level, there was a long covered corridor with six small windows that overlooked the *Forum Romanum*. To the southwest, there were two entrances that connected the

structure. It had a monumental facade that overlooked the Piazza del Campidoglio and two colonnaded galleries that overlooked the Forum. The first level, which joined the *Capitoline Hill* to the *Arx*, looked like a true *via tecta*, and was originally paved in lava stones. Inside, the space was divided into square sectors surrounded by pillars, covered by pavilion vaults, with rooms that may have functioned as shops. On the outside, the surface was dotted with fluted Doric semi-columns, on which there was an entablature (primarily ornamental in nature), surmounted by a Doric frieze with

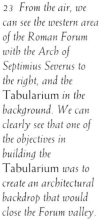

23 *From the air, we can see the western area of the Roman Forum with the Arch of Septimius Severus to the right, and the* Tabularium *in the background. We can clearly see that one of the objectives in building the* Tabularium *was to create an architectural backdrop that would close the Forum valley.*

Forum with the *Tabularium*. The first, at ground level, was blocked off after the Temple of Vespasian and Titus was built; it led to the upper level tunnel through two flights of stairs. The second one, behind the *Porticus Deorum Consentium*, was on a higher level. Here there was an older *Tabularium* building. Perhaps it was the Treasury, which was connected to the Temple of Saturn on one side and to the Imperial Mint (*ad Monetam*), which was on the *Arx*, on the other. In this manner, money could travel protected and unobserved through the hidden path of the covered corridor.

The actual *Tabularium* with its trapezoidal plan was placed on this

metopes and triglyphs. The second level had an arcade about 13 meters high, of which only architectural fragments remain. The structure, an example of late Republican architecture, became a model for all later Roman foundations. The complex was also the first example of a horizontal trabeation combined with the use of arches. This example was so successful that it was subsequently repeated in a number of buildings (such as the Trajan Forum and the Theater of Marcellus).

PANORAMA. From the *Tabularium* portico, now part of the Palazzo del Comune (Via San Pietro in Carcere), there is an excellent view of the entire *Forum Romanum*.

## THE ARX AND THE TEMPLE OF JUNO MONETA

The temple of Juno Moneta ("she who warns") probably stood where the present-day Santa Maria in Aracoeli now stands. It was built on the Capitoline Hill in 343 BC by the son of Camillus, after a victory over the Auruncians. Tradition connects the name to the verb *monere*, used as an epithet for Juno, and the Gauls' attempt to conquer the fortress in 390 BC, which failed due to the actions of Manlius Capitolinus, who was warned in time by honking geese.

Nearby, in an especially sheltered area, was the State Mint, referred to as *ad Monetam* (which means near the Temple of Juno Moneta). The name lives on in the word *moneta*, or money, which was coined here.

24 top  Silver coins from the republican era. In the 6th century BC, Rome established a new political order, the Republic, based on a balanced system of forces and powers, apportioned among consuls, lower magistrates and the Senate. The coins of this period depicted various figures: symbols, deities, historical characters, and buildings, mostly for propaganda purposes.

24 center  Silver coins from the Vespasian era. Only in the mid-first century BC did living persons begin to be depicted on coins. When Caesar used his own portrait as an image, he began a custom that would become common in the imperial era, useful as well for political propaganda.

24-25  This painting, from the house of the Vettii in Pompeii, dating from the first century AD, shows cupids intent on coining money.

# ROMAN MONEY

25 top *Silver coin from the era of Alexander Severus. Beginning in the 4th century BC, coins began to be used as a medium of exchange, regulated by a system based on the ratio between weight*

*and material. Bronze and silver money was coined, but there were also occasional issues in gold. The figures of emperors were most commonly depicted on coins from the imperial era.*

Money as we know it began to be used in Rome only beginning in the 4th century BC. Prior to that, starting in the 8th century BC, *aes rude* (formless copper pieces valued according to weight) were used as a means of exchange, and were then replaced in the 6th century BC by *aes signatum* (copper melted into more or less regular rectangular lumps), which were sometimes stamped on both sides. Before 430 BC, the year of the *Iulia Papiria* law, Romans also used livestock as an alternative type of payment: In fact, the word *pecus*, or livestock, is the root of the words pecuniary and peculator.

Only in the 4th century, however, did Rome begin to feel the need for a more efficient system of monetary exchange, so that it could trade with the flourishing cities of Magna Grecia at their own level. It thus began to produce the first circular coins stamped by the government, which then acquired a monopoly from that time on. The first coins to be minted, known as *Romano-Campanian* coins,

came from mints in southern Italy, especially the Campania region. The city of Rome was later supplied with its own mint, and the monetari, a board created in 289 BC, controlled issues. The other coin Rome issued was the *aes grave*: It was cast, not minted, in bronze, and weighed a pound, with no inscriptions. Silver and gold coins were also minted, but gold was rare and issued only sporadically.

Images printed on coins are a valuable tool for gaining knowledge about people and historical events in ancient Rome. Coins depicted symbols, historical persons, deities, temples and other edifices. Especially in the Republican era, propaganda was quite important, while the imperial coins focused exclusively on the emperors and had a clear celebratory and commemorative function. Only beginning in 45 BC did they also begin to depict living persons. In his senatorial decree, Caesar coined the first money depicting his own image.

25 bottom *Bronze sextant depicting the Capitoline she-wolf (about 217-215 BC) suckling Romulus and Remus. The first figures printed on coins often were scenes taken directly from the legends of ancient tradition, as in this case, where we see the first scene of the myth of the founding of Rome, as Romulus and Remus are abandoned by Amulius and suckled by the she-wolf.*

# THE FORUM ROMANUM

*"Where the Fora now stand, there were once only muddy marshes whose expanse was full of the overflowing river. Lake Curtius, which is now solid ground where dry altars stand, once was nothing more than a lake. Once the Velabrum, where now the triumphal marches to the Circus take place, was nothing more than willows and empty reeds."*
Ovid, Fasti VI, 401-406

**26-27** *Hypothetical perspective reconstruction from the south.*

1. BASILICA AEMILIA
2. SACELLUM OF VENUS CLOACINA
3. CURIA
4. LAPIS NIGER
5. CARCER TULLIANUS
6. ROSTRA
7. UMBILICUS URBIS
8. ARCH OF SEPTIMUS SEVERUS
9. TEMPLE OF CONCORDIA
10. TEMPLE OF VESPASIAN
11. TEMPLE OF SATURN
12. PORTICIS DEORUM CONSENTIUM
13. FORUM SQUARE
14. BASILICA IULIA
15. TEMPLE OF CASTOR AND POLLUX
16. JUTURNA FOUNTAIN
17. TEMPLE OF DIVUS IULIUS
18. AUGUSTAN ARCH (VICTORY AT ACTIUM)
19. REGIA
20. TEMPLE OF VESTA
21. HOUSE OF THE VESTALS
22. TEMPLE OF ANTONINUS AND FAUSTINA
23. TEMPLE OF DIVUS ROMULUS
24. BASILICA OF MAXENTIUS AND CONSTANTINE
25. TEMPLE OF VENUS AND ROME
26. ARCH OF TITUS

For centuries, the *Forum Romanum* had been the center of public life in ancient Rome. But originally, it was only a marshy, inhospitable valley that lay between the Capitoline, the Palatine and the Velia hills. Because of this, the first settlements were on the hills, while between the 10th and 9th centuries BC the valley was used as a burial area. The Forum necropolis (remains have been found between the Arch of Augustus and the Temple of Antoninus and Faustina) was used until the 8th century BC, a date which coincides with the traditional founding of the city (754-753 BC); it was subsequently moved to the Esquiline. The abandonment of this burial ground confirms the expansion of settlements to this area, which by law could thus no longer be used for burials. The first step toward a real and complete use of the area came when Tarquinius Priscus drained the valley by building the *Cloaca Maxima* (7th century BC). In concomitance with this event, the first beaten earth pavement was created. As basilicas, temples, porticoes and votive monuments were gradually built, the forum became the commercial, judicial, religious and political heart of the city. Here, important public acts were performed, religious ceremonies took place and markets were held. Many commemorative statues and monuments were also placed here, which contributed to making the *Forum Romanum* a place for collective memory that remained unchanged for many centuries. Some of the most important buildings that were built on the two ends of the square include the *Regia*, the king's residence, and the first *Comitia*. Around 570 BC, a very important monumental complex was

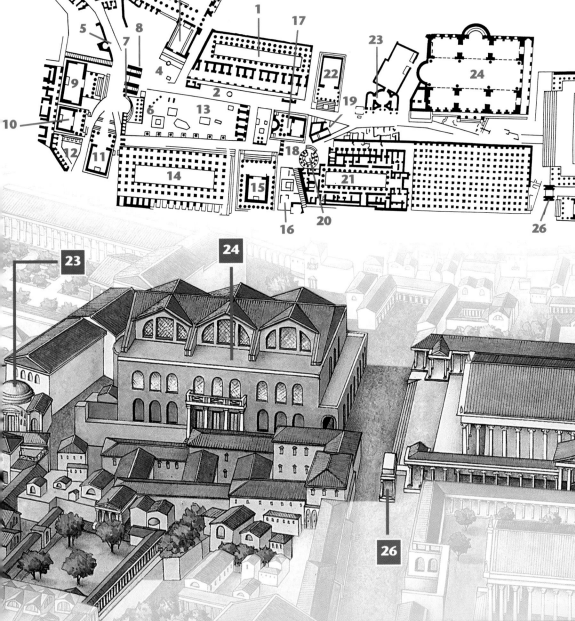

26 bottom General view of the Roman Forum from the east. For centuries, this was the pulsing heart of the city's economic and political activities, with the Arch of Titus in the foreground and the Capitoline Hill in the background.

27 bottom General view of the Roman Forum from the south. Below right, we can see the Curia Iulia, next to the Basilica Fulvia-Aemilia.

built, the so-called *Lapis Niger*, which tradition attributes to Numa Pompilius.

After the kings were driven from Rome (509 BC), new buildings were added in connection with the birth of new Republican institutions: the *Temple of Castor and Pollux*; the *Temple of Saturn*, with an avant-corps in which the Treasury was located; the speakers' platform, which became known as the Rostra after 338 BC, due to the prows (*rostra*) of the ships of Actium hanging here. Beginning in the 4th century BC, open space began to be occupied by so many columns and honorary statues that most of them had to be removed in the second century. The *Macellum* was built in the third century BC. It was a retail market located north of the Forum, and forums, the supremacy and importance of the Forum Romanum gradually diminished. The last construction of any importance dates back to the 4th century AD, when Maxentius again chose Rome as his capital and built the great *Basilica*, the seat of the city prefect, and the so-called *Temple of Romulus*. During the High Middle Ages, many buildings were transformed into churches and fortresses, and the land became pasture for livestock. In the late 18th century, the excavations that led to the current layout began.

INFORMATION FOR VISITORS. You can begin your visit after getting an overall view of the *Forum Romanum* from the *Tabularium* arcades or the street that runs

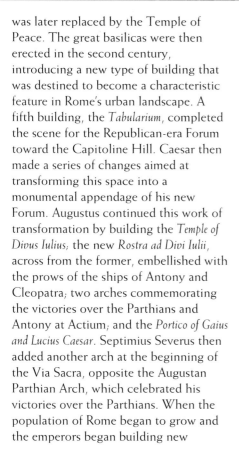

was later replaced by the Temple of Peace. The great basilicas were then erected in the second century, introducing a new type of building that was destined to become a characteristic feature in Rome's urban landscape. A fifth building, the *Tabularium*, completed the scene for the Republican-era Forum toward the Capitoline Hill. Caesar then made a series of changes aimed at transforming this space into a monumental appendage of his new Forum. Augustus continued this work of transformation by building the *Temple of Divus Iulius*; the new *Rostra ad Divi Iulii*, across from the former, embellished with the prows of the ships of Antony and Cleopatra; two arches commemorating the victories over the Parthians and Antony at Actium; and the *Portico of Gaius and Lucius Caesar*. Septimius Severus then added another arch at the beginning of the Via Sacra, opposite the Augustan Parthian Arch, which celebrated his victories over the Parthians. When the population of Rome began to grow and the emperors began building new down from the Capitolium. The buildings have been described here beginning from the entrance to the archaeological zone. If you prefer to follow a chronological route through the monuments, you should begin from the *Regia*, proceed to the Temple of Vesta, the Juturna Fountain, the Temple of Castor and Pollux, the Lapis Niger, the Curia and the Basilica Aemilia.

# THE WESTERN FORUM

## THE BASILICA AEMILIA

The Basilica Aemilia, the remains of which can still be seen on the north side before the Basilica Iulia, was built in 179 BC by Marcus Aemilius Lepidus and Marcus Fulvius Nobiliorus, on the site of an earlier building. It was restored many times by the Aemilii family, becoming a sort of celebratory monument. It is the only remaining example of a Republican basilica, as the others (the Sempronia, the

1. BASILICA FULVIA AEMILIA
2. CURIA IULIA
3. LAPIS NIGER
4. ARCH OF SEPTIMIUS SEVERUS
5. TEMPLE OF CONCORD
6. TEMPLE OF VESPASIAN AND TITUS
7. TEMPLE OF SATURN
8. PORTICUS DEORUM CONSENTIUM
9. SQUARE
10. BASILICA IULIA
11. TEMPLE OF CASTOR AND POLLUX
12. TEMPLE OF DIVUS IULIUS
13. AUGUSTAN ARCH

Porcia, and the Opimia) were demolished to make room for later buildings.

There were three entrances to the south from the square that led to the basilica. Although the structure now has three aisles and a nave due to a later remodeling, it originally had two aisles and a nave. The nave was raised, with large windows to illuminate the inside, and was decorated with relief work showing the mythical origin of the city and the family. During the Augustan era, the *Portico of Gaius and Lucius* was built opposite the Basilica. Its arcaded Doric façade was partially destroyed by a fire in the 5th century AD, but survived until the earthquake of 847. Anyone crossing the Forum probably would not have noticed the Basilica Aemilia, as it was hidden behind a tall building. Behind the façade were a group of shops: the *tabernae argentariae*, an imperial-age reconstruction of the Republican *tabernae novae*, used for money changers and bankers.

*29 bottom All that is visible today of the original Sacellum of Venus Cloacina are the remains of the circular marble foundation, which stood uncovered near the Cloaca Maxima. According to legend, the Sabines and Romans purified themselves here with branches of myrtle before continuing the battle for the abduction of the Sabine women. The altar must have been located inside, along with two statues of the deity in her two aspects: Cloacina – purifier – and guardian of the border (the* Velabrum, *which flowed past here, marked the border between the two warring peoples).*

## THE SACELLUM OF VENUS CLOACINA

In front of the Basilica Aemilia, there was a small, round, marble structure of which only the foundation remains, along with images stamped on coins. It was an ancient open air *sacellum* dedicated to Venus Cloacina, built at the same time as the *Cloaca Maxima*. It had an enclosure around an altar and two statues of the deity in her two aspects as Venus and Cloacina. The term comes from the Latin *cluere* (to clean) and is related to the purifying power of myrtle, which was sacred to the goddess.

Apart from historical memory (Pliny the Elder, *N.H., VII, 60*), which places it south of the Curia, little remains of the *Comitia*, which was the heart of the city's political and judicial action from the age of the kings to the late Republican era. It was the principal meeting place for people's assemblies, a place consecrated by the Augurs and delimited by a series of ritual wells. It was thus a *templum* that was rigidly laid out according to the cardinal points. The *Comitia* included a central square, whose oldest pavement

(eight layers of pavement have been found) dates back to the 7th century BC. The area was surrounded by stairs for citizens only in the third century.

The organization of this area of the Forum closely mirrored Rome's social and political structure. The *Comitia* was used by the *Comitia Curiata*, the people's assembly that represented ancient patricians; the *Curia Hostilia* was used by the Senate; and the *Rostra* tribune was used by the magistrates who expressed themselves here. The brick building that is now visible near the Arch of Septimius Severus is the *Curia Iulia*, an imperial-era reconstruction of an earlier Caesarian structure. In fact, the seat of the Senate was originally the *Curia Hostilia*, which according to legend was built by the king Tullus Hostilius in a different position, probably where the church of SS. Luke and Martina now stands. Caesar rebuilt it

in 53 BC following a fire, and aligned it to the new Forum he had also built. Through remodeling and reconstruction by Augustus, Domitian and Diocletian, as well as its 7th century transformation into the Church of St. Hadrian, it has survived to this day almost intact.

It had a rectangular plan with supporting pillars at the four corners, three large windows and a bronze entry gate, which was originally preceded by a columned portico. The interior had a floor with marble inlay. On the two longer sides, there were three steps on which the seats of the 300 senators were placed, while the magistrates had their seats in the back, on a podium, near a statue of Victory.

The interior now has two reliefs, the so-called *Plutei of Trajan*, which originally may have been used as the balustrades of a tribune or the enclosure around the *Fico Ruminale*. It depicts two scenes related to political events of the Trajan era: the establishment of agricultural loans and tax amnesty. Especially

interesting is the adherence to the topographical definition of the areas, which is typical of the Roman "narrative" technique, with the monuments of the Forum indicated in a simple manner with no spatial intent.

Despite the fact that most of the buildings have been moved or destroyed over time, some features have remained practically unchanged, such as an inviolable area known as the *Lapis Niger*, whose remains are still visible across from the Arch of the Severii. This is a rectangular area that was paved with black marble slabs to mark and delimit the area, when the square was repaved in travertine in the first century BC. Below it are the remains of a small temple. There is a small altar with panels in tufa, part of a column, the base of which is probably a religious statue, a cippus datable to the 6th century BC with an

*30 left In the Forum are the remains of an extremely significant archaic sanctuary (6th century BC), which was located below the Lapis Niger, the black stone that indicated the place where Romulus was killed. It is a memorial stone with a fragmentary boustrophedon inscription in archaic Latin, that has been interpreted as a sacred law, a sort of curse against anyone who dared to desecrate the place.*

boustrophedon inscription in archaic Latin, probably a *lex sacra*, including a curse aimed at anyone who dared violate the sacred area. The religious nature of the site is evident not only from the inscription, but also the fountains, which connect the place with the point where Romulus and Titus Tatius supposedly came to an agreement after the battle between the Romans and the Sabines, and the tomb of Romulus himself. Based on recent theories, it is the ancient *Temple of Volcanal*, Vulcan. In effect, the tradition (Plutarch, *Life of Romulus, 27, 6*) holds that Romulus, the city's founder, was killed right in the center of the forum, where his tomb/temple was erected based on the example of Greek cities.

A symbol of judicial power, the *Carcer Tullianus* (perhaps so named by Servius Tullius) was used for state prisoners. What remains today, visible under the

*30 center  The Curia Iulia was the place Caesar chose to hold Senate meetings during the Republican era. In the foreground, we can see the Decennial Base, depicting a procession of Senators among legionary banners. This is the base of an honorary column placed here to commemorate and celebrate the 10th anniversary of the Tetrarchy (303 AD).*

*30 top right  Sources place the Temple of Janus in the Roman Forum; there are no other traces of the edifice, which tradition attributes to Numa Pompilius, but a few descriptions and figures on coins, like that in the photograph, which we can use to reconstruct its appearance. It was a square, uncovered structure with two doors on opposite sides that were opened during times of war and closed only when peace returned.*

## THE ROSTRA AREA

The first *Rostra*, the platforms from which orators spoke, were built around the 4th century BC on some of the steps of the nearby *Comitia*. They took this name (*rostrum* means "prow") because they were adorned with the prows of the Volsci ships defeated in the battle of Actium. Following the radical changes he made in the Forum, Caesar built the *Rostra* in a different position, on the west side. It was a semicircular marble structure that could be accessed by a stairway, while Augustus added another square structure behind it. Several pillars supported a platform, probably in wood, which was the actual platform. They were known as the *Rostra Vetera* to distinguish them from the *Rostra Actiacae*, built by Augustus opposite the Temple of Divus Iulius.

Behind the imperial Rostra are the remains of other important monuments like the *Altar of Saturn*, from the archaic period, the *Miliarium Aureum*, which Augustus erected in 20 BC to indicate the ideal starting point for all Roman roads, and the *Mundus*, which was the underground portion of the so-called *Umbilicus Urbis*, the umbilicus or center of the city. The *Mundus* is in part connected to the hole Romulus dug when he founded Rome, to indicate its center, and in part to the tradition that it is a sort of open door to the underworld. According to the Roman calendar, this "door" had to be opened three times a year, a period that was considered especially dangerous.

church of San Giuseppe, is only a portion of the ancient edifice, probably the innermost, most hidden part. Other areas must have been dug out along the tufaceous slopes. The travertine façade, dating back to between 39 and 42 BC, hides an older one in tufa from the second half of the second century BC. The interior, accessible through a modern entrance, consists of two superimposed rooms. The upper one, with a trapezoidal plan and a barrel vault, has an opening in the floor that was once the only access to the room below. The latter, with a circular plan with a false blind cupola, was where those condemned to death by decapitation or strangulation were thrown.

Some of the illustrious people who experienced the triumph of victory before being locked in here were Vercingetorix, Jugurtha and the followers of Catilina.

*31 right  Ever since archaic times, an important monument stood behind the Rostra. Connected to the numerous ancient cults of the city, it was known as the Mundus, and was the underground portion of the Umbilicus Urbis. The brick remains visible here are from the Umbilicus Urbis itself, which was considered the center of the city and the door through which the world of the living came in contact with the underworld below.*

*30-31 and 31 left  Inside the Curia are the so-called Plutei of Trajan, two marble reliefs that must originally have been part of a tribune in the*

*Forum area. In the one on the left, we see a scene of the distribution of registers; the one on the right recalls Trajan's establishment of agricultural loans.*

*31 center  The Rostra, the large tribune from which orators spoke, was a large structure with a stairway leading up to a platform. Here were attached the Rostra –*

*the bronze prows of the ships of the Volsci from the battle of Actium. The remains are what Caesar built in the first century BC and the reconstruction by Augustus.*

## The Arch of Septimius Severus

The great Arch of Severus can still be seen near the *Rostra*, on the triumphal road that climbed up the Capitoline Hill. Built in 203 AD in honor of Septimius Severus and his sons Caracalla and Geta (the latter's name was eliminated after his murder, commissioned by his brother Caracalla). The road crosses the great central fornix, while the two side roads, preceded by steps, were used by pedestrians. The triumphal arch is covered in marble, with a core of bricks and travertine, and is decorated by reliefs on each face of the four columns that comprise it: The sculptures depict episodes in the emperor's campaigns against the Parthians. The left pillar has a door five meters up: From here, a stairway led to the attic, in which there were four rooms. Above that was an imposing *quadriga*, or chariot, with the emperor and his sons. From the artistic perspective, the arch has been compared to the Column of Marcus Aurelius, although the relief work here seems to be a sort of three-dimensional interpretation of triumphal paintings that use wartime episodes to portray the generals' successes.

*32 top  The Arch of Septimius Severus, of which we can observe the central fornix with the two winged victories on the sides, had a brick and travertine core covered in marble, with relief work on the sides facing both the Forum and the Capitol.*

*32 center  The Arch of Septimius Severus was built in 203 AD, to commemorate the emperor's victorious campaigns against the Parthians. The parades that marched from here to the Capitol for the final victory ceremonies passed below the central fornix.*

*32 bottom  On the sides of the fornices, the decoration includes a series of panels illustrating the enterprises of the two military campaigns against the Parthians, as well as figures of victories and river deities, while Roman soldiers with Parthian prisoners are depicted on the base of the columns. The most interesting sectors are nevertheless the four larger panels winding all around the monument, showing important episodes in the war.*

## The Temple of Concordia

The Temple of Concordia stood behind the Arch of Septimius Severus as early as the 4th century BC. It was built to celebrate the end of the battles between the patricians and the plebeians. After various restorations, it was reopened by Tiberius in 10 AD and transformed into a true museum, with Greek sculptures from the post-Lysippus period. The new building was larger, and thus took over some of the area previously occupied by a basilica (the

*33 top left* The Temple, built in the 4th century BC and known as the Temple of Concordia, in celebration of the end of the wars between the patricians and plebeians, was later transformed into a museum by Tiberius.

*33 bottom left* The Temple of Saturn is visible to the left, with the Temple of Vespasian and Titus on the right, and the Porticus Deorum Consentium in the background.

*33 top right* Several sacrificial instruments are visible on the architrave of the three Corinthian columns of the Temple of Vespasian and Titus: a knife, a helmet and a bucranium.

*33 bottom right* The Temple of Saturn, with the columns of the pronaos still standing, was the symbol of the Republican period, considered as a new Golden Age, like that when Saturn was ruling.

## THE TEMPLE OF VESPASIAN

A little farther south was another temple dedicated to Vespasian, who was deified by the Senate. The building was begun by Titus, but was completed by Domitian. It was a hexastyle prostyle temple with a large cella that held statues of the two emperors. The colonnade, a few elements of which still remain, was Corinthian, and had a frieze depicting a number of sacrificial instruments. The steps leading to it were located between the columns of the pronaos, a device designed especially to resolve the space problems in this area of the Forum, pressed up against the Capitoline Hill.

## THE CULT OF SATURN

The cult of Saturn is extremely ancient. The god was represented *velato capite* (i.e., with his head covered) holding a sickle in his hand and was also connected to the Greek Kronos. His feast was celebrated on December 17th (*Saturnalia*); on this occasion, the feet of the statue, normally tied with wool, were

unbound (Virg, *Aen.* 7, 179; *Mart.* 11.6.1), marking the day when slaves were allowed to do what they wanted, and when families and friends exchanged gifts (some have theorized that this may be connected to the Christian Christmas). He was the god of sown fields, the protector of treasures held within the earth and the personification of prosperity and well-being. It seems that this aspect was the reason the State Treasury was located in his temple in the Forum.

## THE TEMPLE OF SATURN

## THE PORTICUS DEORUM CONSENTIUM

*Basilica Opimia* - 121 BC). The cella, wider than it is long to utilize as much space near the Capitoline Hill as possible, was preceded by a hexastyle colonnade. Here, at the sides, there were statues of Hercules and Mercury, respective symbols of the security and prosperity of the Augustan regime. The vast cella was also used for Senate meetings. For example, Cicero made his fourth speech against Catilina here, and Sejanus was condemned to death here.

The façade with eight Ionic columns, still partly visible, belonged to the ancient Temple of Saturn: six gray granite columns at the front and two red ones on the long sides. The temple had probably already been built during the era of kings and was opened at the beginning of the Republic. It was completely rebuilt by Munantius Plancus, starting in 42 BC, with a large podium and avant-corps that was originally built to house the State Treasury (perhaps located in the cavities within the great *opus caementicium* podium).

Between the Temple of Vespasian and the Temple of Saturn, are the remains of a portico in the form of an obtuse angle, dotted with Corinthian columns (first century AD). An epigraph dates it to a building that was meant to hold 12 *Deorum Consentium* statues (counselor gods, the most important deities of the Roman pantheon), six gods and six goddesses (Varr. *De Agr.* I, 1, 4), which were probably displayed in groups of two. The six rooms in *opus latericium* behind the columns are part of a late-antique-era remodeling.

# THE FORUM SQUARE

The central area of the Forum contained a number of monuments that gradually began to crowd the square; the so-called *Column of Phocas* was the last monument to be added. Before it was a trapezoidal area with a shaft, the *Lacus Curtius*, commemorating a place enclosed by the consul C. Curtius in 445 BC after a lightning bolt struck here. A little further to the east was the *equestrian statue of Domitian*, about 12 meters high, placed here to commemorate the emperor's Germanic victories.

*34 top The great basilicas of the Forum must have been used for meetings as well as commercial and judicial activities. Some of these great structures were expressly built for the purpose of administering justice, like the Basilica Iulia. To carry out this activity, areas with exedrae were often used, separated by columns, which were found along the smaller heads.*

## THE BASILICA IULIA

*34-35 We know that the* munera, *or gladiator games, were held in the central area of the Forum during the entire Republican era. For example, we have information on games*

*offered by Caesar in 46 BC. Temporary structures were built around the square for spectators, as well as to support the* velarium, *which provided shelter from the sun's heat.*

In 54 BC, Caesar began construction on a large basilica between the *Vicus Iugarius* and the *Vicus Tuscus*, two of the ancient roads running from the Tiber (the work was completed by Augustus). It stood on the site of an older building, the *Basilica Sempronia*, built by Tiberius Sempronius in 169 BC, after he demolished the house of Scipio Africanus, which had

been located here (Livy, XLIV, 16). Recent excavations have revealed the remains of a private home deep below the levels of the two basilicas. The new basilica was bigger than the previous one, and even encroached on the *tabernae veteres* that had stood here. Nevertheless, it is impossible to get an idea of its size, as there is little left but the podium. It was a great hall

35 top  In the center of
the Forum is the tall
honorary column
dedicated to the emperor
Phocas by the exarch
of Italy in 608 AD.

This is a Corinthian
column that was
originally surmounted
by a gold statue. It is
important not so much
for its celebratory

function, but because it
was the last monument
to be built in the Forum.
Thereafter, the slow,
irreversible decline of
this place began.

surrounded by a double row of green
brick and travertine columns; the outer
row had two levels of arcades, while
the central hall rose up three floors.
Inside, in smaller rooms created by
wooden or cloth partitions, there were
various civil tribunals, including the
*Centumviri* tribunal, a special civil court
that dealt primarily with inheritance
problems. The idlers that usually

crowded the square sat on the stairs
outside; they passed the time playing
*tabulae lusoriae* (a game similar to
checkers), with boards scratched right
into the stairs, and drew sketches of the
statues they probably saw as they sat
on the stairs talking. Behind the
basilica, on the longer side, were
several *tabernae* near a *temple of Divus
Augustus*.

35 bottom  Various
civil tribunals were
located in the Basilica
Iulia, including the
Centumviri, which
primarily handled
problems related to

heredity. An assorted
group of Roman idlers
often sat on the steps
outside, passing the
time playing on
tabulae carved into
the stairs.

Three Corinthian columns still standing mark the position of the Temple of Castor and Pollux (or the *Dioscuri*). According to tradition, an earlier temple existed even in the 5th century BC, built by the dictator Postumius Albinus, to commemorate the victory over the Latins at Lake Regillus (499 BC). During the battle, the two demi-gods supposedly appeared in the form of horse soldiers, to lead Rome. What is certain is that the cult, which was connected to the class of mounted soldiers in the Greek areas from which it came, came to Lazio after the 6th century, and spread primarily through the patricians. Some remains of the terra-cotta decoration of this archaic period have been discovered during excavations. In the following centuries, it gradually became the symbol of Roman military success. We also know that the temple housed the office of weights and measures, while bankers' shops occupied the empty spaces carved into the podium. The remains visible today are from a peripteral temple with eight Corinthian columns on the short sides, and 11 on the long sides, attributable to a restoration from the first century BC.

Next to the temple are the remains of the ancient *Juturna Fountain*, where Romans drank until at least 312 BC, the date the first aqueduct was built. The fountain was monumental even in Republican times, with a basin and a group of statues in the center and a small temple nearby.

A little farther south, in the area occupied by *Santa Maria Antiqua* in the 6th century AD, remains have been found of a green brick hall preceded by a portico (from the Domitian period) and a roofless room leading to another one, surrounded by a four-sided portico. The complex may be the entrance to the *Domus Tiberiana* built by Caligula, although another theory holds that it could be the *Atheneum*, a building used for higher education. To the South, other structures have been excavated that have been identified as the *Horrea Agrippiana*, the grain warehouses built by Agrippa near the *Velabrum*.

When Julius Caesar was assassinated on the *Campus Martius* in 44 BC, there was a great public funeral. His body was brought to the *Forum Romanum* to be cremated before the *Regia*, which was probably Caesar's seat when he acted as *Pontifex Maximus*. In 29 BC, on the site of an already existing altar-column, Augustus built a temple dedicated to the deified dictator. Official games were also initiated in his honor. The Temple, of which the base of a column and little else is visible, stood at the east side of the square. The podium, in the front of which a semi-circle had been carved for a circular altar (perhaps where the body had been cremated) was reached by two side stairways. Six columns, probably Corinthian, preceded the cella, within

which there was a statue of Caesar crowned by a star. A star was also found on the outside pediment, a clear allusion to the comet that was said to have appeared during the first celebration of Caesar's games.

Before the podium were the *Rostra ad divi Iulii*, the tribune with the prows of ships in the fleet of Antony and Cleopatra captured in the battle of Actium.

*37 top* Lacus Iuturnae *and sacrificial altar. Near the* Temple of the Dioscuri *there was an ancient spring, perhaps with healing waters, consecrated to Juturna, the nymph who was the sister of Turnus. As early as the 2nd century BC, the place was already marked by a basin, which was rebuilt numerous times until it assumed its present appearance in the Trajan period. In the center, we can see a foundation that must have supported the marble group of statues of the Dioscuri; on the south side is the imprint of an altar, found within the spring, with a depiction of the divine twins on one side.*

*36 top The cult of the Dioscuri, the children of Zeus, had already become part of Roman mythology in the 6th century BC, after a temple in their honor had been built within* the Poemerium, *where, according to law, no foreign cults were accepted. Three of the original columns of the* Temple of the Dioscuri *are still standing.*

*36 bottom Across from the Temple of Antoninus and Faustina are the remains of the* Temple of Divus Iulius, *which Augustus dedicated in 29 BC to* the deified dictator. A semicircular area was found before the podium; enclosed by a wall, it contained a circular altar where the body of Caesar was probably cremated.

*36-37 Behind the spring, toward the south, is a shrine on a high podium, with two columns supporting a marble tympanum, that was the true center of the cult of the* nymph Juturna. The sacellum is from the 2nd century AD; before it was the mold of an altar decorated with two figures (perhaps Turnus and Juturna).

## THE ARCH OF ACTIUM

We know from the sources and a number of pictures that two arches were built south of the Temple of Divus Iulius. The traces of one of them are still visible and can be identified as the Arch of Actium, built in 29 BC by Augustus to celebrate his victory over Antony and Cleopatra at the battle of Actium (31 BC). It replaced an earlier triumphal arch built to commemorate the successful battle of Naulochus against Sextus Pompey in 36 BC (according to some historians, it was the *Parthian Arch*, built to commemorate the return of the Parthian standards taken from Crassus in the battle of Carrhae in 55 BC). This replacement was completely in line with Augustus' attempt to eliminate from the Forum any traces of previous civil wars. Several fragments make it possible to reconstruct its appearance and some of the decorations: It was an arch with three fornices with a long dedicatory inscription. Only the central passageway was vaulted, while the two side passages had flat ceilings and triangular tympanums. The inside may have contained the panels with the *Consular and Triumphal Fasti*, which are now on display at the Museo dei Conservatori.

# THE CENTRAL FORUM AREA

## THE REGIA AND HOUSE OF THE VESTALS

Behind the Temple of Divus Iulius is a group of ancient buildings that may be considered part of a single complex: the *Regia*, the *Temple* and the *House of the Vestals*.

The *Regia* is one of the most ancient edifices of which traces remain in the Forum. It was originally part of the great palatial complex of the kings, which legend states was built by Numa. It was a *templum*, a consecrated space, and during the Republican era was the seat of the *rex sacrorum* and *Pontifex Maximus* (offices that were inherited by the sovereign's religious officials). The *Pontifex* exercised his functions here, and here were kept the archives, the calendar, and the annals of the city. Despite the fact that it was rebuilt numerous times over the centuries (it was rebuilt and its position changed three times from the 7th century BC to the beginning of the Republican era alone), from the Republican era on, its structure remained the same. Its present form dates back to remodeling in 36 BC. It had one part to the south, divided into three rooms in which the temple of Mars and *Ops Consiva* were located. Sources say that the temple of Mars, with its large circular altar, also contained the sacred shield of the god, which supposedly fell from the sky along with 11 replicas, which made its theft impossible. The rooms opened onto a trapezoidal courtyard with a double portico.

The true dwelling of the *Pontifex*

*Maximus* was originally at the House of the Vestals. The complex consisted of the Temple of Vesta and the residence of the priestesses, which were closely connected.

The *Temple of Vesta* was the public hearth of the citizens, a symbol of the community's unity and a synthesis of all domestic hearths. Here were kept the public Penates of Rome, which according to tradition had arrived with Aeneas from Troy. The temple stood on a circular podium covered in marble, with a colonnade of Corinthian columns and a conical roof with a central

*38 top* The remains east of the Temple of Castor and Pollux are from the dwelling of the priestesses of Vesta. The house is arranged around a courtyard, with porticoes on four sides, in the center of which are various fountains. On the ground level are the remains of an oven, kitchen and mill; the lodgings of the Vestals must have been on the upper level.

*38 bottom* Near the Temple of Divus Caesar are the sparse remains of what may be the most important monument in the Forum, the Regia. Formerly the king's dwelling, during the Republican age it was used for functions connected to the Pontifex Maximus. Inside was a circular altar that was part of the ancient sacrarium of Mars.

opening. Inside, the sacred fire burned, constantly fed by the six Vestal Virgins. The still visible remains are from the last restoration of 191 AD, the work of Julia Domna, wife of Septimius Severus.

The *House of the Vestals*, originally modest in size, was rebuilt and expanded after the fire during Nero's reign in 64 AD, incorporating the public *Domus* of the *Pontifex Maximus* as well. Next to the central courtyard, with its porticoes and numerous statues, were a number of rooms on various floors. The ground floor had a *tablinum* and a *triclinium* to the east and west; to the south were the thermal baths, with a heating system that was also used to heat other rooms; on the upper floor were the actual dwellings of the priestesses; and on the third floor were rooms for servants.

*39 top left* The circular Temple of Vesta can still be seen behind the Regia. The sacred fire to the goddess burned inside, and had to be fed continually so that it would not burn out (not surprisingly, the building was destroyed by fire numerous times). Its present appearance is due to late 2nd-century AD remodeling by Julia Domna, the wife of Septimius Severus.

*39 top right and bottom* The statues of the head priestesses of the Vestals, found during excavations, stood in the courtyard of the House of the Vestals. The priestesses that headed the women's community are dressed in flowing mantles. Usually they wore the suffibulum, a long white veil, and the infula, a sort of crown consisting of six fillets of wool.

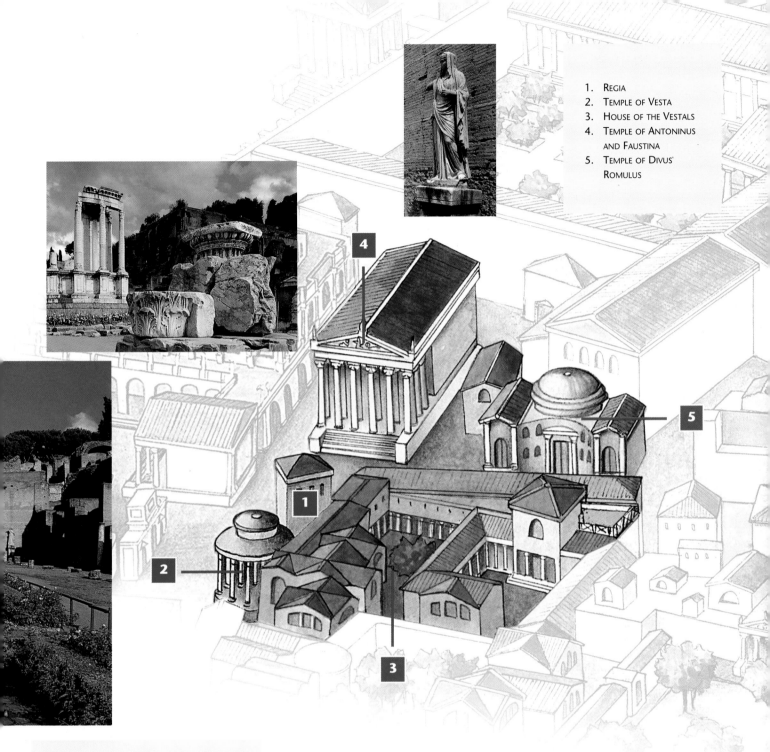

1. REGIA
2. TEMPLE OF VESTA
3. HOUSE OF THE VESTALS
4. TEMPLE OF ANTONINUS AND FAUSTINA
5. TEMPLE OF DIVUS ROMULUS

## THE VESTALS

Six priestesses (this was the only women's priesthood in Rome) were in charge of keeping alive the sacred fire of the temple of Vesta and safeguarding certain extremely important religious objects, such as the *Palladium*, an archaic simulacrum of Minerva, and the Penates of Troy. Only girls between six and 10 years old whose parents were free could enter this order. After taking a vow of chastity, the girls were required to perform their duties as Vestals for 30 years, after which time they were free to marry. This was a very strict obligation, as if they broke their vows,

they were condemned to be buried alive (as their blood could not be spilled) near Porta Collina, while the hapless lover could also be punished with death by flogging in the *Comitia*. Of course, this position gave them many privileges. The Vestals were in fact the only women who were not subject to *patria potestas*, and they could thus own property; outside the walls of their residence they were accompanied by a lictor and they could also drive chariots (which was otherwise permitted only to the empress); they also had reserved seats at shows.

## THE TEMPLE OF ANTONINUS AND FAUSTINA

North of the *Regia*, a large, very well-preserved temple can still be seen, as it was later transformed into the Church of San Lorenzo in Miranda. It was built by the emperor Antoninus Pius in 141 AD, and the inscription bears the still-legible dedication to his wife Faustina (the name of Antoninus was added later, after his death). The façade, preceded by a long stairway with an altar in the center, is adorned by six Corinthian columns and once also had statues at the ends; griffins and plant motifs are sculpted on the frieze. The

40-41 *The Temple of Antoninus and Faustina stood next to the Temple of Divus Caesar. The structure is in nearly perfect condition due to its transformation into the Church of San Lorenzo in Miranda between the 7th and 8th centuries.*

40 bottom *The façade of the Temple of Antoninus and Faustina is interrupted by six cipolin columns, with Corinthian capitals, that supported the architrave. On the shafts, we can still see furrows that have been interpreted as traces of ropes left during an attempt to carry away and reuse the columns.*

cella was covered with slabs of marble, although only the structure in peperino remains today; unfortunately, in fact, as was common practice in medieval times, most of the material was removed and used to build other structures.

## THE ROUND TEMPLE, KNOWN AS THE TEMPLE OF ROMULUS

Even today, access to the Temple of Romulus is still through a bronze gate that was originally framed by a marble cornice. It is above the street level revealed by 19th century excavations, which can be dated to the Augustan era, thus leaving the foundations of the edifice visible.

The structure that still stands before the House of the Vestals was long known to be a temple that Maxentius dedicated to his son Romulus. It is a circular green brick building with a cupola roof, preceded by a semicircular façade with four niches that originally held statues. The entry gate in bronze, preceded by two columns of porphyry, is original. To the right and left, cipolin columns frame two deep, symmetrical apses that lead to the central room

through two doors at the end of the long sides. One of the most accredited theories, strongly supported by the evidence, holds that the main structure is the *Temple of Jupiter Stator*. The ancient cult of this deity was supposedly restored by Constantine, after Maxentius had dedicated the monument to Romulus for a brief time. The statues of the Penates, which in the 4th century AD had been moved from their original position, were placed here in the two side rooms.

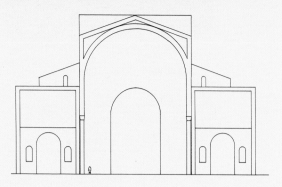

## THE BASILICA OF MAXENTIUS AND CONSTANTINE

In the early 4th century, Maxentius built a magnificent judicial basilica that held the prefecture, which from that time on became a single organ for the whole city administration. The structure replaced an earlier complex from the Flavian era, the *Horrea Piperataria*, which were warehouses for pepper, spices, herbs and medicines.

The building had a large central nave that ended in an apse to the west. It was covered by three immense cross vaults, supported by eight columns almost 15 meters in size. The two aisles were covered with barrel vaults and caisson ceilings. The first entrance was to the east and preceded by a horizontal vestibule, thus giving the monument an east-west orientation that was changed when it was completed by Constantine, who added a second entrance to the south onto the *Via Sacra*; here, a stairway led inside,

through a porticoed entry preceded by four Corinthian columns. Inside, on the opposite side, another apse was built, embellished by numerous statues; closed by a gate, it gave privacy to a new form of trial reserved for the senatorial class. The floor was embellished by geometrical designs made of different types of marbles. Slabs of marble covered the inside walls as well, making it appear truly magnificent and imposing. This image was also reinforced by the presence of the statue of the emperor Maxentius, which after his death was replaced with an enormous marble and bronze statue of Constantine located in the west apse. To get an idea of the size of the entire statue, look at what remains of it in the courtyard of the Palazzo dei Conservatori on the Capitoline Hill: the emperor's foot, which alone is 2 meters long, and his head.

42 top *This drawing of the interior of the Basilica of Maxentius clearly shows the high central nave with its barrel vault, and the two side aisles.*

42 center *Maxentius built a magnificent civil basilica, later remodeled by Constantine, on the site of the Temple of the Penates and the spice warehouses, the* Horrea Piperataria. *The basilica housed the Urban Prefecture. The north side aisle of the Basilica of Maxentius* still remains, and is in excellent condition. The great edifice was originally divided into a nave and two aisles, with the central nave higher, interrupted by gigantic columns in Proconnesio marble. These columns have all been lost, except for the one on Piazza Santa Maria Maggiore in Rome.

42 bottom *The Basilica of Maxentius has two entrances. The original entry was to the east, while the second one, built in the late 4th century, was to the south. The latter was much more monumental in appearance, preceded by an avant-corps with four porphyry columns.*

43 top left *A large apse on an axis with the southern entrance has survived, covered by a caisson vault. This area was originally fenced off to permit trials of Senate members to take place.*

43 top right *The interior of the Basilica had three crosses, supported by square brackets inserted* into the supporting walls that formed the roof of the central nave. The columns below the corbels were primarily decorative in nature. The side aisles had spans covered with barrel vaults, decorated with caissons.

43 center *The Basilica of Maxentius also had a* typical basilica structure, with the hall divided into a nave and two aisles by rows of columns with architraves. As the drawing shows, the central nave was higher than the aisles. This way, it was possible to illuminate the interior using claristoria, large openings in the upper walls.

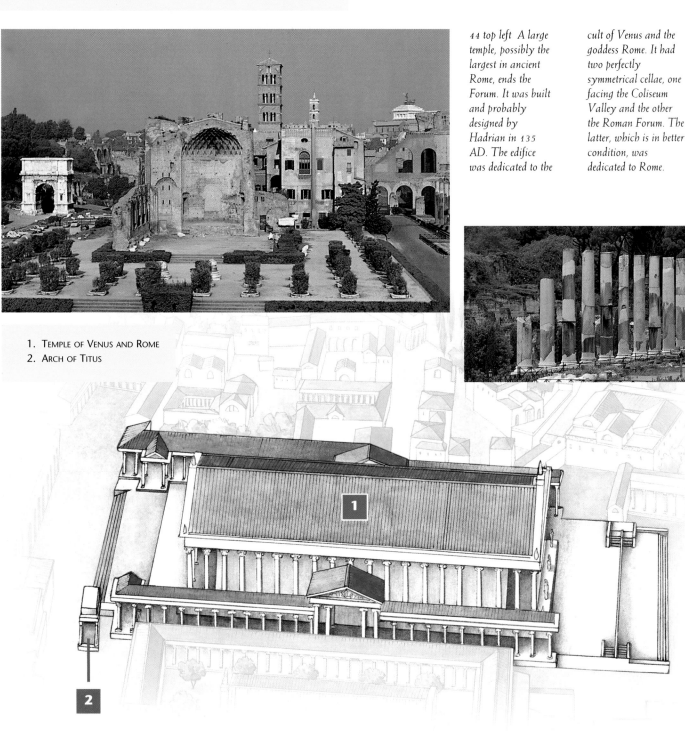

44 top left A large temple, possibly the largest in ancient Rome, ends the Forum. It was built and probably designed by Hadrian in 135 AD. The edifice was dedicated to the cult of Venus and the goddess Rome. It had two perfectly symmetrical cellae, one facing the Coliseum Valley and the other the Roman Forum. The latter, which is in better condition, was dedicated to Rome.

1. TEMPLE OF VENUS AND ROME
2. ARCH OF TITUS

The largest religious structure of ancient Rome was built at the back of the *Forum Romanum*, on the Velia. It was 100 by 145 meters in size, and to build it, Hadrian (in 135 AD), using his own design, had to construct a large artificial podium, where the atrium of Nero's *Domus Aurea* had once stood. The temple was dedicated to Venus and the personification of Rome, and its two opposite cellae had a perfectly

symmetrical structure, with adjacent back walls. The main entrance was to the west, facing the *Forum Romanum*. The cella dedicated to the goddess Rome was located on this side; it has survived in better condition. Two double colonnades, with a propylaeum in the center, delimited the sacred area to the north and south. The temple stood on a stylobate with Greek-style stairs

typical of the Hadrian period, on which was a row of columns that surrounded it completely. Following a fire, Maxentius modified the interior in 307 AD. Two apses were carved into the back of the cellae, in which the statues of the deities were placed. A barrel vault with stuccoed caissons was also built, while the side walls with porphyry columns framed niches for statues. The floor had geometrical designs of colored marble.

# THE ARCH OF TITUS

*44 top right Two double colonnades, with a propylaeum in the center, marked the sacred area north and south of the Temple of Venus and Rome. Above the stylobate on which the temple stood was a colonnade that completely surrounded it.*

*45 top The Arch of Titus, as the inscription on the portion of the attic facing the Coliseum notes, was built by the Senate in honor of the emperor after his death in 81 AD. The monument has a single fornix surmounted by a high attic with four engaged composite columns.*

The arch that stands on the col between the Velia and the Palatine is almost fully intact, in part because it was part of the fortified structures of the Frangipani family. The monument, with its single fornix in Pentelic marble, was built by Domitian in honor of his brother Titus, who was deified after his death in 81 AD. Four fluted semicolumns frame the outer sides of two pillars, which in turn support a tall attic on which the dedicatory inscription can still be seen. The keystones and archivolts depict the Genius of the Roman people, Rome and winged Victories. The arch commemorated the triumph of Vespasian and his son Titus over the Jews in 71 AD. The most noteworthy decoration is on the interior of the arch, with two episodes depicting the important moments of the Judaean triumph. The scene on the vault, showing Titus' apotheosis as he is carried to heaven by an eagle, utilizes a surprising perspective from below. These reliefs are part of the neo-Hellenistic trend and show a three-dimensional intent, introducing the spatial dimension of depth. Indeed, of the scenes portrayed, the depth perspective of the curve described by the movement of the procession toward the triumphal door (panel on the south pillar) is quite original. The spectator is almost drawn into it, participating firsthand in the scene, alongside people who are sometimes shown from the back. Although a certain classical effect persists, it truly seems as if the artist is trying to use a new concept of space.

*45 bottom A large portion of the relief work that adorned the Arch of Titus still survives, celebrating the emperor's victories over the Judaeans. Above the architrave we can see the victory ceremony celebrated in 71 AD. Inside the passageway are two panels depicting some highlights of the triumph. To the left (in the photo) is a group of people carrying the seven-branched candlestick and silver trumpets on their shoulders as spoils of war; on the right, a quadriga carries the triumphant Titus, preceded by the goddess Rome.*

# THE IMPERIAL FORUMS

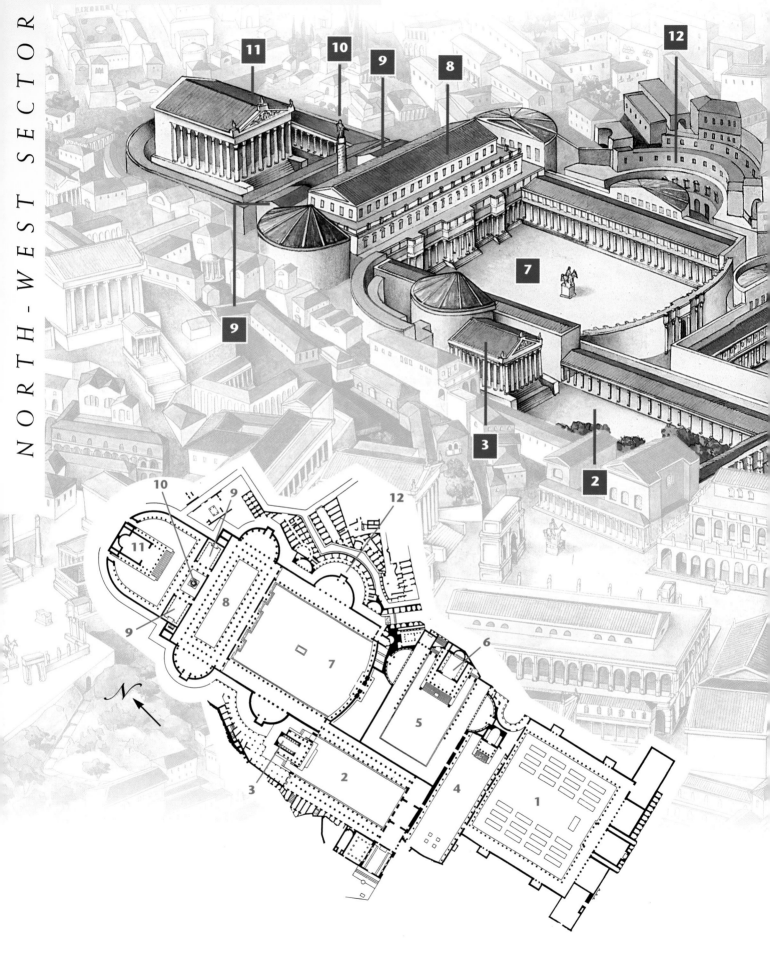

The present-day Via dei Fori Imperiali was built in the 1930s under fascism, with the goal of creating a broad avenue for military parades that would run from the Coliseum to Piazza Venezia. This work thus cut right through one of the richest and most important archaeological areas of Rome: the Imperial Forums, making them extremely difficult to understand for present-day visitors. Nevertheless, numerous excavations have made it possible to reconstruct the complex history of this large area used for forensic, judiciary and commercial activities. The structure of the Roman Forum had a particular significance precisely because it was connected to the political system of the Republic, and thus to a public life strongly influenced by the great discussions and "parliamentary" battles in the Senate and comitia. The new Forums, however, built in rapid succession between about 50 BC and 115 AD, to some extent represent the change that took place as power passed into the hands of the emperors and their collaborators. Political battles took on a different form from those of the past, and the Forum areas were also especially designed to exalt the figure and exploits of the emperor who had ordered them. Architects carefully planned structures to make them true manifestos of imperial ideology: a reflection of the emperor and his benevolence and an expression of his program. In addition to the judicial edifices, where numerous cases continued to be heard, new areas were also opened and used for teaching, culture, and commerce. Suffice it to consider the two large libraries in Trajan's Forum, one Greek and the other Latin, the honorary column, or the large Market complex.

*46-47 Hypothetical perspective reconstruction of the Forum area.*

1. TEMPLE OF PEACE
2. FORUM OF CAESAR
3. TEMPLE OF VENUS GENETRIX
4. FORUM OF NERVA OR FORUM TRANSITORIUM
5. FORUM OF AUGUSTUS
6. TEMPLE OF MARS ULTOR
7. TRAJAN'S FORUM
8. BASILICA ULPIA
9. LIBRARIES
10. TRAJAN'S COLUMN
11. TEMPLE OF DIVUS TRAJAN
12. TRAJAN MARKETS

## The Temple of Peace

Built by Vespasian between 71 and 75 AD, with the goal of commemorating his victory over the Jews, the Temple of Peace stood where the Republican-era *Macellum*, the great public market, had been located. The complex had a large open space completely surrounded by an arcade with four exedras (two to the northeast and two to the southwest). On the back side, opposite the monumental entrance, was the façade of the Temple

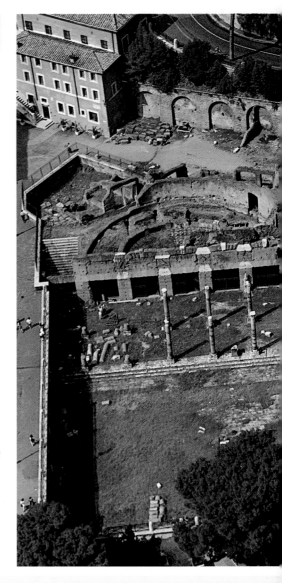

of Peace, which people approaching as they crossed the square could identify only by its larger columns and the presence of a pediment. It had a simple apsidal hall preceded by a colonnade. There were two halls on each side; the *Forma Urbis* was found in the first to the right, while the second one housed one of the two libraries in the complex. The candelabra with seven branches and silver trumpets brought from Jerusalem as spoils of war, depicted on the Arch of Titus in the *Forum Romanum*, must also have been kept here. Little remains of the actual Temple of Peace (the area only began to be called a Forum in the late imperial era). The best preserved sector is to the southeast, for reasons that include the fact that it was incorporated into the church of SS. Cosma and Damiano,

founded by Pope Felix in 527 AD.

Nevertheless, due to the discovery of the so-called *Forma Urbis*, one of the most precious testimonies to ancient urbanization, it has been possible to make a very faithful reconstruction of the complex. The *Forma Urbis* was a marble relief from the Severian era that showed the city of Rome at a scale of about 1:240. The original on which it must have been based dated back to the Augustan era, and was created by order of the emperor when the city was reorganized into 14 districts, or *regiones*. It occupied the entire south wall of the room next to the Temple of Peace (the holes used to support it can still be seen), while it is theorized that there was a large painted map of the country on the opposite wall. It is believed that this place was originally used for the *Paefectura Urbis*, which would explain the presence of the maps, which would have been used for cadastral purposes as well. After being damaged numerous times, the complex was abandoned by the 5th century AD.

## Caesar's Forum

Caesar was the first to understand that the growing city of Rome needed another space in addition to the *Forum Romanum*. He designed a large complex, aligning it with the new Curia that he himself had built facing a different direction. The Forum was destined to become a new political center in which the figure of the dictator acquired a decisively central role. His own equestrian statue was located in the center of the square, part of a sort of "sacred axis" that ended right at the temple dedicated to *Venus Genetrix*, mother of Aeneas and mythical progenitor of the Julia offspring. The message was thus clear: In Rome, a new individual power now existed alongside the traditional power of the Senate. The long open space (150 x 75 meters) was delimited by a double colonnaded portico, which was reached directly by the *Argiletum* to the southeast. Access to

the Forum is midway up Clivo Argentario, a path that flanks the southwest side. To the left of the entrance, a vast semicircular hall is visible, above the Forum level and its *tabernae*: This was a latrine from the Trajan period, equipped with a double floor, for the heating system, and a counter that runs along the entire curved wall. Inside the Forum, on the southwest side, there was a group of *tabernae* in tufa and travertine, with two levels, possibly where the goldsmiths had their workshops. At the back of the arcade, excavations have revealed a green brick structure with two rows of columns, identified as the *Basilica Argentaria* built by Trajan and restored by Constantine. The discovery of a series of graffiti (some with verses from the Aeneid), still visible inside and protected by transparent sheets, shows that this structure was the school that sources mention.

*49 bottom  The few visible remains of the Forum of Caesar include several columns from the Temple of Venus Genetrix, the mother of Aeneas and mythical progenitor of the Iulia offspring, a portion of the portico that surrounded the central square, and the square's pavement.*

*49 right  The area originally occupied by the Forum of Caesar was rather elongated, 160 x 75 meters in size. The central square was surrounded by a double colonnaded, covered arcade on one side, while the short side to the west ended with the Temple of Venus Genetrix.*

*48  One of the most precious testimonies to the history of the city of Rome is the Forma Urbis, found in a hall of the Temple of Peace. Unfortunately, only a few fragments remain of this great marble map from the Severian era. The entire city of Rome is carved on it on a scale of 1:240, probably as of the Augustan era.*

*48-49  Caesar was the first to understand the needs of a city that continued to grow, including economically. Thus, in 46 BC, he built a new area in the Roman Forum, arranged around a central square, with his large equestrian statue in the center and the temple dedicated to Venus Genetrix in back, to the west.*

## THE TEMPLE OF VENUS GENETRIX

The night before the battle of Pharsalia against Pompey, Caesar vowed to build a temple in honor of Venus. After the victory, the temple, a *peripteros sine postico* in Italic tradition with eight columns in front and nine to the side, was built and dedicated in 46 AD. It was located in the back of the Forum in an extremely scenic position, and was based on Hellenistic models for temples dedicated to deified sovereigns. It stood on a high podium that was originally covered in marble, with access from two small side stairways. Steps then led to the colonnade and from there to the cella. Inside, there were two rows of antique yellow columns along the sides, while in back there was an apse, in which there was a statue of Venus, done by the famous Arcesilaus. The cella was also decorated with a frieze sculpted with figures of Eroti playing with the spoils of war (some fragments are preserved at the Palazzo dei Conservatori). Numerous works of art from various areas are on display here, including a statue of Cleopatra, paintings by Timomacus, gems and other objects.

Suetonius (*Life of Caesar*, 78) recounts that one day the dictator actually received the Senate while seated in the center of the podium of his temple. This seemingly unimportant episode is actually clear evidence of how Caesar contributed to creating a deified image of himself.

Imperiali. Behind it was a large horseshoe-shaped exedra, a porticus absidata facing the Subura district.

LATEST INFORMATION: Recent excavations (1996) in the Argileto area behind the Curia have revealed that even before the construction of the monumental Forum of Nerva, starting in the mid-first century AD, the road already had a colonnade, which the Forum colonnade replaced.

*50 top left  The two Corinthian columns that were part of the Temple of Minerva, visible from the street, have always been part of the urban landscape, and have been baptized the "colonnacce." Only the shafts remain, along with the architrave and attic*

*with sculpted decoration and part of the back wall, toward Via Cavour.*

*50 right top  On the portion of surviving frieze above the "colonnacce," are scenes of women at work. Minerva was the patron goddess of handicrafts.*

Two Corinthian columns, the so-called *"colonnacce,"* still connected to the back wall and complete with an attic with a relief work depicting Minerva, mark the position of the ancient Forum of Nerva. The forum, also known as the *Forum Transitorium*, indicating its function as a passageway between the Forum of Peace and the Forum of Augustus, was built by Domitian and completed by Nerva in 97 AD. It replaced the first stretch of the *Argiletum*, the road which in the Republican era led from the forums to the working class district of *Subura*. It had a rather elongated form, dominated, as were the earlier forums of Caesar and Augustus, by the presence of a temple dedicated to Minerva at the back. The forum was surrounded by a colonnade located a short way from the enclosure wall (in fact, a true arcade would not have been possible due to the limited space). Only vestiges remain of the original nucleus of the Temple of Minerva, a guardian deity of handicrafts particularly dear to Domitian. The *Cloaca Maxima* passed below it, and the rest of it still lies below the present-day Via dei Fori

*50 right center  The Imperial Forums were built in rapid succession between about 50 BC and 115 AD. Although they were not planned together and do not have a single design,*

*they nevertheless were built organically. Today, only a portion of them can be visited, as for the most part they are hidden by the present-day Via dei Fori Imperiali.*

*50 bottom  The figure of Minerva, a deity to whom the Temple on Nerva's Forum is dedicated, is sculpted on the attic of the columns.*

## THE FORUM OF AUGUSTUS

Augustus had decided to build a forum as early as 42 BC, following a vow he had made before the battle of Philippi against Brutus and Cassius, who murdered Caesar. Still, the work was not completed until 2 BC. Private parties purchased the land, while war booty was used to build it. The area he was able to utilize and expropriate from the landowners was not large. Built a little later than the Forum of

podium of the Temple dedicated to *Mars Ultor*, or the avenger. To the right and left of the temple were two large exedrae, inserted into the two-story arcade that surrounded the square on two sides. Niches carved into the two cipolin semicolumns held marble statues of historical and mythological persons: Aeneas with Anchises and Ascanius and the ancestors of the *gens Iulia* on one side, and Romulus with the *Summi Viri*, the great personages of the Republic, on the other.

Outside on the upper portion of the arcade were statues of caryatids (copies of those in the Erectheum of Athens), symbols of conquered nations, alternating with heads of

Jupiter Ammon. In the center of the space was the great statue of Augustus on his triumphal chariot. There was also an imposing statue of the emperor in the square room in back of the north portico. Here there were also two famous paintings by the painter Apelles, portraying Alexander the Great.

Nothing was left to chance in the iconography and organization of space. An expression of Augustan compromise, even the position of the statues revealed an effort to link Republican history with the history of the Julia family; within this framework, the empire fit perfectly as the supreme culmination of the Republic.

## THE TEMPLE OF MARS ULTOR

To indicate a certain political continuity, the Temple of Mars occupied the same position as the Temple of Venus in the Forum of Caesar. A large central stairway with an altar in the center led to the podium. The cella was entered through a row of columns (eight in the front and a double row of eight on the sides). The interior had columns on two levels against the walls; there were niches between them for statues. In the back, in the apse, were the two religious statues of Mars and the goddess Venus. The famous Parthian Standards that Augustus took back

Caesar, it was meant to create a new space for trials and commercial affairs, but primarily exalted the figure of the emperor. The organization of space and the forum's decoration should be interpreted in this way, as a true political message, designed to transmit the image of Augustus as a conqueror and peacemaker who was respectful of *mos maiorum*, or ancient tradition.

A 33-meter-high wall of peperino and *lapis gabinus* completely surrounded the area, isolating it from the Subura district. Two flights of steps led down from this district and the forum area below and led to the two entrances to the Forum of Augustus, next to the

*51 left Augustus began building his forum after 42 BC and the battle of Philippi against Brutus and Cassius, Caesar's murderers, but it was not completed until 2 BC. It has a central square surrounded by a high wall of peperino and lapis gabinus; the Temple of Mars Ultor was at the back, and to the right and left were two large exedrae in the two-story arcade.*

*51 right The Temple of Mars continued the tradition Caesar had begun with his Forum, as Augustus set himself to carry out the dictator's policies. The Temple dominated the Forum with its long stairway leading to the podium and the cella.*

from the Parthians may also have been located here.

While the continuity of Roman tradition is evident, there is also a clear inspiration from the classical Greek world. We know that the Senate met here a number of times to make important decisions, such as whether to declare war or sanction a peace accord.

# TRAJAN'S FORUM

Built between 107 (the year the Dacian wars ended in victory) and 113 AD, the great Forum of Trajan was the last of the great squares of the imperial epoch, designed to expand the civic and political center of the city of Rome. Over the centuries, the forum elicited the admiration of visitors due to its imposing size and the masterful compositional equilibrium, especially designed to become a homogenous complex by the famous imperial architect, Apollodorus of Damascus. He accomplished the great work of cutting the col that joined the Capitoline Hill to the Quirinal, without which there would have been no room to build it, given the density of buildings in that area. Even today, Trajan's Column is an extraordinary testimony to the original height of the col.

Overall, the complex was built using slightly raised terraces on which the monuments were placed. The square, about 300 meters long, was accessible from the Forum of Augustus through an arch with one fornix surmounted by an attic and flanked by walls dotted with semicolumns. On the two long sides was a colonnaded portico preceded by two flights of steps and embellished with statues of various personalities. On the high attic, sculptures of Dacian prisoners alternated with shields with heads. Behind the portico, one before the other, were two large semicircular exedrae, while in the center the equestrian statue of the emperor dominated the area. To the back, the view was blocked by the imposing façade of the *Basilica Ulpia*. Trajan clearly used the Forum of Augustus as

a model, thus presenting himself as continuing Augustus' political enterprises. The *Basilica Ulpia*, however, was somewhat of an innovation over previous models. The scheme used closely followed the emperor's militaristic policy: This included the arrangement of the buildings, which resembled the structure of military camps, with a square in the center (the forum's open area); a basilica (the *Basilica Ulpia*) next to the sanctuary of the legionary standards (Trajan's Column); and a place for the military archives (the two libraries). We know from various sources that the Forum served multiple functions. Laws were promulgated here, emperors bestowed so-called *congiaria*, monetary donations to the populace, and schools and reading areas were located here.

**6**

**1**

1. TRAJAN'S FORUM
2. BASILICA ULPIA
3. LIBRARIES
4. TRAJAN'S COLUMN
5. TEMPLE OF DIVUS TRAJAN
6. TRAJAN MARKETS

*52-53 With its magnificence and originality, Trajan's Forum stands out in the general plan for the Imperial Forums. It has a large porticoed square, with markets held on the semicircular terraces, the Basilica Ulpia, two libraries, the column and the large Temple.*

*53 Trajan's Forum was built at the end of the victorious Dacian wars. It was the last and most well-organized square of the imperial era. The famous architect Apollodorus of Damascus designed it, and even cut the col that joined the Capitol to the Quirinal, leaving Trajan's Column as a reminder of the hill's original height.*

# TRAJAN'S COLUMN

"Senatus populusque Romanus
Imp(eratori) Caesari divi Nervae f(ilio) Nervae
Traiano Aug(usto) Germ(anico) Dacico Pontif(ici)
Maximo trib(unicia) pot(estate) XVII, Imp(erator)
VI co(n)s(ul) VI p(ater) p(atriae)
ad declarandum quantae altitudinis mons et locus
tantis operibus sit egestus."

In 113 AD, Trajan's Column, nearly 40 meters high, was built between the two halls. It had a high foundation with 18 large tympana covered in Carrara marble, a Doric capital, and the statue of Trajan at the top. Between the plinth and the cornice, the base was decorated with relief work depicting Dacian weapons and, on the corners, eagles bearing festoons. Inside was the golden urn with the ashes of the emperor.

The column, within which was carved out a narrow spiral staircase that rose to the "terrace," was completely decorated with a frieze that spiraled up for about 2 meters. Through various scenes, the relief work recounted the Dacian wars from which Trajan emerged as victor. It was both a celebratory and documentary work that originally could be admired from close up as well, from the terraces of adjoining buildings. But even in ancient times, it was impossible to follow the story completely (like a true monumental *volumen*, located between the two libraries), and it took on an almost absolute, symbolic value independent from any hypothetical spectator. The author, probably just one person, given the work's unitary concept, who is known as the "Master of Trajan's enterprises," admirably combined Roman narrative tradition (which was characterized by narrative continuity with the insertion of exemplary scenes) with elements from Hellenistic tradition (such as the depiction of the landscape and the superimposition of various levels). In 500, Sixtus V replaced the statue of Trajan, which had looked down from the top of the column, with the present-day statue of St. Peter.

In 121 AD, after the Forum was completed, Hadrian built a temple dedicated to the deified emperor and

his wife Plotina. Probably even the original plan had provided for construction of the temple, but it was never completed due to Trajan's death. Nothing remains of it but a few fragments which nevertheless give us a glimpse of the magnificence of this structure as well, with its columns 20 meters high.

*54 top The emperor Trajan built a tall decorated column between the two libraries, to commemorate the wars against the Dacians. The column also served as a funerary monument, as the emperor's remains were to be buried in a golden urn at the base.*

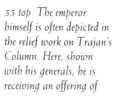

55 top The emperor himself is often depicted in the relief work on Trajan's Column. Here, shown with his generals, he is receiving an offering of two heads of Dacian leaders. Some openings illuminate the interior of the shaft, where there was a spiral staircase cut into the marble that ascended to the top of the monument, where a statue of the emperor Trajan originally stood. In the 16th cent. it was replaced with a statue of St. Peter.

54 bottom Some of the numerous details we can observe in Trajan's Column, a constant, inexhaustible source of information of every type for experts on the history and customs of ancient Rome, include reliefs depicting Roman and barbarian weapons and armor.

54-55 The long frieze on Trajan's Column tells of events in the two Dacian wars, using exemplary, recurring episodes such as marches, the construction of encampments, battles, and sieges. The relief seen here shows a crossing of the Danube on a bridge of boats.

55 right center Trajan's Column is completely decorated with a long, spiral frieze that describes in detail the various phases of the Dacian war. Probably not even in ancient times was it possible to view the relief in its entirety, although it was possible to approach it more closely by ascending the terraces of the two libraries or the Basilica Ulpia.

55 bottom Trajan's Column stood on a high plinth with the exterior decorated by a very low bas-relief depicting piles of weapons. Two small rooms were found inside. The urn with the emperor's ashes must have been placed on a marble bar in the one to the north.

## THE TRAJAN MARKETS

East of the Forum, Apollodorus built a series of green brick structures on various levels of terraces, the so-called Trajan Markets. They served a purely functional purpose as warehouses for foodstuffs and as a retail sales area. The complex, which was built just before the actual Forum, also had the purposes of concealing as well as supporting the cutting of the Quirinal.

To make the best use of available area and at the same time create a certain uniformity, a single monumental façade was built, consisting of a large,

there were other *tabernae* facing the ancient *via Biberatica* (the name may come from the fact that *thermopolia* were found here). Beyond the road was an important rectangular room, with a six cross vault supported by travertine piers lined with shops on each of the long sides. On the upper floor there was also a series of *tabernae* opening along a long corridor. It was probably a large warehouse for foodstuffs and may have been connected to rooms to the south that could house the management of the entire Market complex.

semicircular exedra, preceded by a colonnade that separated it from the portico on the opposite square. On the sides, two smaller exedrae, covered with a half cupola and illuminated by large windows on two floors (eight to the left and three to the right) may have been auditoriums or lecture halls. Beyond the exedra were 11 vaulted *tabernae* that rested directly on the wall of the hill. There are traces of graffiti in some of them. Above the area on the ground floor was a corridor illuminated by a series of windows, also vaulted, over which there were another ten *tabernae*. To the north was another exedra, located above the one on the left on the lower floor. Finally, on the third floor,

56 top  Unlike other squares, Trajan gave his forum a large mercantile area, arranged on a series of terraces. The complex looked out over the square through a monumental façade consisting of a large brick exedra, in the bottom of which were eleven tabernae. Above, a series of windows illuminated a vaulted corridor.

56 bottom  On the third level of the semicircular Trajan Markets, was a terrace with a series of tabernae opening onto a street known as the Via Biberatica, perhaps because this was the area of thermopolia, or bars.

57 top right  We can still visit the inner corridors of the great Trajan Markets, which the various shops generally faced.

57 bottom right  Two semicircular halls covered with a half dome stood on the sides of the great exedra overlooking the Forum. The northern hall (in the photo) has a façade with five large windows. The areas were probably used as halls of higher education or auditoriums.

56-57  The Trajan Markets were boldly arranged in a semicircle on various terraces, created by cutting the Quirinal hill, and housed about 200 shops. Halfway up, the Via Biberatica served distribution needs within the complex, acting as a true service road.

# THE CAMPUS MARTIUS

The *Campus Martius* originally included a rather large area between the Capitoline Hill, the Tiber, the Quirinal and the Pincian. It was laid out precisely under Augustan organization, when it was given the name of *Regio IX* (*Circus Flaminius*), as distinguished from *Regio VII* (*via Lata*), with which it was originally connected. Over the course of the centuries, it was inhabited without interruption, and even today it is possible to identify the ancient

a vast open area, marshy in some places, used for military exercises (hence the name Mars, the god of war) and horse and chariot races. It was also the *Diribitorium* and *Saepta*, where male citizens gathered to vote in their "century comitia" (the "centuries" to which they belonged) and later also in "tribute comitia."

One of the oldest edifices of which traces still remain is the *Terentum* or *Tarentum*, located at the far west side at the height of the present-

tribe and military duty), known as the *Relief of the Altar of Domitian Enobarbus*, now at the Louvre and the Gliptoteca in Monaco. The temple of Mars was a homogenous complex with a series of buildings, located near today's Piazza Venezia and Via del Corso. It included the *Villa Publica*, where the five-year censuses of the Roman people and citizen enlistment took place, and the *Saepta*, a large rectangular square over 300 meters long, where the *comitia* met.

Beginning in the second century BC,

structure of a road, a square or an entire quarter. Suffice it to note how Piazza Navona is almost an exact imprint of the ancient *Stadium of Domitian*, or how the Piazza di Grotta Pinta resembles the form of the *Theater of Pompey*.

It is possible to reconstruct at least some of the original *Campus Martius*, at least from the time when, according to tradition, it belonged to the Tarquinians as the *Campagna di Roma*, until it became a public area after the kings were driven out.

The *Campus Martius* was originally

day Vittorio Emanuele Bridge. It was probably a sort of solfatara, a place where sulfur emerged through cracks in the earth. For this reason, it was considered an entry to the underworld and was connected to a sanctuary dedicated to Dis and Prosperpina. Nearby was also the *Trigarium*, an area used for horse races (the *triga* was an archaic chariot drawn by three horses). In the central area, there was an important temple dedicated to *Mars*. This area has revealed the famous reliefs recounting a census (assigning a citizen a class,

1. THEATER OF MARCELLUS
2. PORTICUS OCTAVIA
3. THEATER OF BALBUS
4. LARGO ARGENTINA SACRED AREA
5. THEATER OF POMPEY
6. AGRIPPA'S BATHS
7. PANTHEON
8. SAEPTA
9. THEATER OF HADRIAN
10. NERO'S BATHS
11. STADIUM OF DOMITIAN
12. COLUMN OF ANTONINUS PIUS
13. COLUMN OF MARCUS AURELIUS
14. HOROLOGIUM
15. ARA PACIS
16. MAUSOLEUM OF AUGUSTUS

a series of construction works heightened the monumental appearance of the *Campus Martius*. A number of mostly state buildings were constructed over a short time. Architects, sculptors and Greek painters competed to embellish the area with their works. They built the *Porticus Octaviae, Porticus Metello,* and *Porticus Pompeo,* and the *temples of Juno Regina, Diana, Hercules* and the *Muses.* Caesar began construction on a large number of monuments, including the future *Theater of Marcellus* (he even wanted to divert the course of the Tiber to make a larger area). During the Augustan period, steps taken by

Agrippa continued this work of urbanization, concentrating on the central area, with new buildings harmoniously added to already-existing structures, many of which were restored. The *Theater of Marcellus* was completed, and construction was completed on the *Agrippa Baths,* the *Pantheon,* and the new *Saepta Iulia* and *Ara Pacis.* Augustus also built his *Mausoleum* here, continuing the tradition whereby victorious generals could request to be buried in this area. To supply the thermal baths, the *Aqua Virgo* was built, and water and aqueduct administration was also reorganized (*Porticus Minucia*). Following the great

fire of 80 AD during Nero's time, more monuments were built on the *Campus Martius,* including the *Stadium* and the *Odeon of Domitian,* as well as the *Porticus Minucia Frumentaria.* The Antonines completed this intensive work of urbanization in the northern sector (beyond the present-day vie Coronari, S. Agostino, and delle Coppelle), where they built the columns of Antoninus Pius and Marcus Aurelius, and the temples of Matidia and Hadrian. The monuments that were erected here had a different orientation, as they followed the course of the *via Flaminia.*

59 *The* Porticus Octaviae, *named after Augustus' sister, was one of the monuments that delimited the* Circus Flaminius. *Built by the emperor in the mid-first century BC, it had* *a vast rectangular area delimited by a double colonnaded arcade and a monumental entrance in the form of a propylaeum, of which some traces remain from a Severian-era restoration.*

# THE SOUTHERN CAMPUS MARTIUS

## PORTICUS OCTAVIAE

The area east of the *Circus Flaminius* was originally delimited by a number of porticoes, such as that of Octavian, Philippus and Octavia. The only traces that remain are those of the latter, however, which are visible as you go along the Via del Portico d'Ottavia. The edifice was built by Augustus between 33 and 23 BC and replaced the earlier *Portico of Metellus,* opened by the censor Caecelius Metellus Macedonicus around 131 AD. The new portico, dedicated to Octavia, the emperor's sister, had a rectangular area surrounded by a double colonnade supported by a low podium. The main entrance was on the short side, facing the Tiber. It looked like a great protruding propylaeum, with two identical faces with four fluted Corinthian columns placed between antae, surmounted by a high architrave and joined by two arches in green brick. On the back side there was a structure with an apse, the

A. MAIN ENTRANCE
B. TEMPLE OF JUNO REGINA
C. TEMPLE OF JUPITER STATOR

*Curia Octaviae,* and a *library.*

Within the enclosed area were the *temples of Juno Regina* (the only temple with any visible remains, on Via di Sant'Angelo di Pescheria) and *Jupiter Stator.* The latter, a *peripteros sine postico,* was the first temple in Rome to be built entirely of marble; it was the work of the famous Greek architect Hermodorus of Salamis. The *Temple of Juno Regina* stood farther to the west and was a hexastyle prostyle edifice, although originally it was probably peripteral in the Greek style, similar to the other (Vitr. *De arch.* III, 2, 5). We know that the portico was embellished by numerous works of art, many of which were spoils of war from the Greek world. For example, this is the case of the 34 bronze statues by Lysippus, depicting Alexander and his officials.

The remains that have survived to this day are from a Severian period restoration.

60 top The Theater of Marcellus, named for Augustus' nephew and heir who died prematurely, was opened in 13 BC, and is one of the best-preserved theaters in Rome, especially the exterior of the cavea. It was first encompassed by a fortress in the 13th century, then, in the 16th century, by Palazzo Savelli (later Orsini and Caetani).

Begun by Caesar, the theater was opened by Augustus in 13 BC and dedicated to his nephew Marcellus, the emperor's designated successor, who died prematurely. Different techniques and materials were used for the various parts of the monument: travertine for the cavea, *opus quadratum* in tufa for the radial walls and ambulatories, *opus caementicium* for the interior parts, and *opus reticulatum* for the faces.

On the outside, the cavea was originally over 30 meters high and consisted of 41 arches framed by pillars, on three levels with three different architectural styles: Doric on the first level, Ionic on the second and Corinthian on the attic, which terminated the theater at the top and unfortunately has not survived. The architectural orders served a primarily aesthetic purpose, as the arches provided the primary support. Marble theater masks were placed among the fornices. Little has remained of the interior: We know that the scene had a deep exedra in which there were two small altars, perhaps replacing two temples (Diana and *Pietas*) that were torn down to make room for the theater. There were two apses on the sides.

It has been estimated that this important performance hall, one of the three permanent theaters of ancient

60-61 As can be seen from the design, there were originally three architectural orders in the outer face of the cavea: Doric, Ionic and probably Corinthian. From the bleachers, accessible through a system of stairs visible in the cross section, one could originally see not only the orchestra, but also the magnificent stage, of which nothing now remains.

Rome, could hold up to 20,000 people. Inside, spectators were separated according to a strict hierarchy imposed by Augustus. The farthest section, above, was reserved for women, foreigners and slaves, while the part nearest the scene was for Roman citizens. The cavea was thus a true cross-section of Roman society.

What we can now see of the Theater of Marcellus from the street is only a part of the original outer façade, which was first transformed into an urban fortress in the 13th century, and then into a palace by Baldassarre Peruzzi, in the 16th century.

Two temples stood near the site of the Theater of Marcellus even before it was built. The one to the west, the *Temple of Apollo Sosianus*, was the older one. It was built around 431 BC, probably by the Tarquinians, perhaps on the site of an earlier altar dedicated to *Apollo Alexikakos* ("who keeps away evil"). We know that it was dedicated to *Apollo Medicus* in concomitance with the outbreak of a plague. The temple was, however, completely rebuilt by C. Sosius (hence the name), one of Caesar's lieutenants, in 34 BC and moved farther north, near the *Porticus Octaviae*, due to construction work on the theater. This is when a number of modifications were made, such as the use of side stairways

instead of the central flight of steps leading to the podium. The columns of the pseudoperipteral temple (six in the front and three on the sides) were Corinthian and had alternately wide and narrow fluting. Inside, seven semicolumns stood against the walls; according to a frequent custom in the Republican era, to save on marble, they were made of stuccoed travertine. In the cella were numerous works of art by well-known Greek artists, such as an Apollo with lyre, an Artemis, a Latona and nine Muses. On the pediment were 5th century BC sculptures from a Greek temple, depicting an Amazon attack against Hercules and Theseus in the presence of Athena.

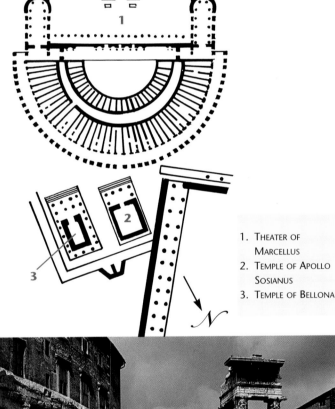

1. THEATER OF
   MARCELLUS
2. TEMPLE OF APOLLO
   SOSIANUS
3. TEMPLE OF BELLONA

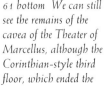

*61 bottom We can still see the remains of the cavea of the Theater of Marcellus, although the Corinthian-style third floor, which ended the series of arcades, has not survived. On the first floor, the fornices are framed by Doric columns, with Ionic columns on the second floor.*

# THE CENTRAL CAMPUS MARTIUS

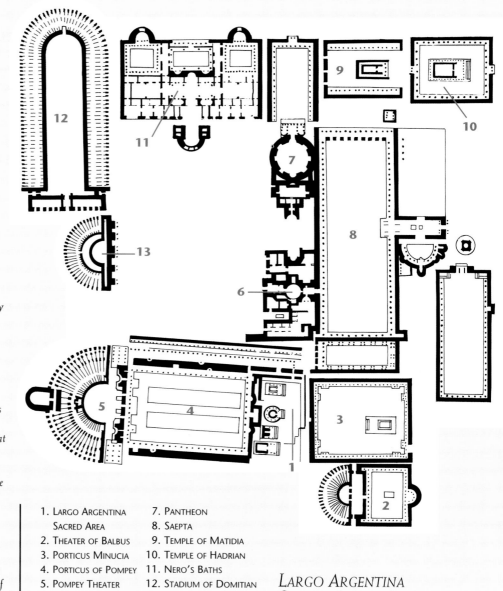

*62 bottom The square area in front of the Pantheon originally had a long portico that visually continued with the pronaos of the temple. Behind the Pantheon was the so-called Basilica Neptuni, with the Saepta to the left.*

*63 top left Between the present-day via Florida, Torre Argentina and Largo Argentina, is an important religious area with four temples from the Republican age (A, B, C, and D), built in successive phases from the end of the 4th century BC (C) to the early 2nd century BC (D). The last in time is temple B, shown in the photograph, which was probably dedicated to Fortuna Huiusce Diei. It is a circular edifice on a podium, with a cella surrounded by a Corinthian colonnade and a stairway to the east.*

*63 top right The Theater of Pompey was the first masonry theater that first century BC Rome could finally boast. It was imposing in size, its dimensions increased by the vast colonnade that opened behind the stage, which was exceptionally large (about 180 x 135 meters) and adorned with splendid statues. This is where Julius Caesar was killed on the Ides of March in 44 BC.*

N

1. LARGO ARGENTINA SACRED AREA
2. THEATER OF BALBUS
3. PORTICUS MINUCIA
4. PORTICUS OF POMPEY
5. POMPEY THEATER
6. AGRIPPA'S BATHS
7. PANTHEON
8. SAEPTA
9. TEMPLE OF MATIDIA
10. TEMPLE OF HADRIAN
11. NERO'S BATHS
12. STADIUM OF DOMITIAN
13. ODEON OF DOMITIAN

## LARGO ARGENTINA SACRED AREA

The Largo Argentina Sacred Area is an archaeological complex between the present-day via Florida, Torre Argentina and Largo Argentina, which was discovered between 1926 and 1928 when some work was being done there, and was immediately identified as an important religious site. In addition to the *Hecatostylum* (a portico with 100 columns) and the *Agrippa Baths*, this area of the *Campus Martius* also contained four temples from the Republican era, which scholars have named temples A, B, C and D. The travertine floors now visible, dated to 80 AD, cover earlier floors in tufa from the second century BC with another even older one a meter below. Temples A, B, C and D were erected at this level.

When the new tufa floor was put in, probably after a fire, the three temples were joined into a single complex. Only later was the fourth temple (D) built, to

fill in the gap.

The remains now visible are for the most part from a restoration by Domitian.

*Temple C*, a *periptero sine postico*, was the oldest edifice, from the late 4th to the early 3rd century BC. It was probably a temple dedicated to Feronia. *Temple A*, the northernmost temple, followed immediately thereafter and can be dated to the mid-3rd century BC. The edifice, identified as the Temple of Juturna (another theory holds that it was dedicated to Juno *Curtis*), was probably built by Lutatius Catulus after the battle against the Carthaginians, and later underwent

some radical changes. As it currently appears, it is a peripteral hexastyle, with fluted tufa columns and travertine Corinthian capitals.

*Temple D*, the largest of the four temples, is dated to the early 2nd century BC, and stands on the far east side of the area. It has been hypothesized that it is the Temple of the Lares Permarini, but this theory is still questioned. The current structure, entirely in travertine, is from a late Republican remodeling.

The last in time is *Temple B*. It is a circular edifice with a flight of stairs leading to the podium. The Corinthian columns are in tufa, while the bases and capitals are in travertine. It is almost certainly the Temple of *Fortuna Huiusce Diei* ("of that day"), dedicated by another Lutatius Catulus following the battle of Vercelli against the Cimbri.

## THE THEATER OF BALBUS

The Theater of Balbus (about 11,000 spectators), was the smallest .of the three theaters on the *Campus Martius*. It was dedicated by Cornelius Balbus, a Roman banker friend of Augustus, in 13 BC but, on the day it was opened, the Tiber flooded and the theater could only be reached by boat. Its remains were found beneath the Palazzo Mattei-Paganica. Behind the scene was a large rectangular area known as the *Crypta Balbi*, surrounded by a portico with pillars and completed by a large exedra. From a funeral inscription, we know that the portico was used for commercial activities, such as the sale of high-quality bronzes. In the Middle Ages, the crypt was used by ropemakers, hence the name to the nearby church of Santa Caterina dei Funari (from the Latin *funis*).

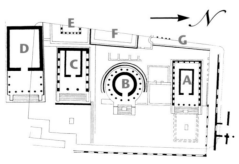

*PLAN OF THE LARGO ARGENTINA SACRED AREA*
A. TEMPLE OF JUTURNA
B. TEMPLE OF FORTUNA HUIUSCE DIEI
C. TEMPLE OF FERONIA
D. TEMPLE OF LARES PERMARINI
E. PUBLIC LATRINE
F. CURIA OF THE PORTICOES OF POMPEY
G. LATRINE

## THE THEATER AND PORTICO OF POMPEY

The Theater of Pompey was the first permanent theater of the city of Rome. Work on this complex began around 61 BC, on land that probably already belonged to C. Pompey. In 55 BC, the year of the second consulate of Pompey,

great games were organized to celebrate the opening. The cavea was 150 meters in diameter and could hold up to 18,000 spectators. On the top (*summa cavea*) was a *temple of Victory*. Temple buildings and performance structures were often associated in the Roman world. Behind the scene was a large portico (180x135), which Atticus, Cicero's friend, embellished with statues of the most famous Greek artists, depicting subjects related to the world of theater or to Venus. There were works of art on the scene as well, some of which have been found (two large sculptures are now at the Louvre). In the center of the portico were two groves of plane trees with fountains.

On the opposite side, behind the circular temple on Largo Argentina, there was a large rectangular exedra, a *Curia* used for Senate meetings, decorated with a statue of Pompey. It was here that Julius Caesar was assassinated in 44 BC. After the murder, the *Curia* was walled up (32 BC) and later transformed into a latrine. The theater survived over the centuries, and in fact the houses that were built in this area followed its inner curve exactly (Piazza di Grotta Pinta). For example, Palazzo Righetti stands where the Temple of *Venus Victrix* was located.

## AGRIPPA'S BATHS

Agrippa's Baths were the most ancient public baths of Rome. They were originally private baths that were only donated to the Roman populace later, through a will. They were built by Agrippa, Augustus' son-in-law, between 25 and 19 BC, between the Pantheon and the Theater of Pompey, north of the Largo Argentina area (the present-day Via di Santa Chiara and Corso Vittorio Emanuele). The facilities, which extended over a surface area 120 x 80/100 meters in size, had the traditional structure of the most ancient baths, with rooms placed irregularly around a circular central room, 25 meters in diameter. We know that the baths were embellished by numerous works of art by famous Greek artists, such as the

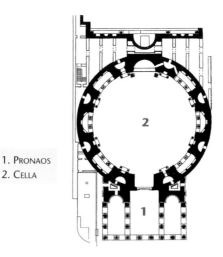

1. PRONAOS
2. CELLA

*64 right top  The Pantheon consists of a deep pronaos, divided horizontally into three naves, and a large circular cella, into which are carved numerous niches and circular and rectangular openings.*

## THE PANTHEON

With Hadrian, there was a return to classicism, which had once also characterized Augustan political and artistic decisions. Here, however, the style is new, more eclectic, and tends to blend Greek and Roman models. Considered the emperor of consolidation more than of expansion, Hadrian's political orientation was also reflected in his artistic decisions, which he followed personally with great interest. This was also part of an attempt to seek a common identity for all regions of the empire, with the goal of holding it together in this way. And

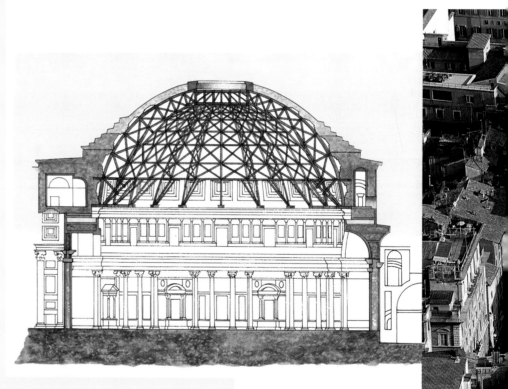

PATTERN OF THE PRESENT-DAY VIA DELLA CIAMBELLA

*64 bottom  In addition to the numerous porticoes, beautiful statues by Greek artists or replicas of the famous originals adorned thermal edifices as well. The subjects of these works of art often used bath motifs, like the Apoxyomenos by Lysippus, of an athlete cleaning himself.*

famous statue of *Apokyomenos* by Lysippus (an athlete scraping himself with a strigil), a 50 AD replica of which fortunately remains. To the west was the *Stagnum Agrippae*, a man-made lake that was probably used as a swimming pool for the baths and was fed by the *Virgo aqueduct*. Overall, it was a large recreational complex that completed the performance district. Today, the only portion remaining is the masonry structure of the circular hall from a Severian-era remodeling, over which the Via dell'Arco della Ciambella now runs (nos.9 and 15).

*64 center right and bottom  The Pantheon structure is quite complex and could be termed "self-supporting." The cylinder at the base consists of 16 niches carved into the walls. The empty spaces thus radially formed act as supporting pillars, connected by safety arches. The cupola is placed about halfway up and includes a reinforcement ring that contains the oblique pressure of the vault. The lacunars that decorate the vault also help lighten the weight, as does the use of increasingly lightweight materials (such as layers of concrete alternating with tufa and volcanic slag for the upper portion).*

classicism met this need, even though it used new technical solutions, especially in architecture.

The reconstruction of the Pantheon is part of this picture. Located between Agrippa's Baths and Nero's Baths, this circular temple was built by Agrippa (*M. Agrippa L. F. Cos tertium fecit*) in 27 BC. It was consecrated to all the deities, but especially Mars and Venus, protectors of the *Gens Iulia*. Hadrian made radical changes in the earlier edifice, changing not only its orientation (the façade was probably rotated 180° to the north), but also its overall appearance, which has survived to this day. It has a deep pronaos, with a colonnade surmounted by a pediment, and a round cella covered by a high vault. In front of the edifice was a vast porticoed square,

curved, and the wall is dotted with three superimposed sectors, emphasized by cornices. In the base there are numerous niches, alternately circular and rectangular. The central exedra is preceded by two columns; between one exedra and another there are eight niches framed by small columns supporting tympana, which are alternately triangular and semicircular. The second order has blind windows framed by Corinthian columns with pilasters. Above, the curved surface ends with the cupola. This is supported by a wall six meters thick and a structure that uses progressively lighter construction materials, down to the volcanic material of the cupola. It was made with a single casting on a large wooden centring. It is decorated by five orders of concentric caissons that narrow to the final circular aperture (9 meters), accentuating the curved appearance of the interior.

Overall, the monument is highly innovative from a technical perspective: The structure can in fact be considered self-supporting, fully resting on the base ring and solid foundations, while the internal niches and arches serve more to distribute pressure. The Pantheon has survived almost perfectly intact due primarily to its later transformation, in 609 AD, into the *church of Santa Maria Ad Martyres*, after the emperor Phocas donated it to Boniface IV.

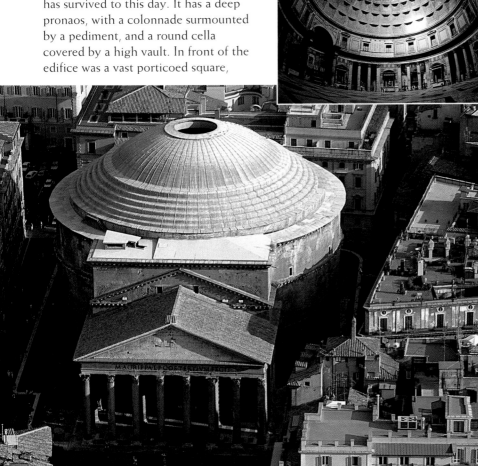

whose pavement was originally a meter lower than it is today. The view of anyone crossing the square was thus different from what we see today. For example, one could not completely see the circular element at the back of the pronaos, while this pronaos fit in perfectly as a functional element joining to the other porticoes. The inner circular portion must thus have come as a surprise to anyone approaching, set against the exterior.

The pronaos, which dated to around the time of the first temple of Agrippa, has a façade with eight gray granite columns on the outside and four in two rows on the inside, forming a nave and three aisles. The pediment was originally decorated with an eagle with a crown. To the back, there was a green brick construction with two side stairways leading to the vault, that connected to the cella. Access to the inside was through a large bronze door.

The rotunda itself is a concrete cylinder 150 Roman feet in diameter (about 44 meters), while the cupola is inserted geometrically as a perfect sphere inscribed in the cylinder. The balance of these proportions is impressive. Inside, all surfaces are

## The Saepta

The *Saepta Julia*, which in ancient times was a voting precinct, was a vast rectangular porticoed space (310x120 m) located east of the Pantheon. Begun by Caesar in 54 BC to replace the first *Republican Saepta*, Agrippa completed it after his death, in 27 BC. The area was enclosed (*Saepta* means "fences") and the inner area divided into passageways. Voters cast their ballots within their respective centuries, according to procedures that were also based on their economic status, which also determined their type of military service and participation in political life. Each century constituted one voting unit. Beginning in the second century BC, there were many changes made in this system, primarily because the importance of the individual citizen was diminishing against the power of political groups and the masses of "clients" maneuvered by the dominant oligarchies. With the establishment of the principate, the *comitia* also lost their importance and became a mere formality. Thus, even the *Saepta* became practically useless, until it was transformed into a porticoed square, embellished with statues and later occupied by an art and antiques market.

## The Temple of Matidia

Hadrian dedicated the Temple of Matidia to his mother-in-law in 119 AD, immediately after her death (it is probably the only historical example of a monument dedicated to a deified mother-in-law). It was located near Piazza Capranica and must have been quite large (the columns were 1.7 meters in diameter and no less than 17 meters high). Unfortunately, we can reconstruct its appearance only through a depiction on a coin.

## The Temple of Hadrian

The Temple of Hadrian was built in 145 AD, east of the Temple of Matidia, by Antoninus Pius, who dedicated it to the deified emperor. The Stock Exchange has been built on the site where the ancient temple stood, now known as Piazza di Pietra. It incorporates 11 Corinthian columns that belong to the earlier edifice. The peripteral temple originally had a row of 13 columns on the long sides and 8 on the short ones. A stairway led to the peperino podium, four meters high, which modern excavations have now brought to light. The inside of the cella was dotted with semicolumns against the walls and was covered by a barrel vault with caissons. On the base, on which the columns rested, were sculpted allegorical figures from the Roman provinces (the reliefs are now at the National Museum in Naples and at the Palazzo dei Conservatori).

*66 bottom left Inside the courtyard of the Palazzo dei Conservatori, on the Capitol, are several relief works surviving from the Temple of Hadrian in the central Campus Martius portraying Roman provinces alternating with monuments.*

*66 center The interior of the cella of the Temple of Hadrian was dotted with engaged columns standing against the walls, which rested on a base. Here there was an allegorical decoration with relief work alternately depicting monuments and provinces, now in the courtyard of the Palazzo dei Conservatori.*

ELEMENTS OF THE STRUCTURE STILL VISIBLE

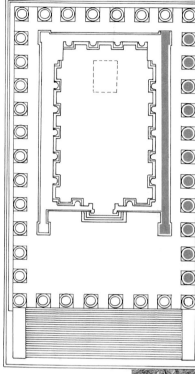

DOMITIAN STADIUM

PLAN OF THE STADIUM

SANT'AGNESE CHURCH

## THE ODEON OF DOMITIAN

The present-day Piazza Navona, a splendid example of urban continuity, follows the circumference of the *Stadium of Domitian*. It is in fact perfectly preserved as an imprint, the rectangular form elongated with a slight curve north of the complex. Built by Domitian before 86 AD, it was meant to be used for athletic games in honor of Jupiter Capitolinus (the *Certamen Capitolium*). It has been estimated that the structure could hold about 30,000 spectators.

It was a completely open arena 275 meters long. The outside of the façade had a series of arches resting on travertine pillars with Ionic semicolumns. There may have been Corinthian semicolumns in the upper part of the cavea. Access to the stairs was through two large entrances on the long sides. A third one, preceded by a colonnaded portico, was located in the center of the side curving to the north.

Behind the Stadium was the Odeon of Domitian. This was a small indoor theater built by Domitian in close connection with the stadium, and could hold about 10,000 spectators. The *Certamen Capitolium* games were held here as well, but it was primarily designed for musical performances and poetry contests.

*66 bottom right  As can be seen from the drawing, Piazza Navona almost perfectly retraces the area once occupied by the Stadium of Domitian. The square is where the arena was located, and the buildings stand on the remains of the bleachers in the cavea. The obelisk in the center comes from the Circus of Maxentius.*

*66-67  The Stadium, whose remains are where Piazza Navona is located today, was built by Domitian in 85 AD. Every year, athletic events were held here in honor of Jupiter Capitolinus, the Certamen Capitolinum. Fully 275 meters long, the edifice could hold up to 30,000 spectators.*

*66 top right  A portion of the colonnade that once surrounded the cella of the temple dedicated to Hadrian in 145 AD still remains. It was a periptery that had 13 columns on the long sides and eight on the short ones.*

## NERO'S BATHS

Nero's Baths were built in 62 AD in the central area of the *Campus Martius*, between the *Stadium of Domitian* and the Pantheon. The complex was later restored by Alexander Severus in 227 AD, and therefore known as the *Alexandrine Baths*. The plan, which can be reconstructed from Renaissance designs, shows a large complex with rooms symmetrically organized around a central axis. It is probably the first and most ancient example of baths with this sort of distribution of space, and was destined to become a model for all other thermal facilities. Some remains are still visible under Palazzo Madama.

*67 right  We can see the imposing remains of the Stadium below the level of the square. On the ground level there were pillars and walls that supported the bleachers in the cavea, along with a series of brick rooms with stairs that connected this area to the upper levels.*

## THE COLUMN OF MARCUS AURELIUS

In the center of Piazza Colonna is the column that the Senatus erected between 180 and 196 AD to commemorate the emperor Marcus Aurelius and his military campaigns against the Germans and Sarmatae. The monument consisted of a shaft 100 Roman feet long (about 30 meters), entirely sculpted, and a high plinth, placed on a foundation that emerged three meters over *via Flaminia*. The ancient level is 3.86 meters below the present-day street level.

The frieze on the column depicts the two principal campaigns of 172-173 and 174-175 AD, separated by a Victory about halfway up. The narrative begins

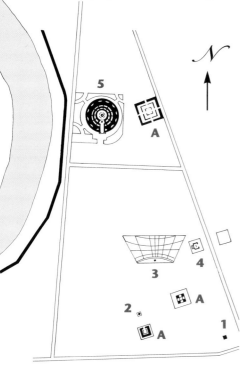

1. COLUMN OF MARCUS AURELIUS
2. COLUMN OF ANTONINUS PIUS
3. HOROLOGIUM
4. ARA PACIS
5. MAUSOLEUM OF AUGUSTUS
A. USTRINA

*Monuments to funeral pyres, ustrina had a marble enclosure with a foundation in the center. They were religious in nature and were used to commemorate the pyres on which the emperors and their families were cremated.*

with the army's trip up the Danube to *Carnuntum*: This long-celebrated episode was a decisive moment in the offensive against the Germans and Sarmatae; it was also meant to be a reference to the tale of the Dacian wars on the Trajan's Column, a reference point for the creator of the Column of Marcus Aurelius. The first part shows characteristic episodes such as the miracle of the lightning that destroyed an enemy war machine, and that of the rain that overcame the Quadi, but benefited the thirsty Romans. Compared with Trajan's Column, however, this

work uses new iconographic solutions. The frieze is higher, and the figures are less dense and detached, and thus more visible. Despite a tendency toward general simplification, the artist wanted to give the images a certain pathos, endowing the frieze with new spiritual content and a new compositional concept. While the compositional scheme is generally poor, the quality is still high. The triumphant emperor, for the most part portrayed from the front, is shown as the historically real man.

In Rome, historical relief had already created precise iconographic schemes

68 *The Column of Marcus Aurelius has a tall, completely sculpted shaft. The frieze, like that of Trajan's Column, depicts his two primary military campaigns, separated* *approximately halfway up by the figure of a Victory. While Trajan's monument was clearly used as a model, the result here is substantially different. For example, the frieze is* *higher, the figures more detached from the background. In general, we can see a tendency toward simplification, accompanied by an attempt to give a certain pathos to the scenes.*

that were best exemplified in Trajan's Column. It was thus inevitable that these motifs would be interwoven in this narration as well. The style of the frieze draws increasingly less inspiration from Hellenistic experience and uses more typically Roman motifs, such as in the triumphal paintings that ever since the Republican period had described

mature in the 3rd and 4th centuries and emerge in medieval art as the culmination of a series of encounters with different cultural trends. Above all, it was the result of the success of an exclusively Roman art style, with expressionistic trends that would fully develop over the course of the third century.

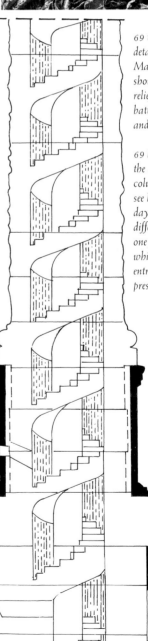

69 *top right This detail of the Column of Marcus Aurelius shows one of the many relief works depicting battles between Romans and barbarians.*

69 *bottom right From the design on the column section, we can see how the modern-day pavement level differs from the original one from Roman times, which, along with the entrance, was below the present-day street level.*

episodes in the wars of victorious generals. These didactic paintings of the common people, however, had nothing of the tone of the friezes in honorary columns. Even before Trajan's Column, the column of Marcus Aurelius acted as a supporting axis for the imperial statue; the base is in fact twice as high, to encourage a view of the column itself. Following is a high plinth marked by a horizontal frieze. This work could perhaps evidence a final break with official art, which from Augustus on had been marked by classical experience. This transformation in style would

68-69 *A column erected to commemorate the wars against the Germans and Sarmatae stands on Piazza Colonna. Like Trajan's Column, this was also designed to memorialize an event and at the same time celebrate the emperor responsible for it, in this case Marcus Aurelius.*

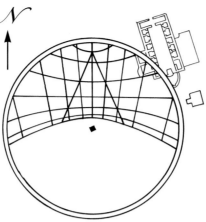

# THE COLUMN OF ANTONINUS PIUS.
# THE HOROLOGIUM
## AND THE OBELISK ON PIAZZA MONTECITORIO

In front of the *Ustrinum* (the enclosed area, with a foundation in the center commemorating the funeral pyre of emperors and their families) found on the Via degli Uffici del Vicario, are the remains of the *Column of Antoninus Pius*, built to commemorate the emperor, who died in 161 AD. The actual column was probably Corinthian. Of particular importance, however, is the sculpted base, now on display at the Vatican Museums. One side depicts the apotheosis of the emperor and his wife Faustina, transported to heaven by a winged Genius. At the scene is Mars, holding the obelisk of the nearby *Horologium* in his hand, and the goddess Rome. The style is rather academic and shows some hardness and rigidity typical of allegory. The other sides have two almost identical reliefs; using a completely different, more narrative style, they depict a *decursio*, the ritual cavalcade around the pyre and the military parade that concluded funerals.

Piazza Montecitorio now has an

*70 top The "needle" of Augustus' clock was set into the ground near the present-day Piazza del Parlamento, and cast its shade on great bronze letters inserted into a marble pavement.*

*70 center left A column was erected to commemorate the death of the emperor Antoninus Pius (106 AD), near the altar where he was cremated. The Vatican Museums*

hold the marble plinth of this column. One side depicts the emperor's apotheosis with his wife Faustina, transported into the sky by a winged Genius, and the other side shows a ritual procession of cavalry soldiers (decursio).

*70 center right Symmetrically placed to the left and right of the main entrance to*

the Ara Pacis, are two allegorical panels depicting, respectively, the goddess Rome and the Earth (in the photographs), portrayed by a seated woman with two children; next to Tellus, or Earth, are two other female figures representing other elements – air on a swan and water on a sea monster.

Obelisk that belonged to Psammeticus II (594 - 589 BC) and was brought to Rome from the great temple of Heliopolis in 30 BC after Egypt was annexed by the Empire. It was used by Augustus as part of a great sundial built in 10 BC, for the 20th anniversary of the conquest of Egypt. The *Horologium*, designed by the mathematician Novius Facundus, occupied a rather vast area opposite the *Ara Pacis* (between the present-day Piazza S. Lorenzo and Piazza del Parlamento). A travertine pavement contained the engraved Greek letters and signs of the Zodiac, in bronze characters, that used the shadow of the obelisk at noon to indicate the hour, day and month.

*70 bottom Several fragments from the Column of Antoninus Pius were used to restore the Egyptian obelisk on Piazza Montecitorio. The obelisk came from Heliopolis and was brought to Rome by Augustus, to become the needle of a gigantic sundial.*

*71 top The outer sides of the Ara Pacis show a long procession of figures. The south side depicts the most important members of the imperial family.*

# THE ARA PACIS

The first discovery of the *Ara Pacis* dates back to 1568, when several sculpted blocks from it appeared below the Palazzo Peretti (now Palazzo Almagià). In 1879, Von Duhn first identified the monument as the *Ara Pacis*. The first official excavations then began in 1903, leading to the discovery of the altar's structures and the recovery of other reliefs. Excavations were finally concluded in 1937-38. The altar was then pieced back together (no longer facing east-west, but north-south) in the special pavilion built near the Mausoleum of Augustus and the Tiber. It was reopened in 1938. This monument is perhaps the most representative of Augustus' policy and the man himself. It was to stand on the place where later, in 14 AD, Tiberius built the *Ara Providentiae*, standing symmetrically on the other side of the road. Voted in by the Senate in 13

BC and dedicated by Augustus in 9 BC, it must have been something of a symbol of reconciliation between the two political forces in play, the emperor and the senate. There was also a clear attempt to exalt that *pietas augustae*, through which Rome finally obtained a long-coveted peace. The monument consists of a monumental rectangular enclosure on a high base, with access by a stairway. There are two entrances, of which the main one faced the Via Flaminia. The complex's structure replicates the original, temporary *templum*

even in its interior decoration, which depicts a palisade hung with garlands. On three steps, within the enclosure, is the altar itself. On it is a depiction of the annual sacrificial ceremony that took place here each year. Still visible are the Vestal Virgins, the *Pontifex Maximus*, priests, and *camilli* with the pig, sheep and bull (the sacrifice was called the *suovetaurilia*). The whole enclosure is richly decorated with highly symbolic reliefs. The lower area is decorated with volutes of acanthus that probably symbolize the Augustan family tree that is explicitly depicted farther up (in Greek, *stemmata*, related to the modern Italian word for "coat of arms," means "branches"). The upper area, on the sides of the entrance, has four panels, two with mythological themes and two allegories, showing

the *Lupercal* (the cave where the wolf is said to have suckled Romulus and Remus); Aeneas sacrificing a white sow to the Penates, flanked by two *camilli*; the *Tellus*, mother earth in time of peace, shown as a woman with two children; and another female figure who may represent the goddess Rome, but which has unfortunately been almost completely lost. There is a sort of ideological continuity among the four scenes, as Aeneas and then Romulus and Remus constituted the necessary foundation for the later prosperity of

Rome. On the south and north sides are "historical" scenes showing a procession of people, almost all of whom can be identified as members of the imperial family, as well as priestly figures. This is the *gens Iulia* that step by step led the Roman people to the goal of the *pax augusta*. The south side faced the city and was thus the most important. Indeed, Augustus himself is depicted here.

Overall, this is a quite eclectic work. The relationship with Greek art is evident. Classical art is the model for the procession (the frieze of the Parthenon itself), while the volute decoration and panels with Aeneas and the Earth are clearly based on art from the Hellenistic era. The decoration on the altar is more closely related to a more typically Roman tradition.

*71 bottom The Ara Pacis is perhaps one of the most beautiful and significant monuments of Augustan classicism. Consecrated in 13 BC, it has a marble enclosure that reproduces a provisional templum, within which is the actual altar. The whole monument is decorated with extremely symbolic relief work.*

The Mausoleum, the *Horologium* and the *Ara Pacis* appeared to be aligned to anyone entering Rome from Via Flaminia. The Mausoleum, probably inspired by the great tombs of Greek kings, perhaps that of Alexander the Great himself, was built by Augustus in 29 BC. The name itself connected it to dynastic tombs and the custom of naming them in this manner, beginning with King Mausolus of Caria. It must also have used the model of noble Roman tombs with a tympanum, which

the emperor: the *res gestae divi Augusti*. A copy of this, which we can consider Augustus' spiritual and political legacy, has survived through one of the numerous copies reproduced throughout the empire, found in Ankara (*Monumentum Ancyrarum*). A modern reproduction can be seen on the side of the *Ara Pacis* pavilion.

"I restored the Capitolium and the Theater of Pompey, both of which were very costly works, without inscribing my name on them. I restored

The first ring in tufa was 4.35 meters thick, with a series of niches carved out and filled with earth. The second and third were in *opus reticulatum* and connected by radial walls that created inaccessible rooms. Going on to a further wall, five meters thick, it extended to the outside, constituting the second floor. From here began a corridor that surrounded the cella, in the center of the entire structure. The cella, which was also circular, was reached by an entry on an axis with the

were widely used by families in the second century BC (suffice it to consider the *Monument to Cercilia Metella* on the Appia Antica).

The structure changed over the centuries and was used for the most varied purposes. It was transformed into a fortress by the Colonna family in the 1600s, into a travertine quarry, into vineyards, a theater, a garden, and a concert hall in which Toscanini performed. In 1936, its remains finally began to be uncovered and the surviving structures studied. Although it could not be reconstructed without some guesswork, we have a general idea of its appearance. On the outside, it had a foundation/enclosure in travertine that was about 12 meters high. To the south was the entrance, preceded by two obelisks. Here was affixed the famous autobiography of

the aqueducts, which time had damaged in many places, and doubled the carrying capacity of the Water known as *Marcia*, after adding a new spring to its course. I completed the *Forum Julium* and the basilica between the Temple of Castor and Pollux and the Temple of Saturn, works begun and almost completed by my father; and when this basilica was destroyed by a fire, I began to rebuild it on a larger area, dedicating it to the names of my children; … Consul for the 6th time, by will of the Senate I restored 82 temples of the gods in the city, … Consul for the 7th time, I restored the *Via Flaminia* from the city to *Ariminum*, and all bridges, …"

The internal structure, a cylinder 87 meters in diameter, was rather complex. It consisted of a series of concentric walls, most of which were not passable.

*72 The entrance to the Mausoleum of Augustus must originally have been preceded by two obelisks. In addition, we know that what must have been the emperor's spiritual testament was affixed near the entrance – the so-called* Res Gestae Divi Augusti.

outer one. The inner walls contained three niches in which were buried the emperor's family, including Marcellus, Octavia, Agrippa, and Lucius and Gaius Caesar. In the center, a large pillar, into which a small square room was carved to hold the ashes of the emperor, emerged on the outside. This external part must have supported the statue of Augustus as well as indicated the position of the tomb. There must have been a large green area above and around the monument.

*72-73 Augustus wanted to build a large circular tomb for himself, modeled after the tombs of Greek rulers. The structure was rather complex and included an outer enclosure and a cylindrical central structure several floors high, with concentric walls and a large pillar in the center that supported the bronze statue of the emperor.*

PLAN OF THE MAUSOLEUM OF AUGUSTUS
1. ENTRANCE
2. OBELISKS
3. ENTRANCE TO FUNERARY CELLA
4. NICHES
5. TOMB OF AUGUSTUS

# THE FORUM BOARIUM AND THE HOLITORIUM

1. FORUM BOARIUM
2. HOLITORIUM
3. PONS AEMILIUS
4. PONS SUBLICIUS
5. TEMPLE OF PORTUNUS
6. ARA MAXIMA
7. SANTA MARIA IN COSMEDIN (STATIO ANNONAE)
8. TEMPLE OF HERCULES VICTOR
9. SANT'OMOBONO SACRED AREA
10. ARCO DEGLI ARGENTARI
11. ARCH OF JANUS

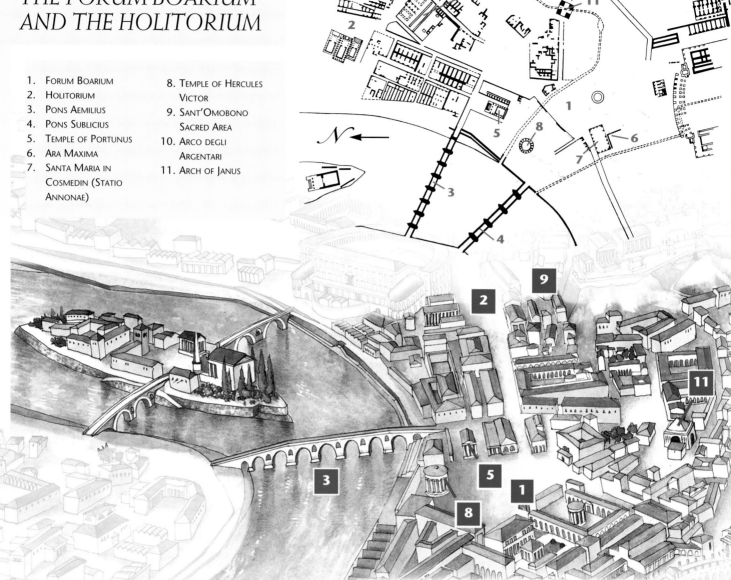

74 *The Pons Aemilius, known as the "Broken Bridge," is located near the Vegetable Market. It was built in the 2nd century BC, at one of the most important points of transit and fords across the river, along with the Pons Sublicius. The Broken Bridge was built in two phases, between 179 BC, when the piers were built, and 142 BC, when the arches were added through the work of the two censors for that year, one of whom was Scipio Aemilianus. The arch we can see today, however, is from a reconstruction from the mid 1500's.*

The area between the Tiber, the Capitoline, the Aventine and the Palatine hills has always been extremely important, even in pre-urban times. According to tradition, the area, which was originally marshland, was reclaimed by the Etruscan kings. The *Forum Boarium*, the ancient livestock market, and the *Forum Holitorium*, the vegetable and herb market, were located near the Tiber; this was a crucial feature, as the area had been a focal point for trade since ancient times. It was here, in fact, that two important trading routes

75 top right *The Temple of Portunus now visible is from a first century BC restoration. It is a rectangular edifice that stands on a podium in sack work, with four Ionic columns on the façade and a travertine cella covered in stucco.*

intersected: the Tiber itself, which was navigable up to Orte, and a road that connected Campania to Etruria. Here ran the ancient *Via Salaria*, the salt road, whose trade, coming from the salt marshes at the mouth of the Tiber, had been fundamentally important ever since prehistoric times. Today we can say for certain that the area was utilized as early as the 8th century BC by the Greeks, due to discoveries that have allowed us to confirm what we knew from the legends of Evander, Hercules and Aeneas. In reality, the actual monumental arrangement of the forum came only under the domination of the Etruscan kings. Servius Tullius is believed to have laid out the *Portus Tiberinus*; the port occupied the area between the *Temples of San Nicola in Carcere* and the *Temple of Portunus*, near the present-day Palazzo dell'Anagrafe.

Related to the port, near the *Ponte Emilio*, was the *Temple of Portunus*, improperly known as the *Temple of Fortuna Virile*.

The edifice was actually consecrated to the god Portunus, protector of sailors and ports. Built as early as the 6th century BC, the monument that stands today, which is extraordinarily well preserved, is from a first-century BC restoration. It is a rectangular, pseudoperipteral, tetrastyle, Ionic structure surrounded by a sacred enclosure and covered with stucco. The frieze, also in stucco, shows candelabras and festoons; the cornice is decorated with leonine protomae.

Ancient cults related to the world of trade were celebrated at the port. Around the mid-6th century BC, the *sanctuaries of Mater Matuta and Fortuna* were built (Sant'Omobono Sacred Area).

During the 4th century BC, there was a great deal of restoration and remodeling of already existing temples. But only between the 3rd and 2nd centuries BC did a new phase begin, as the conquest of the Mediterranean was completed. Thus, work on embanking the Tiber began; a new defensive system was adopted, including a portion of the *Transtiberim*; and the temples of the *Forum Boarium* and the *Ara Maxima* were built.

The *Ara Maxima* was a monument built in the first half of the 2nd century BC in honor of Hercules, located near the present-day *Church of Santa Maria in Cosmedin*, in whose portico is the *Mouth of Truth* (the low relief that is famous primarily for the legends that surround it). According to legend, Hercules came here with the cattle of Geryon, which were then stolen by Cacus, the gigantic son of Vulcan who lived in a cavern on the Aventine. The hero then killed the giant and was for this reason honored by the Arcadians, who lived on the Palatine. Following this episode, the altar was said to have been built and dedicated to Hercules.

## THE CIRCULAR TEMPLE OF HERCULES VICTOR

The circular temple that stands near the *Mouth of Truth* is improperly known as the *Temple of Vesta*, due to its similarity to the circular edifice of the *Forum Romanum*. But thanks to an inscription, the edifice has been identified as the *Temple of Hercules Victor*, also known as *Olivarius*, the patron of the guild of *olearii*. It was built at the end of the 2nd century BC by a merchant, M. Octavius Herrenus, who probably grew rich through the oil trade. The architect in charge of building it must have been the Greek, Hermodorus of Salamis.

The building is still in excellent condition, due in part to recent restoration work that has returned some of its original splendor. It is in fact the most ancient temple preserved in Rome made almost entirely of marble. It stands on a circular podium with stairs, on which stand 20 Corinthian columns. Behind them is the wall of the cella, covered with marble on the outside and travertine inside. The entrance is on the east. The statue of the deity was sculpted in the 2nd century BC by a famous Greek artist, Scopas the Younger, as confirmed by an inscription on the base of the statue. Unfortunately, the upper portion of the monument, which was later transformed into a church, has not survived. The remains of the frescoes inside are from the 15th century.

*75 bottom right The circular temple located a short distance from the Temple of Portunus, was probably dedicated to Hercules Victor, also known as Olivarius. With its cella surrounded by 20 columns, resting on a foundation with steps, it is Rome's most ancient surviving temple built almost entirely in marble.*

*75 bottom left The famous relief work known as the Mouth of Truth is under the portico of the Church of Santa Maria in Cosmedin. It is a marble disk that may have been a drain cover, sculpted to depict a mask.*

# SANT'OMOBONO SACRED AREA

THREE TEMPLES OF SAN NICOLA IN CARCERE

1. TEMPLE OF SPES
2. TEMPLE OF JUNO SOSPITA
3. TEMPLE OF JANUS

*76 left Near the Church of Sant'Omobono are the remains of an important sacred area that tradition tells us dates back to Servius Tullius. It was a large, square temple with a single cella divided into two wings, dedicated to Mater Matuta, the patron goddess of navigation. The temple was later destroyed and rebuilt after the Tarquinians were driven out. The two temples that were built in its place are close to each other but distinct, each one with its own cella. One is dedicated to Fortuna and the other to Mater Matuta.*

In the Thirties, near the ancient *Forum Boarium*, a square foundation in tufa blocks was found, with the remains of two cellae inside, along with two large altars, an underground room, shafts and pavements that created a rather complex stratigraphy. Under the apse of the church of St. Omobono were found remains of an archaic temple, the oldest example of a Tuscan temple in the world, that can be dated

SAN NICOLA IN CARCERE AND THE THREE TEMPLES IN THE FORUM HOLITORIUM

to the mid-6th century BC. In fact, as early as the late 7th century, there was an altar in the area that was probably dedicated to *Mater Matuta*, whose cult was connected to the trading center on the river. According to mythology, with the aid of water nymphs, Leucotea, a goddess of Theban origin, landed here on the banks of the Tiber with her son Portunus, and took the name of *Mater Matuta*, the tutelary deity of sailors. According to tradition, Servius Tullius built the temple on that site. It had a square plan and stood on a high podium of tufa about 12 meters wide. It could be entered through a front stairway, which led to a pronaos with two columns and a single cella divided into two *alae*. The temple was destroyed by fire, and when it was rebuilt, again in the second half of the 6th century BC, a counterpodium was added. Most of the terra-cotta and covering slabs are from this period (conserved at the Antiquarium

Comunale in Palazzo Caffarelli). An altar in blocks of tufa stood before the temple.

At the end of the 6th century, after the Tarquinians were expelled from Rome, the *Temple of Mater Matuta* was destroyed. In the early 5th century, two nearby but distinct temples were built, each with its own cella. The one to the west was dedicated to Fortuna, while the one to the east was to *Mater Matuta*. They were destroyed by a fire in 213 BC and rebuilt late in the century. During the Severian era, a number of *tabernae* were added to the back, the sides and the front of the temple. Traces of an arch have been found in the center, probably the *Triumphal Gate*, through which the parades of victors marched. From the 6th century AD on, Christian edifices were added to the Pagan temple until, in the 1700s, it was finally dedicated to Saints. Omobono and Anthony.

The San Nicola in Carcere area is where the ancient herb market, the *Forum Holitorium*, once stood. In the Republican era, three temples were built here, facing the Capitoline Hill. Their remains are part of the present-day church.

THE SOUTHERN TEMPLE. The smallest building is also the oldest. It was probably a temple dedicated to *Spes*, Hope, built during the First Punic War and then restored numerous times. The temple, a Doric peripteral structure, had a stairway that led to the podium, where there were columns, originally in travertine, with a covering in faux marble. Six are still visible in the outside wall on the left side of the church.

THE CENTRAL TEMPLE. The building in the center is probably the most recent of the three, and was added last. It was a large peripteral, hexastyle, Ionic temple (30 x 15 meters), with a double row of columns on the back side and a triple row at the front. An altar stood in the center of the stairway that led to the podium. Some remains are still visible below the church, near the apse. Very probably the temple was dedicated to Juno Sospita, Juno protectress of births.

THE NORTHERN TEMPLE. The Ionic temple to the north is the best preserved. It is located to the right of S. Nicola in Carcere. It was a peripteral hexastyle building *sine postico*, with a triple row of columns on the façade and a colonnade on the long sides (two columns remain on one side and seven on the other; they were about 26 x 15 meters in size). It stood on a podium covered with blocks of travertine, preceded by a stairway. The temple was presumably dedicated to Janus, and according to sources was located *iuxta Theatrum Marcelli*, that is, near the Theater of Marcellus. Built in the Republican period, during the First Punic War, by Duilius, the winner of the battle of Mylae, it was rebuilt a number of times until the time of Hadrian.

*76 right Three temples from the Republican era stand within the church of San Nicola in Carcere. The southern temple is smaller and more ancient, and was probably dedicated to Spes. The central temple, which may have been built last, was consecrated to Juno Sospita (in the photo), and finally, the Ionic, peripteral, hexastyle temple to the north was dedicated to Janus.*

*77 top left On the Piazza di San Giorgio in Velabro is an arch (which was most probably an entry gate to the forum) decorated with splendid relief work. It was built in 203 AD by cattle merchants and silversmiths, the bankers of the time, in honor of Septimius Severus.*

*77 bottom Elaborate vegetal decoration almost completely covers the Arco degli Argentari. There is a frieze in the lower portion of the pillars depicting the sacrifice of bulls. Above, to the left, is a larger scene, probably portraying Caracalla. On the outer portion of the arch, in the photo, are military soldiers leading a barbarian prisoner.*

*77 top right Near the descent of the Velabrum is a large four-faced arch known as the Arch of Janus. It was built around the 4th century AD by Constantius II, in honor of the emperor Constantine.*

## THE ARCO DEGLI ARGENTARI

In 203 AD, livestock merchants and bankers, known as *argentarii*, built an arch in honor of Septimius Severus on Piazza San Giorgio al Velabro. More than an arch, it was probably a monumental gate leading into the *Forum Boarium*. Almost seven meters high, it has two masonry pillars with a marble architrave, where the statues were originally located. The pillars were decorated with sculpted panels, framed by pilasters with military standards and volutes of acanthus. Between the pillars one can see friezes with Victories and eagles, the sacrifice of a bull in the lower section, and a depiction of sacrificial tools on the upper section. The largest panels show a standing male figure that can be identified as the emperor Caracalla, two soldiers with a barbarian, and Caracalla once again, preparing a libation. Next to

him, in an empty space, must have been the figure of Geta, which was later removed. Inside the arch, Septimius Severus is depicted with his wife Julia Domna; on the architrave is Hercules with the lion skin and club, and next to him the figure of a Genius.

## THE FOUR-FACED ARCH OF JANUS

At the feet of the descent of the Velabrum is a large monument, a four-faced arch known as the Arch of Janus, dating to the 4th century AD and built in honor of the emperor Constantine. It had four pillars covered in marble that supported a cross vault. On the outside, two rows of three niches ending in hemispherical shell calottes were used to hold statues. The four keystones of the arches are sculpted with figures of Rome and Juno, seated, and Minerva and Ceres, standing. The attic, now lost, must have been located above. Fragments of the inscription have been preserved in the nearby church of San Giorgio in Velabro.

According to legend, after the Tarquinians were driven from Rome, the grain of the *Campus Martius*, land that was once owned by the Etruscan kings, was cut and thrown into the river. This supposedly created Tiber Island (the Isola Tiberina), although it is now believed to date back to a much earlier period. Another legend states that due to a terrible pestilence, a delegation was sent to the temple of Aesculapius (the god of medicine) in Epidaurus. The delegation returned to Rome with a

porticos used to house the ill. The island was long a place for healing, and even today the hospital Fatebenefratelli, dating back to 1548, is located here.

There were two ways to get to the island, the *Pons Fabricius* (Fabricius Bridge) that connected it to the *Campus Martius*, and the *Pons Cestius* (Cestius Bridge) to Transtiberim. Originally, a ferry or wooden barge was probably used to cross the river.

The *Pons Fabricius* was built in 62 BC by Lucius Fabricius, as the inscription

states. It was 62 meters long and had two large arches resting on a central pier, within which was a small arch, useful for lowering water pressure in the case of floods.

The *Pons Cestius*, built in 46 BC, was originally about 50 meters long and had a large central archway and two smaller ones on the sides; it was completely rebuilt in the 1800s. The inscription that commemorates a remodeling in the 4th century AD is located in the center of one of the bridge's abutments.

serpent, symbol of the god, which when set free supposedly jumped into the Tiber and swam to the island, thus indicating the place where a temple dedicated to Aesculapius should be built. The present-day *Church of San Bartolomeo* stands right on the spot of the ancient *Temple of Aesculapius*, of which no trace remains, except perhaps the medieval well in the center of the stairs, which could be the primitive sacred font, just as the 14 columns within the church may belong to the temple. Within the sanctuary, like that at Epidaurus, there must have been

*78  Isola Tiberina is in the middle of a bend in the Tiber, in an area of great historical significance. This had been an almost mandatory river crossing from the very earliest times, and thus controlling it was originally of crucial importance.*

*79 left  The Pons Fabricius, built in 62 BC, was 62 meters long. It still has the two large spans resting on the central pier, where there was a small arch that helped decrease water pressure in the event of flooding.*

## THE VATICAN AREA. THE AGER VATICANUS

The area between the Vatican Mountains and the Tiber, the so-called *Ager Vaticanus*, was not exactly a part of the city. Rather, it was considered a suburban area, characterized by a succession of villas and tombs that lined the roads. The imposing *Mausoleum of Hadrian* stood here along the Tiber, as well as the so-called *Meta Romuli*, a pyramid-shaped tomb similar to the sepulcher of Cestius. Here was also the *Villa of Agrippa*, which is probably the remains found near the Villa della Farnesina, and the *Villa of Agrippina*, which was originally also part of the *Circus of Caligula*. Remains of the *Horti Agrippinae* have been found below the Santo Spirito hospital (Corsia Sistina 3) and can be dated to the earliest phase in

the first century BC. We know that the *Villa of Agrippina*, the wife of Germanicus and mother of Caligula, was richly decorated. What remains includes polychrome mosaic floors and a basin with marine scenes, now at Palazzo Massimo.

In the area of the nearby St. Peter's Square and the Vatican Basilica, where there was once also a sanctuary dedicated to Cybele, stood the *Circus of Caligula*. It was a large area, originally private, built by Caligula and expanded by Nero. The curved side was to the west, while the *carceres*, the starting stalls, were to the east. In the center was a large obelisk with no hieroglyphs. It was 25 meters high, and a special, exceptionally large ship had to be built to carry it

back from Egypt. The ship was then sunk by Claudius in front of his port at Fiumicino, to serve as the foundation for a wharf. In the 1500s, the obelisk was brought to the present-day St. Peter's Square, where it can still be seen. The circus had already fallen into disuse by the 3rd century AD. In a sector bridging the spina, a mausoleum with a cupola was built that was transformed into a church between the 5th and 6th centuries.

Below St. Peter's Basilica, where the right aisle is located, is a large, important burial area known as the *Vatican necropolis*. It is a series of tombs in green brick, all rather similar, opening onto a funeral way. They were built here, mostly by rich freedman families, from the 2nd century AD to the 4th century AD. They had rectangular rooms with vaulted ceilings, often with niches in the sides. A rich decoration with paintings and stucco covered the walls, while mosaics embellished floors and walls. To the north is a rectangular square 7x4 meters in size, with a series of mausoleums. The area must have been considered particularly important, as the tombs surrounded it completely, and in fact it was known as the *tomb of St. Peter*. In the 2nd century, the original grave was celebrated with the construction of the so-called *Trophy of Gaius* (from the name of the apologist that mentions it). It was a monument with a shrine and two superimposed niches, the lower one covered with a sheet of travertine and preceded by two columns. Constantine rebuilt the shrine in 313 AD and included it in a new monument, the *Martyrium*, which was then added to the center of the presbytery of the basilica that was built here. In fact, *St. Peter's Basilica* was built precisely with the intention of honoring the apostle in the place where he was buried. The hilly area on which it was to be built was terraced on one side for this purpose, while the hill had to be cut to the north. Constantine's basilica had a nave and four aisles, separated by four rows of 24 columns, a long, narrow transept and an apse at the back. In the central portion of the transept, 36 centimeters deep, was the monument to Peter.

N

PLAN OF THE
VATICAN
NECROPOLIS

7

6

5

4

3

2

1

1.  MAUSOLEUM WITH RICH ARCHITECTURAL DECORATIONS AND PAINTING
2.  MAUSOLEUM OF TULLIUS ZETHUS (WITH STUCCO DECORATION)
3.  MAUSOLEUM OF TYRANNUS AND URBAN, HADRIAN'S FREEDMEN
4.  MAUSOLEUM OF THE FREEDMEN OF THE TULII AND CAETENNII
5.  MAUSOLEUM OF THE VALERII (WITH STUCCO DECORATION)
6.  MAUSOLEUM OF THE GIULII (DECORATION WITH CHRISTIAN THEMES AND MOSAIC WITH CHRIST AS APOLLO)
7.  TOMB OF PETER (TROPHY OF GAIUS)

Later, an additional monumental structure was built on this spot, covered with a baldachin supported by four spiral columns in Parian marble. There was no altar, as the basilica was only used for funeral purposes at that time. In the 6th century, the floor of the presbytery was superelevated and preceded by two rows of six spiral columns. The edifice remained this way until the 15th century, when it was rebuilt by Nicholas V.

A. HADRIAN'S MAUSOLEUM
B. PONS AELIUS

ROMAN MASONRY
STRUCTURES

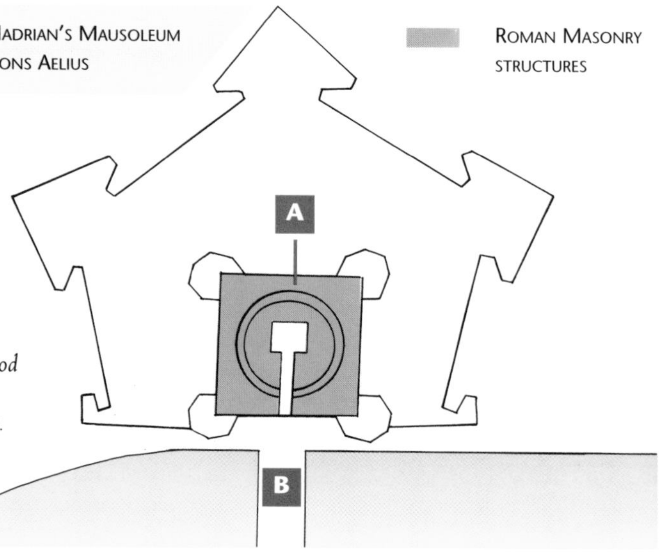

80  In 134 AD, Hadrian completed a magnificent new funerary monument, inspired by the mausoleum of Augustus, that would become the tomb for almost the entire Antonine dynasty. A new bridge was specially constructed to connect Hadrian's Mausoleum to the Campus Martius. Called Pons Aelius, it is now known as Ponte Sant'Angelo.

81  An aerial view allows us to admire the mausoleum's structure. A large cylinder stood on a square foundation, surmounted by a tumulus on which stood a bronze quadriga driven by the emperor.

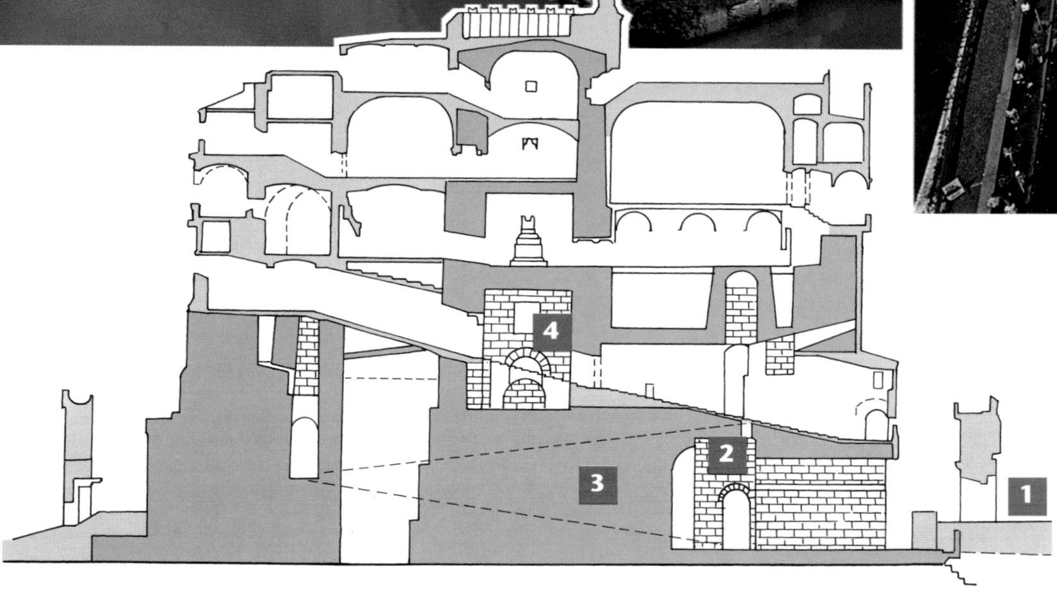

A

B

MODERN STRUCTURES
ROMAN MASONRY
STRUCTURES

1. ENTRY
2. VESTIBULE
3. BEGINNING OF ORIGINAL RING CORRIDOR
4. BURIAL CHAMBER

4

3

2

1

In 123 AD, in the *Horti of Domitia*, Hadrian began construction of a monument that was not opened until 134, and was destined to become the dynastic tomb for the Antonines. To connect the mausoleum with the *Campus Martius*, a new bridge was built, the *pons Aelius*, the present-day Ponte Sant'Angelo. The original construction, inspired by the Mausoleum of Augustus, must have rested on a square foundation 89 meters long and 15 meters high, in *opus latericium* and with radiating rooms with vaulted ceilings all around. On it capped by friezes with bucranes and festoons. The four corners of the foundation were decorated with groups of bronze statues, while on an outside enclosure there were probably gilt bronze peacocks, now at the Vatican Museums (della Pigna courtyard). The present-day entrance is three meters above the original entry with three fornices, which unfortunately have not survived. A short corridor leads to a square vestibule, whose back wall contains a semicircular niche where a statue of Hadrian probably originally stood (the and Severine emperors down to Caracalla. Earlier emperors, from Augustus to Nerva, were buried in the Mausoleum of Augustus, while the ashes of Trajan were placed at the base of Trajan's Column. Above the burial room, and on an axis with it, are two other rooms (and perhaps a third). In 403, the emperor Honorius fortified the mausoleum, transforming it into a bastion of the Aurelian walls. In 537 the edifice resisted the assaults of Vitige's Ostrogoths, but fell soon thereafter when attacked by Totila. In the 10th century it was transformed

stood an enormous cylinder 64 meters in diameter and 21 meters high, surmounted by a tumulus that supported an imposing bronze quadriga driven by the emperor. On the outside, the wall was covered with marble slabs. On the foundation tympanum were inscriptions with the epitaphs of the people buried within. Pilasters dotted the surface and were head is in the Vatican Museums). Continuing, you reach a helicoidal ramp illuminated by four vertical shafts that rise to the burial room in the center of the structure. In the hall, originally covered in marble, with its square layout with three arched niches on the three sides, were the burial urns of the emperor Hadrian and his wife Sabina, and those of all the Antonine into a castle and was also used as a prison and sanctuary. Gregory VII, Cola di Rienzo, and Clement VII all took refuge here. The edifice, named Castel Sant'Angelo, thus became the principal stronghold of Rome. Between the 10th and 14th centuries, it fell into the hands of the most powerful families until, under Nicholas III, it became property of the popes.

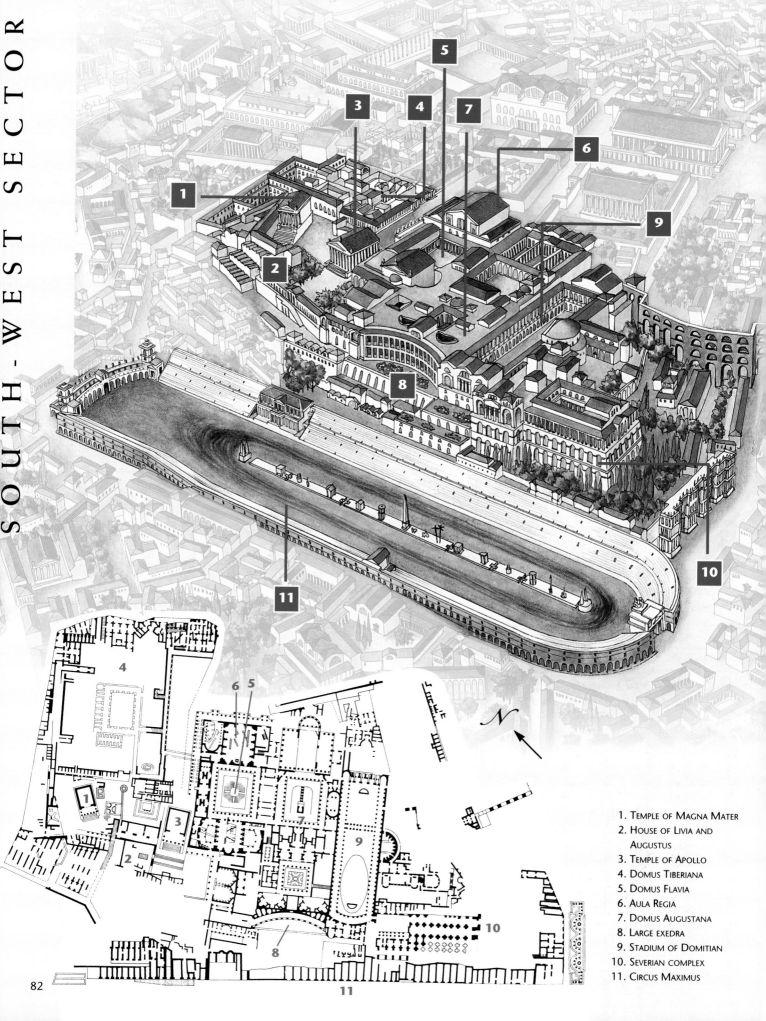

SOUTH·WEST SECTOR

1. TEMPLE OF MAGNA MATER
2. HOUSE OF LIVIA AND AUGUSTUS
3. TEMPLE OF APOLLO
4. DOMUS TIBERIANA
5. DOMUS FLAVIA
6. AULA REGIA
7. DOMUS AUGUSTANA
8. LARGE EXEDRA
9. STADIUM OF DOMITIAN
10. SEVERIAN COMPLEX
11. CIRCUS MAXIMUS

82-83 *The Palatine Hill still retains traces of the sumptuous dwellings that gradually covered the entire hill: the house of Augustus and Livia, the* Domus Tiberiana, *the* Domus Augustana *and* Flavia, *the* Stadium, *and the* Domus Severiana.

83 *If we note the Palatine Hill's position from the Tiber, which was very close by, and from the other hills, from which it stood in a central position, we can understand why it was chosen by the first peoples who settled here.*

According to legend, in ancient times the Palatine Hill was occupied by Greeks who had left Arcadia under the leadership of Evander. When Aeneas arrived here after his long voyage from Troy, this same king welcomed him.

This and other tales in Roman tradition were long considered nothing more than fables, but archaeological excavations have actually been able to confirm at least some of them. In fact, remains have been found on the hill from a settlement prior to the time of Romulus (9th century BC), which was followed by an actual village of huts, traceable to the legendary epoch of the founding of Rome (8th century BC). According to the ancients, the dwelling of Romulus (*House of Romulus*) was a hut in the southwest area, where Augustus' house was later built. The traces that several huts left on the tufa surface of the hill are still visible. Indeed, the location was excellent, and quite suitable for a human settlement. According to sources, the primitive city, which was enclosed by walls, could be entered through three gates (Pl. *Nat. Hist. 3,5,66*): the *Porta Mugonia*, which led to the *Via Sacra*; the *Porta Romana* or *Romanula*, near *Via Nova*; and finally, the *Scalae Caci* (named after the legendary giant killed by Hercules).

What is certain is that the area was always religious in nature, as evidenced by the existence of numerous cults, some of which were extremely ancient. An important festival was the *Lupercalia*, a fertility festival connected with the city's totem animal and the *Lupercal*, a cave at the foot of the Palatine from which a procession of wolf priests dressed in goat skins would emerge, harassing anyone who passed, especially women.

Postumius Megellus built a *Temple of Victory* at the top of the hill in 294 BC, probably on the site of an earlier cult to the deity. Near it was the *Temple of Magna Mater*.

The religious and historical importance of the Palatine made it the preferred residence for Roman ruling classes. Numerous *domus* of illustrious persons were built here during the Republican era. Lutatius Catalus, Marcus Livius, Drusus, Clodius, Milo, Cicero and his brother Quintus, Mark Antony, Silla Messalla Corvinus, Agrippa, and Hortensalus chose the hill as their residence. When Augustus, who was born here, decided to move to the Palatine as well, he bought numerous dwellings, including that of the orator Hortensius, so that his *domus* would be built in an especially significant location. This was all part of a policy aimed at reviving the cult of origins in Roman spirit, with a return to the *mos maiorum*, or the traditions of the ancestors. Consequently, other emperors moved to the Palatine as well. Tiberius built his palace, the *Domus Tiberiana*, in the northwest corner, where the Farnesian

Gardens are today. Caligula extended the construction to the forum. Nero reorganized the urban landscape of the area by building the *Domus Transitoria*. In 64 AD, a fire gave the emperor the opportunity to design the *Domus Aurea*, which stretched from the Esquiline to the Velia and the Palatine. Domitian made a further radical transformation of the hill when Rabirius, his architect, leveled the valley between the Cermalus and the summit, the *Palatium*, building such a vast *domus* that the site on which it stood *itself* became known as the *Palatium*, i.e. *the palace* par excellence. An aqueduct, the *Aqua Claudia*, was extended to the hill to provide water for this enormous complex and all its gardens. From the forum side, the emperor also created a sort of monumental vestibule to the imperial palaces. Thereafter, Septimius Severus further expanded the complex by adding thermal baths. To build them, he erected a foundation supported by arches that looked out directly onto the Circus Maximus, almost suspended in the air. In this way, the imperial family could enjoy a privileged view of the shows. To make it even more magnificent, he also built the *Septizodium*, a sort of monumental scene. There were also several service areas, such as the *Schola Praeconum* and the *Pedagogium*. The last significant work was the construction of the *Temple of Elagabalus*, after which the Palatine went into a decline. In the Middle Ages, Odoacer and Theodoric lived here. Later, there was a proliferation of churches and monasteries.

# THE WESTERN PALATINE HILL

## THE TEMPLE OF MAGNA MATER

The *Temple of Magna Mater*, the goddess Cybele, was built in 191 BC, after the Second Punic War, in an attempt to regain the favor of the gods, which seemed to have slipped away. Its high podium can be seen and has been positively identified through

*84 top  Very ancient traditions are tied to the Palatine, such as that of the goddess Pales, whose name may be etymologically connected to the name* of the hill and what was called Palatium, *the complex of Imperial Palaces, whose remains still strongly characterize the place.*

the discovery of a beautiful statue of the seated deity, now at the Palatine Museum. The sources say that the Sybilline Books were consulted during the war, and that they suggested that the aniconic symbol of the goddess, a long black stone, should be brought to Rome from Pessinunte in Asia Minor. A temple on the Palatine was then built to hold the similacrum. The structure stood on an artificial tufa terrace, in which a group of rooms were carved, probably shops, facing a covered road. A large stairway led to the foundation, and through a Corinthian hexastyle colonnade, to the square cella. When it was dedicated, the *Ludi Megalenses* were celebrated on the foundation across from the pronaos, and included some of the best comedies of Plautus and Terentius. Augustus restored the edifice in 3 AD following a fire.

*84 bottom Of the remains of the first imperial era, and not surprisingly located above the Republican residential area, we can visit a complex known as the House of Livia, in the western zone of the Palatine, east of the Temple of Magna Mater, which still has beautiful style II frescoes.*

85 right
*The House of Livia
still has numerous
frescoed rooms.
Particularly beautiful
are the* tablinium*,
with two wings, and a*
triclinium*. The
painted surfaces are
dotted with*

*architectural elements,
such as columns that
seem to stand out from
the walls, framing
monochrome or
figurative panels.*

## THE HOUSE OF LIVIA AND AUGUSTUS

*84-85 top
Spectacular
architecture, such as
in the* tablinium *of
the House of Livia,
includes doors that
half open onto
frescoed scenes of
mythological
episodes. Some may
have been replicas of
the more famous
Greek originals, such
as Mercury coming
to free Io as she is
guarded by Argus.*

The first nucleus of the house of Augustus consisted of the house of the orator Hortensius, and was then expanded with the acquisition of neighboring dwellings. The *Domus* on the Palatine included both a public and a private section. The *domus* of Livia, which dates back to the first century BC, should also be considered a private area reserved for his wife, and an integral part of the emperor's home. The dwelling was accessible through a descending corridor decorated with a mosaic floor, that led to a large covered atrium. Three rooms opened to the east, of which the central and most important one was used as a *tablinium*, or receiving area, and was decorated with elegant paintings in the second Pompeiian style. On the right wall is a figure of a colonnaded portico, in the center of which is a niche showing a mythical episode in which Io, beloved by

Jupiter and forced into prison by the jealous Juno, is freed by Mercury. To the right is a depiction of Argus, whom Jupiter's wife used as a prison guard. The fresco must have been part of a well-known painting from the 4th century BC by the painter Nikias. The back wall shows another mythological episode with the nymph Galatea fleeing from Polyphemus. The room to the left has a painted decoration of columns and pillars, stylized figures, and winged griffins. The room on the right has festoons tied to the columns and a yellow frieze above, with incredible impressionistic-style landscapes. Even the *triclinium*, or dining room, was decorated with frescoes in the second style: False architecture and windows open onto landscapes. This type of painting was particularly popular and was used when there was no view of real gardens nearby.

The House of Augustus had rooms on two terraces. Overall, it was a rather simple dwelling, as the sources tell us: The *private section* to the northwest was in fact characterized by a series of modest rooms. The rooms are named after the various frescoes that are still visible, such as, for example, the Room with the Masks and the Room with the Pine Festoons. To the northeast was the *public* section, near the temple of Apollo. There were two libraries on this side for Latin and Greek literature. One of them is the so-called Black Room. The decoration of the so-called Room with Perspectives, where the wall is frescoed with a two-story architectural structure, is especially beautiful, with an extraordinary sense of depth. To the southeast was a large colonnaded room with a stucco vault and inlaid floor. The wall decoration includes a painted architectural structure with paintings of figures and masks. The most elegant room in the entire *domus*, however, is a *cubiculum* known as Augustus' Bedroom, which has recently been restored. It was a small room decorated with complex painted structures, illustrated panels, friezes and small squares. As in the other rooms, the predominant colors are red, yellow and black.

In 12 BC, when Augustus was elected *Pontifex Maximus*, a temple dedicated to Apollo was built in the public section of his house. It was one of the most important buildings on the Palatine, and famous poets like Horace and Propertius dedicated their poetry to it. The temple was built entirely of white marble, and the doors, which led to the cella, were covered in gold and ivory. The edifice was connected to the so-called Portico of the Danaids, a portico in *giallo* (yellow) *antico* columns embellished with 50 statues of the daughters of Danaus. It probably also contained numerous slabs of polychrome terra-cotta depicting scenes related to the cult of Apollo. We also know that the famous Sybilline Books, which once had been kept on the Capitol, were also conserved in the base of the cult statue of Apollo.

86 *bottom* Another beautiful example of style II painting is the Room of the Festoons in the House of Augustus, with delicate decorations characterized by pine festoons hanging from slender pillars.

86-87 The emperor Augustus, who was born on the Palatine Hill, built his home here, including and expanding the house of the orator Hortensius Hortalus. By political choice, he did not want an especially luxurious dwelling, but the rooms nevertheless had sumptuous painted decorations. Here, for example, is the Room of Masks, with its complex architecture inspired by stage settings.

87 *top* The façade of the palace of Tiberius had a series of arcades that led to an inner street known as Clivus Victorius, and to some shops below. The rooms discovered are vaulted and have stucco and painted decorations.

87 *center* Tiberius was the first to build a large palace on the Palatine, continuing the tradition Augustus had begun. The Domus Tiberiana, of which remain only the vestiges of the walls that supported the actual palace, is on the west side of the hill and faces the Forum.

87 *bottom* Nero continued the tradition by building the Domus Transitoria on this section of the hill. After 80 AD, it was rebuilt by Domitian and connected to his palace, which was located higher up, by a vaulted cryptoporticus 130 meters long.

# THE DOMUS TIBERIANA

Tiberius built his *domus*, the first of the Imperial Palaces, in the northwest corner of the Palatine, according to an organic project. The structure covered a surface area 120 x 150 meters in size, which Caligula later extended toward the Forum. Unfortunately, all that is visible today is the portion that supported the upper floors. The actual palace was above it, but has not survived. We nevertheless have an idea of its great magnificence, as the remains visible on the north side are up to 20

overlooking the Forum that was transformed into an appendage of his palace, built higher up. A cryptoporticus was built to connect the two sections.

Beginning your visit from the podium of the *Temple of Magna Mater*, the rooms in green brick that can be seen are from the time of Nero. The graffiti on the walls identifies them as service areas, the site of a guard corps. Continuing on, there are still visible remains of a vat with steps, probably a

meters high. The most recent excavations have shown that the complex was not built all at one time, but formed gradually and uniformly with a series of successive expansions that encompassed a number of *Republican domus*.

A true palace did not appear until the time of Nero. Known as the *domus Transitoria*, it was designed to be part of the majestic *Domus Aurea* project. Following the fires of 64 and 80 AD, Domitian rebuilt the *domus*, with the addition of a monumental façade

fishery. A 130-meter-long cryptoporticus ran from here toward the Forum, illuminated by wolf's mouth apertures. The vaulted roof was decorated with geometrical stucco work (a replica can be seen near the House of Livia) and mosaic floors.

The front of the palace overlooking the Forum had a series of arches that led to an inner street, the Clivus Victorius, and several shops below; the vaulted rooms were decorated with stucco work and paintings; on the ground floor is more graffiti carved into the plaster, with lewd phrases, game tables and lists of accounts, indicating the passage of guards. After the depredations the *Domus Tiberiana* suffered during medieval

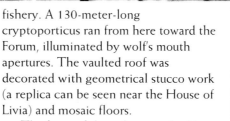

times, the area was occupied by the Farnesian Gardens. Actually, it appears that this part of the Palatine was a "green" area from the beginning, with alternating edifices and park areas, gardens, and pavilions. The Farneses probably perceived the original function of the house as a hanging garden, blending perfectly with the ancient topography.

# THE EASTERN PALATINE HILL

## DOMITIAN'S PALACE.
## THE DOMUS FLAVIA AND DOMUS AUGUSTANA

*88-89 After Augustus decided to build his home on the Palatine, all of his successors chose the hill for their dwellings as well, building a series of palaces that, to some extent integrated, gradually occupied the entire surface of the hill. First came the palace of Tiberius, then the Domus Aurea, the Domus Flavia and Tiberiana, and finally, the palace of Septimius Severus.*

*88 bottom From the wide windows of the dining room of the Domus Flavia, guests could admire the jets of water produced by nymphaea, or elliptical fountains, with the brick central structure of the western one still visible.*

In the year 81 AD, Domitian commissioned his architect Rabirius to build a large palace on top of the Palatine. In 92, he built a structure entirely of green brick, with complex architecture that revealed remarkable technical skill. This same skill is reflected in the decoration and incredible variety of plans. The structure filled the depression between the Cermalus and the *Palatium*. It is probable that the nucleus also included the public section of Augustus' *Domus*.

We can identify three distinct zones in the Palace: a public section, the *Domus Flavia*; a private section where the emperor lived, the so-called *Domus Augustana*; and the *Stadium*.

The *Domus Flavia* was reached through a colonnaded portico to the north that overlooked a vast open area, and stood on a podium, with three protruding sections. Behind the portico were three state rooms used for official ceremonies. To the left was the so-called *Lararium*, which may have been the emperor's private chapel or the headquarters of the praetorians responsible for guarding one of the entrances of the *Domus*. In the center,

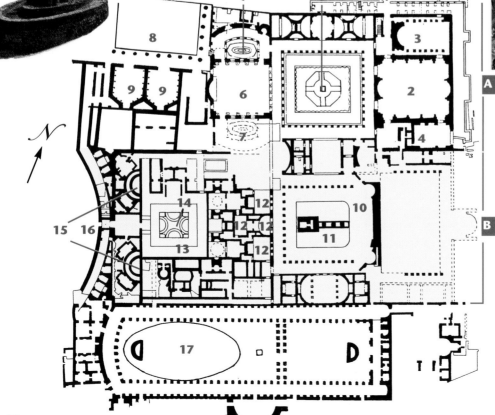

A. DOMUS FLAVIA
1. ENTRANCE
2. AULA REGIA
3. BASILICA
4. LARARIUM
5. PERISTYLE
6. COENATIO IOVIS
7. NYMPHAEA
8. ACADEMY
9. LIBRARIES

B. DOMUS AUGUSTANA
10. PERISTYLE ON THE UPPER TERRACE
11. FOUNTAIN AND TEMPLE
12. CUBICULA AND SERVICE AREAS
13. PERISTYLE ON THE LOWER TERRACE
14. FOUNTAIN
15. DIETAE
16. LARGE EXEDRA
17. STADIUM

89 top  The Lower
Peristyle of the Domus
Augustana, which
originally had a
portico, was the
emperor's true private
residence. A large
fountain in the center,
with a basin inserted
into the greenery, had
opposing concave
walls.

89 right  North of the
Peristyle were several
rooms that were
probably used for
reading.
This southern area
seems to have been built
after the Domus
Flavia.

the *Aula Regia*, the largest room, had magnificent decorations, niches with statues and pavonazzetto marble columns against the side walls, and, in the back, a large apse for the throne. From here the emperor, *dominus et deus*, set apart from the throngs, gave audiences, received ambassadors and presided over meetings. To the right was the so-called Basilica, which was probably used for Domitian's council. It was divided into an aisle and three naves by two rows of columns, with an apse at the back. Here, firm decisions were made regarding policies of the Empire. The apses, carved out throughout the most important rooms of the Palace, were especially for the Emperor, who was thus isolated from the common people, while at the same

time attention was focused on him alone. Going south, we come to a large peristyle that was originally surrounded by a portico, whose inner walls were covered with slabs of Cappadocia marble. This marble, which was especially reflective, may have allowed the emperor to watch his back and avoid any attacks as he passed through here. In the center of the peristyle, the remains of a large, octagonal fountain are still visible. To the south is a large triclinium, the so-called *Coenatio Iovis*, known for its opulent banquets. Domitian's table, slightly raised, must have been located in the center of the hall. From here, while they enjoyed elegant food, guests could admire the luxuriant gardens and beauty of the fountains and nymphaea. It was a

winter *triclinium*, as shown by the surviving hypocaust, i.e. the double flooring system used to heat the rooms. To the sides of the *triclinium* were two elliptical nymphaea, of which the western one is still standing. In back of the *triclinium*, past the apse, is a porticoed area called the Academy; farther to the south are two parallel rooms, probably two libraries.

The eastern side of the Palace, the *Domus Augustana*, was strictly reserved for the imperial family. It was on two levels and generally had smaller rooms. On the upper terrace, a series of rooms opened onto another colonnaded peristyle with a pool of water and a small temple in the center, perhaps dedicated to Minerva, which could be reached over a small foot bridge. In back of the peristyle were *cubicula*, baths and rooms.

The other level is almost 12 meters lower. Here as well, rooms are organized around a large peristyle surrounded by porticoes on two levels. In the center was an imposing fountain, decorated with a motif of opposing Amazon peltae shields; around it were living rooms and nymphaea that ran to the monumental façade facing the *Circus*

*Maximus.* It was a large colonnaded semicircular exedra behind which there are still remains of some rooms with odd architecture, probably *dietae* used for rest or meditation.

The great Stadium, built around the end of Domitian's reign, is still visible on the eastern side. It is a large, long area (160 x 48 meters), with a short curved side, surrounded by an arcade with pillars on two levels. Halfway up the east side was the imperial platform,

a large exedra surrounded by a vaulted, two-story corridor. To the north, remains have been found of a series of structures that were used as storerooms or dressing rooms. The Stadium was not used for spectacles or games, but was rather designed as a large area for walking and riding, inspired by the hippodromes of suburban villas. The complex was also decorated with numerous works of art to make it more pleasant.

90 bottom  An older floor, with colored marble decorations, was found below the triclinium of the Domus Flavia. It must have been part of an edifice on top of which Domitian built his palace, perhaps Nero's Domus.

91 top  To the southwest was a large banquet hall facing two elliptical nymphaea, of which the western one has been preserved; its fountains impressed guests at opulent official dinners.

91 bottom  In the center of the Domus Flavia is a vast rectangular peristyle surrounded by a colonnaded portico. In the center, we can still see the remains of the octagonal fountain, with low walls arranged to form a labyrinth.

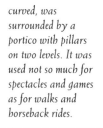

92 top left
The complex's structures were originally covered in marble. The decoration was also sumptuous, due to the numerous works of

art that made the place even more pleasant.

92 top right
The Stadium, fully 160 meters long with one of the short sides

curved, was surrounded by a portico with pillars on two levels. It was used not so much for spectacles and games as for walks and horseback rides.

92 center  The remains of a Republican house were found below the Domus Flavia, at the level of the Basilica. One of the rooms is frescoed with late style II

architectural-type paintings.  The decorations on the ceiling, with interwining ribbons that frame scenes with symbols of Isis, gave the place its name.

Under the Basilica, in an area not open to the public, were found the remains of a rich Republican house. A large rectangular space revealed advanced style II frescoes datable to the mid-first century BC, now on exhibit at the Loggia Mattei. The decorative scheme is of a traditional architectural type, while the decoration of the vault, which has given this hall its name, is particularly original. It consists of two ribbons, one red and one blue, that interweave in a complicated pattern and frame scenes with symbols of Isis and objects sacred to her cult (lotus flowers, garlands of roses, and asps). This type of decoration became fashionable at the time of Augustus after the battle of Actium, when it was used in dwellings for its ornamental value, with no special religious significance.

92 bottom  The Stadium is on the eastern side of the complex of Domitian palaces. Halfway down the east side is a large exedra that was originally surrounded by a corridor on two levels; this was the imperial family's box.

Below the *Lararium* is another Republican *domus*, the House of the Griffins, named after a fresco with two griffins on the lunettes of a room. It is the oldest Republican residence on the Palatine. It was on two floors resting on a natural slope of the hill, with two separate entrances. The rooms on the upper floor were arranged around an atrium; on the lower floor there were eight rooms. The walls were decorated with paintings in the oldest phase of style II, and can be dated to between the end of the 2nd and the first century BC. Of particular note are the frescoes in the *cubiculum*, whose walls have survived completely intact, with figures of a three-story architecture. The first has columns on a protruding plinth, the second has a podium, and the third has orthostatic walls and intarsia panels, framed above by a cornice. The painting in the next room to the west is also remarkable, and shows the same type of architectural scheme and a stucco vault with fasciae divided into lozenges and squares. The colors of the lunettes on the vault stand out: On the red background are two stucco griffins before a tuft of acanthus.

*93 top Below the Lararium of the Domus Flavia are the remains of a Republican domus, the oldest on the hill, known as the House of the Griffins, so called due to the stucco decoration of two griffins on the lunettes of one of the rooms. The walls are decorated with early style II paintings. Here, in fact, for the first time we see figures of architectural elements, which appear to stand out from the walls.*

*93 bottom Most of the frescoes in the House of the Griffins, from the late 2nd to the early first century BC, were pulled off and taken to the Antiquarium on the Palatine. Nevertheless, some style I and early style II frescoes still remain in situ, along with the remains of the mosaic floor.*

*92-93 The southern portion of Domitian's palace, the Domus Augustana, held the emperor's private apartments, with smaller rooms on two levels. There were two peristyles on the upper and lower levels of the Domus Augustana. The lower peristyle was surrounded by porticoes on two levels, and had a large fountain in the center decorated with peltae, opposing Amazon shields.*

The *Domus Severiana* is a series of structures, some of which have now been identified as part of the work by Domitian. For example, the thermal baths seem to have been part of Rabirius' design, which also included baths for the Palace. Work began again under Septimius Severus and continued until the time of Maxentius. Vats and channels have been found, as well as the normal systems for heating water and air that were used to heat rooms and swimming pools. A vast artificial terrace was built in front of the Baths, using a series of vaulted arcades on two levels supported by green brick pillars, which were intended to expand the hill's

rooms arranged along a peristyle, in which graffiti has been found containing the phrase *"exit de paedagogio"* and then the name of a slave. One of the best known ones shows a crucifix with the head of an ass and the Greek inscription, "Alexandros loves his god."

"As soon as he entered the city, Elagabalus built a temple on the Palatine in his own honor as the Sun god …and here transferred all sacred Roman objects…so that no other god would be venerated in Rome…" The remains of the Temple of Elagabalus have been found beside the *Domus Augustana*, near the Vigna Barberini area.

*94 top A vast terrace was built in front of the Baths, supported by a series of vaulted arcades with brick pillars. This area also had the purpose of increasing usable space.*
*On the lower level, toward the Circus Maximus, was the Pedagogium, the school for imperial slaves, and the Schola Praeconum, the college of heralds.*

usable surface area.

The famous *Septizodium* once stood in the southeast corner of the Palatine, toward the *Circus Maximus*, until it was destroyed by Sixtus V in 1588. It was a monumental façade-nymphaeum about 90 meters long, on a number of levels with columns, fountains, exedrae and statues. It was probably built to impress visitors coming to Rome on the Via Appia.

Farther north were the small *Maxentius Baths*, and then the *Pedagogium*, the school for imperial slaves, and lower down the *Schola Praeconum*, the site of the college of heralds, identified through a floor mosaic portraying a procession of people carrying a standard. The *Pedagogium*, which dates from the Domitian era, had a series of

94 bottom  A large, colonnaded semicircular exedra faced the valley overlooking the Circus Maximus. This was the monumental façade of Domitian's palace. Behind it were the remains of rooms that have been interpreted as rest and meditation areas (dietae).

95 top left  Septimius Severus built his Palace in the eastern area of the Palatine, but only a few remains of this complex survive. It must also have included thermal baths, from which tubs and channels have been found.

95 top right  Unfortunately, little remains of the Domus Severiana: There are some brick arcades on two floors, which primarily served to support the upper part of the palace.

95 bottom  In the southeast corner of the Palatine, toward the Circus Maximus, was a famous, monumental nymphaeum, the Septizodium, which unfortunately has not survived. Remains of the arcades of Claudius' aqueduct, the Aqua Claudia, are visible from Via San Gregorio.

*96 bottom left*
*While the upper portion of the walls was decorated with checks on a white background, the central area often continued to be dotted with broad, even areas with a red background, placed over a yellow molding.*

*96-97 We know little about domestic painting in Rome, as few examples of frescoed domus and villas have survived. One of the most beautiful is the Villa of Livia, which preserves a summer triclinium entirely*

*frescoed with illusionist garden paintings (20-10 BC). In fact, to protect its illustrious guests from the heat, the room was completely closed off, and the painted decorations were used to give the illusion of being outdoors.*

"The ancients first imitated marble facing; later the distribution of festoons, *baccellature* [molded designs of pod-shaped grooving] and cornices; later they tried to imitate figures of edifices with columns and fastigia detached from the background and in perspective; in open places as well, as in exedrae…, they depicted tragic, comic or satirical scenes; but in the cryptoportica, given the length of the spaces, painted decoration portrayed various types of landscapes: ports, promontories, beaches, rivers, springs, canals, sanctuaries, sacred groves, mountains, herds and a few shepherds; simulacra of gods or mythological episodes or battles of Troy or Ulysses' wanderings from land to land. But all these themes are now ignored, and nonsensical things are painted on the plaster rather than normal and definite objects: instead of columns, striped walls, instead of pediments, grapevines and candelabras that support figures of little temples, on tympana on which stand delicate flowers, like roots among volutes, that senselessly show little statues seated on their calyxes; as well as steles in the form of statues, some with human heads, others in animal form. Now, all these things do not exist, cannot exist and have never existed.

How can a reed truly support a roof or a candelabra the structures of a pediment, or a soft volute support a seated statue, or steles and branches spring from flowers and busts? And even knowing that these things are false, men enjoy them!… While the ancients sought public approval by using their intellect, now they seek to obtain the same effect using colors and illusory fictitious figures." (Vitruvius, *De Architectura* VII,5,1-8)

Vitruvius was the first author to discuss Roman painting in depth,

although he was critical of the art of his period. Through passages like this one, experts have been able to reconstruct the development of styles of wall decoration, at least until the first century AD (i.e., until Vesuvius erupted). The work of August Mau is particularly important in this regard. Mau created a development theory, still valid and authoritative today, that distinguished four different painting styles.

The first style, which is almost completely absent in Rome, became popular in the second century BC, and

podiums or paintings in frames. Splendid examples are found in Rome, like the frescoes of the *Villa di Prima Porta of Livia*, the *Villa Farnesina* (at the Palazzo Massimo) and the House of the Griffins on the Palatine.

The third style, which began with Augustus, is less marked than the others. The walls are overall rather unitary, with a small number of openings onto landscapes and scenes, which, when present, are still drawn in an illusionist manner. Slender elements, miniaturistic, spare details, and exotic and Egyptianized forms are added. The paintings in the underground basilica of Porta Maggiore, the pyramid of Cestius, and the Auditorium of Maecenas are examples of this third style.

A fourth style of decoration emerged

*97 top  In the villas of Farnesina, even the cryptoporticoes and corridors were decorated with small scenes of figures emerging from a light background, like little squares separated by ornamental motifs.*

imitated the wall decorations of Hellenistic palaces, like those of Alexander in Pergamum. This style emulates marble encrustation and wall hangings enriched by stucco work that emphasizes its elements.

The second style developed over the course of the first century BC and introduced a new, richer and more complex system. It is characterized by figures of bold architectural structures that allow glimpses into other spaces and at the same time frame works of art, like "settings," such as statues on

during the period between the reign of Claudius and the eruption of Vesuvius. Architectural structures continued to characterize walls, but became less fantastic and spacious. Famous examples include the Domus Transitoria, the Domus Augustana on the Palatine and Nero's Domus Aurea. Later developments led to a further stylization and simplification of false architectures in the era of Constantine: Isolated figures stand out against brown, yellow or red monochrome spaces, within simple, slender frames.

*97 center Although the House of the Griffins shows early architectural perspective, the illusionist background of the wall typical of full style II is not yet present.*

*97 bottom  The bedrooms, or cubicula, of the Villa della Farnesina, now at the Palazzo Massimo alle Terme, have splendid style II paintings, characterized by the typical division of spaces using architectural elements and niches, and scenes with figures.*

# THE CIRCUS MAXIMUS

The area between the Palatine and the Aventine was occupied by a *circus* used for chariot races, especially *quadrigae*. These races have been traced back to Tarquinius Priscus, although legend states that Romulus himself began them, starting with the celebration that followed the infamous rape of the Sabine women. Later, races became a fixture during the *Roman Games* or *Magni*, between September 4 and 18. The circus occupied an extremely vast space: It was over 600 meters long and over 100 meters wide and could seat 150,000 spectators, a number that rose to 380,000 during the 4th century AD. This is clear testimony to the enthusiasm these games elicited.

Initially, the structure must have been quite provisional, with spectators sitting on simple wooden chairs. But quite soon, after the river that crossed the valley was channeled, actual masonry bleachers were built. In the 4th century BC, the so-called *carceres*, or starting stalls for chariots, were added, first in painted wood and then in marble. The cavea consisted of three floors, the last one probably in wood, with a series of arches that supported the bleachers.

In the center of the circus was an extremely long spina (a wall separating the arenas), which over the centuries was enriched with works of art and monuments. The obelisk of Ramses II from Heliopolis (now in the Piazza del Popolo)was placed here in 10 BC, and in the 4th century AD the obelisk of Thuthmosis III from Thebes was added (visible in Piazza di San Giovanni in Laterano). The center also contained seven eggs that were used to count the laps the quadrigae completed; Agrippa also had seven bronze dolphins added that performed the same function. With time, numerous monuments, niches and small sanctuaries were placed on the

spina. At the end, Claudius built bronze metae, conical structures that marked the point around which the chariots were to turn. In the center of the southern curved side was a door, which in the second century BC was replaced by the Arch of Stertinus; later, around 81 AD, it was replaced with another arch that the Senate dedicated to the emperor Titus in commemoration of his victories against the Jews.

On the east side, below the Palatine, Augustus built the *pulvinar*, a

platform that was originally designed as a sacred area, used not so much by the emperor and his circle as by the gods who attended and protected the games.

What is still visible today is a vast field that shows the perfect imprint of the circus, as well as some remains of the short sides and the *carceres*. Excavations that were underway here had to be interrupted due to heavy flooding.

*98 top and 98-99* *According to legend, even in the Etruscan age there was an area between the Palatine and the Aventine used for chariot races. Tradition and interest in these races grew over time, and between the 4th century BC and 4th century AD, a better constructed, more practical complex was built: the Circus Maximus.*

1. PLAN OF THE CIRCUS
2. FIRST FLOOR
3. SECOND FLOOR
4. THIRD FLOOR
5. CIRCUIT ROAD

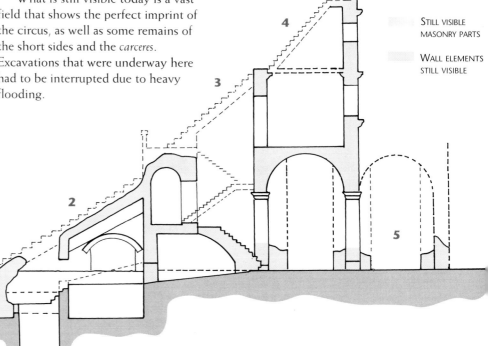

STILL VISIBLE MASONRY PARTS

WALL ELEMENTS STILL VISIBLE

*99 right* In the 3rd
century AD, the
headquarters of the
Secretarium Circi
Maximi, *which was
behind the Circus, was
changed to include a
Mithraeum. After*

*entering from the east,
one came to the inner
sanctum, the* spelaeum,
*or grotto. A large relief
work was found here
depicting the god killing
a bull, a typical scene in
the Mithraic cult.*

*99 bottom What is
still visible today of the
Circus Maximus is
its imprint on the grass.
We can also see a few
remains of the short
sides, with the walls
that supported the*

*masonry bleachers in
the cavea and the
carceres, the starting
gates for the chariots.
Unfortunately,
excavations here had to
be discontinued due to
flooding.*

## THE MITHRAEUM

In the 2nd century AD, the structure
that can be seen at the level of Via
dell'Ara Massima, behind the north side
of the *Circus Maximus*, was probably a
public building, the *Secretarium Circi
Maximi*, seat of a tribunal of the *praefectus
urbi*. Five parallel, rectangular, rather
elongated rooms can be identified,
which could be entered through two
long stairways on the Circus side. In the
3rd century AD, the complex was
remodeled to hold a *Mithraeum*, as shown
in a dedicatory inscription that can be
seen in one of the east rooms. The

faithful, most of them freedmen, also
left their testimony here.

"Tiberius Claudius Hermes,
following a vow, offers the image of the
god to the Sun god, the mighty
Mithras"

*Deo Soli Invicto Mithrae Ti(berius)
Cl(audius) Hermes ob vptum dei typum d(ono)
d(at)*

The *Mithraeum* had an east entrance;
an *apparatorium*, a sort of sacristy; and
the actual sanctuary, the *spelaeum*, or
grotto. Two niches held the statues of
the torch-bearers, *Cautopates* and *Cautes*.
The following rooms to the east were
more important, and the great relief
found of the god Mithras may have
been here; it depicts him killing a bull,
with *Sol*, *Luna*, *Cautopates* and *Cautes* at
his side, and lower down shows Mithras
with the bull behind him.

# THE AVENTINE HILL

The Aventine is the northernmost hill of the city. It stood outside the *Pomoerium*, at least until the time of Claudius. Its proximity to the Tiber and its geological conformation have in some ways shaped its history. According to legend, the area was inhabited by Ancus Marcius, who led the inhabitants of numerous conquered cities here. From the beginning, the hill has always been bound to the history of the plebeians, especially after the new port of Rome, the *Emporium*, was built at its feet. It then became a commercial district, frequented by merchants of various nationalities who in time established the class of plebeians who finally obtained political equality after the wars with the patricians in the 4th century BC. When a law was promulgated in 456 BC that provided for the distribution of lands on the hill to the plebeians, the area became predominantly working class. One can thus imagine how the district developed, growing ever more populous and chaotic. Remains of dwellings have been found in the Santa Sabina area. Here, some portions of the *Servian Walls*

have been found, dating to the 4th century BC. Ancient edifices were built up against the wall, and in Republican times structures were also added outside them, with passages that connected them, showing that the walls had lost their original defensive function by that time.

There were numerous religious centers on the Aventine: Some of the most ancient sanctuaries include the *Temple of Diana*, a peripteral octastyle surrounded by porticoes, and the *Temple of Minerva*, in the center of the hill, where Via San Domenico is located (it appears that from the 3rd century BC on, this temple was the headquarters of the guilds of scribes and actors). Other temples were built next to them, like those of *Ceres, Liber and Libera, Luna* and *Libertas*.

During the imperial age, the district gradually transformed into a residential quarter: Here were the homes of the poets Ennius and Nevius, of Trajan, before he became emperor, and of Vitellius and L. Sura. The remains of the Surane Baths from L. Sura's home are under the church of Santa Prisca. A

*THE AVENTINE AREA*

1. PORTA OSTIENSE
2. PYRAMID OF CAIUS CESTIUS
3. MT. TESTACCIO
4. PORTICUS AETTILA
5. HORREA GALBANA
6. WHARVES

imposing *Porticus Aemilia*, a storehouse for incoming materials, made of tufa in *opus incertum*, by Lucius Aemilius Lepidus and Lucius Aemilius Paulus. The complex was almost 500 meters long. It was divided into 50 aisles by pillars (seven deep) and was covered by a series of small vaults jutting out one over the other. Some parts of the walls are still visible between vie Branca and Vespucci.

When Rome's population began to increase in the 2nd century BC, free distributions of grain to the populace also increased, and as a consequence more space was needed. There were many of these food warehouses, or *Horrea*, between *Porticus Aemilia* and Mount Testaccio. The best known were the *Horrea Galbana*, which consisted of three buildings with a central courtyard and a series of rooms all around. Recently, however, these areas have also been identified as the dwellings of the numerous slaves employed here.

## THE TESTACCIO

few rooms of a *Mithraeum* have also been found over these structures.

The *Mithraeum* of Santa Prisca, from the 2nd century AD and destroyed in the 1400s, is accessible through the church's left aisle. Through a crypt, you reach a *spaeleum*, preceded by an atrium. Near the entrance, two niches were used for statues of Mithras' helpers, *Cautes* and *Cautopates*; in the back was another niche showing a rather common scene of Mithras killing a bull, with a reclining Saturn visible below; both figures are made of amphorae covered in stucco. On the side walls are paintings of people in procession carrying objects/symbols of the various levels of their initiation: the crow, the *nymphus*, the soldier, the lion, the Persian, the *Heliodromos*, the father.

The remains of another thermal facility, the *Decian Baths*, built by the

emperor Decius in 252 AD, were found below the square of the Temple of Diana. The plan has survived due to a design by Palladio.

Beginning in the 2nd century BC, the cattle market was no longer large enough to meet the needs of trade, which required more and more practical features and space for commodities, and housing for the multitudes employed in the various operations. Thus, a new river port was built in a still-vacant area at the foot of the Aventine, the so-called *Emporium*. The paving was completed, and barriers, wharves and stairways descending to the Tiber were built, along with a pier fully 500 meters long, in front of which were large blocks of travertine with mooring rings for the ships.

In the area behind it were numerous service buildings like the

The *Testaccio* — the hill of potsherds — is an artificial rise on the left bank of the Tiber, between the Aurelian Walls and the present-day Via Galvani. It is about 30 meters above street level and has a total surface area of about 20,000 square meters.

The present-day name comes from the Latin *testa*, which means shard. It was here, in fact, that broken amphorae were customarily tossed after being unloaded from ships moored at the nearby port. Most were oil amphorae of the "Dressel 20" type, bearing the factory mark on the handles and an indication of origin and the various controls on the body. The majority of the containers came from Spain, especially Betica, the present-day Andalusia, while others came from North Africa. Most of the amphorae can be dated to a period between the mid-2nd and the mid-3rd century AD.

# THE PYRAMID OF CAIUS CESTIUS

*C(aius) Cestius L(uci) f(ilius) Epulo, Pob(lilia tribu), praetor, tribunus plebis, (septem)vir epulonum*

*"Caius Cestius Epulus, son of Lucius, of the Poblilia tribe, praetorian, tribune of the plebeians, septemvirate responsible for the sacred banquets"*

This inscription comes from a pyramid-shaped monument that can still be seen on Piazza Ostiense. Added to the Aurelian Walls in the 3rd century, in the Middle Ages it was known as the *Meta Remi*; it is a funeral monument built for Cestius. On the bases of the bronze statues of the deceased, now in the Musei Capitolini, were other inscriptions that named the illustrious heirs, including Valerius Messalla and Agrippa, Augustus' son-in-law. We know that these statues were made with money from *attalica*, i.e. precious vellum tapestries, which could not be placed inside due to a recent law (18 BC) against extravagance. The pyramid was originally surrounded by four columns, and was based on models from Ptolemaic Egypt, like the pyramids of Meröe. The monument, made in *opus caementicium*, is covered in marble slabs. It was almost 30 meters at the base and was 36.40 meters high. The inner chamber, accessible through a modern entrance, was rectangular and had a barrel vault. The brick facing is one of the oldest examples of this type of technique (*opus latericium*) that has survived to this day. The style three pictorial decoration was especially rich, featuring panels framed by candelabras with seated and standing female figures in the center. There were four Victories at the four corners of the vault.

102 *An imposing pyramid stands on Piazza Ostiense – the burial monument of Caius Cestius. In the Middle Ages it was known as the* Meta Remi, *and was related to another structure, the* so-called Meta Romuli. *The statue of the deceased that stood here is now on view at the Capitoline Museums. The original pyramid of Cestius was to be surrounded by columns; the architect* certainly modeled his work after pyramids in Ptolemaic Egypt. The outer surface of the monument is covered with sheets of marble, while the structure itself is in opus caementicium.

# TRASTEVERE

The Trastevere was the last of the 14 Augustan regions and included, in addition to Isola Tiberina, the right bank of the river to the Janiculum hill. Originally, however, the Trastevere was outside the urban area (separated by the *Pomoerium* until the time of Vespasian), but had nevertheless been an extremely important area ever since the age of the kings.

The Janiculum hills were a natural bulwark against Etruria, and thus indispensable for Rome's defense. Tradition states that a red flag was raised here when *Comitia* were held in the *Campus Martius*. When, during the Republican era, the new port was built (in the present-day Testaccio quarter),

PLAN OF THE EXCUBITORIUM
OF THE 7TH COHORT

A. CHAPEL (LARARIUM) DEDICATED
   TO THE GENIUS OF THE BARRACKS
B. BASIN OF FOUNTAIN
C. EXEDRA
D. GUARDS' LODGINGS

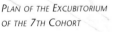

the area began to fill with service buildings and the dwellings of port workers and merchants. This was accentuated during the imperial period, when artisans, potters, millers, porters and workers, along with a large number of immigrants from the Orient, chose this place for their homes. Below the *church of Santa Cecilia* (Via della Lungaretta), at the level of the nave, structures have been found from Republican-era *horrea* and a hide-tanning workshop from the Antonine age, identified through the presence of seven hemispherical vats.

On Viale Trastevere, between Via Montefiore and Via della VII Coorte, eight meters below street level, is the *Excubitorium of the VII cohort of guards*, the barracks used for the guards who, like modern policemen and firefighters,

were in charge of supervising two of the Augustan regions (IX and XIV).

The working-class nature of the quarter can also be seen in the cults that arose here. There was a large Jewish community in this area, and it appears that the ancient synagogue stood near the present-day Porta Portese. There were also numerous temples dedicated to the *Goddess Dia*, *Fors Fortuna* (three of them, two on Via Portuense) and the *Divae Corniscae*. Several more of these religious buildings have also been found in the area of Porta Portese, Viale Trastevere, and near the Ministry of Public Education. There was also a large number of sanctuaries for

Oriental cults that served as meeting places for foreign communities and new Roman followers. They included an important *Syriac sanctuary* discovered on the Janiculum.

# THE JANICULUM

On the southern slopes of the Janiculum, as early as the 2nd century BC, there was a religious edifice dedicated to *Zeus Keraunios* and the Furies. Around the first century AD, this cult was connected to the Syriac deities, for whom a sanctuary was built (the present-day remains, however, date back to a 4th century AD reconstruction). It has a rather elongated plan in three sections. The entrance, halfway down one of the long sides, led to a large rectangular courtyard. This led into two other rooms: To the left was an atrium with two side cellae; through them one reached a basilica-type hall with a nave and two aisles, with a triangular altar in the center and at the back a large apse, for the main religious statue, in the form of a seated Jupiter. To the right, two doors led to another quite original room with a mixtilinear plan. It consisted of two smaller rooms at the sides and a larger one, with a more or less octagonal shape, with an apse at the back. Here as well, a triangular altar was found at the center, in a cavity in which several eggs and a small bronze statue were found. This *simulacrum* depicted a

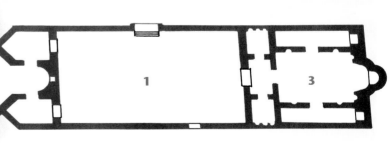

PLAN OF THE SANCTUARY TO ISIS

1. RECTANGULAR
   COURTYARD
2. MIXTILINEAR AREA
   WITH APSE
3. BASILICA STRUCTURE

male figure wrapped in the coils of a snake, and represented the god Osiris, who was buried each year to be reborn again through seven celestial spheres (the seven coils of the serpent), symbolizing the initiation of the faithful.

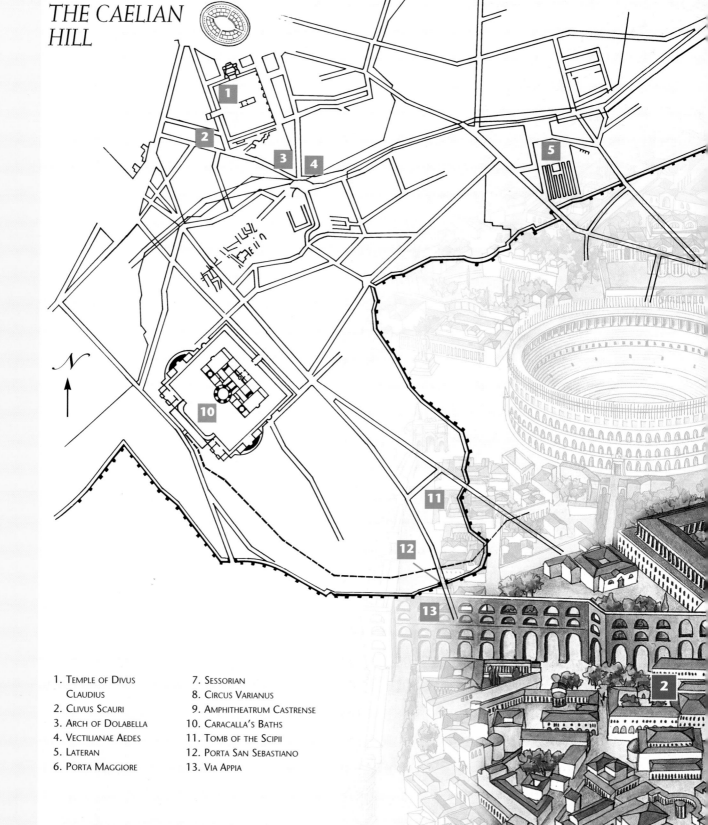

# THE CAELIAN HILL

1. TEMPLE OF DIVUS
   CLAUDIUS
2. CLIVUS SCAURI
3. ARCH OF DOLABELLA
4. VECTILIANAE AEDES
5. LATERAN
6. PORTA MAGGIORE
7. SESSORIAN
8. CIRCUS VARIANUS
9. AMPHITHEATRUM CASTRENSE
10. CARACALLA'S BATHS
11. TOMB OF THE SCIPII
12. PORTA SAN SEBASTIANO
13. VIA APPIA

The Caelian is the hill between the
Coliseum, present-day Via San Gregorio,
and Viale delle Terme di Caracalla. It
was the point where two important roads
converged: the Via Appia and the Via
Latina, to which Porta Capena led. The
oldest monuments known are sanctuaries
dedicated to primitive cults, tombs, and
a series of structures related to the
departure and arrival of magistrates and
emperors.

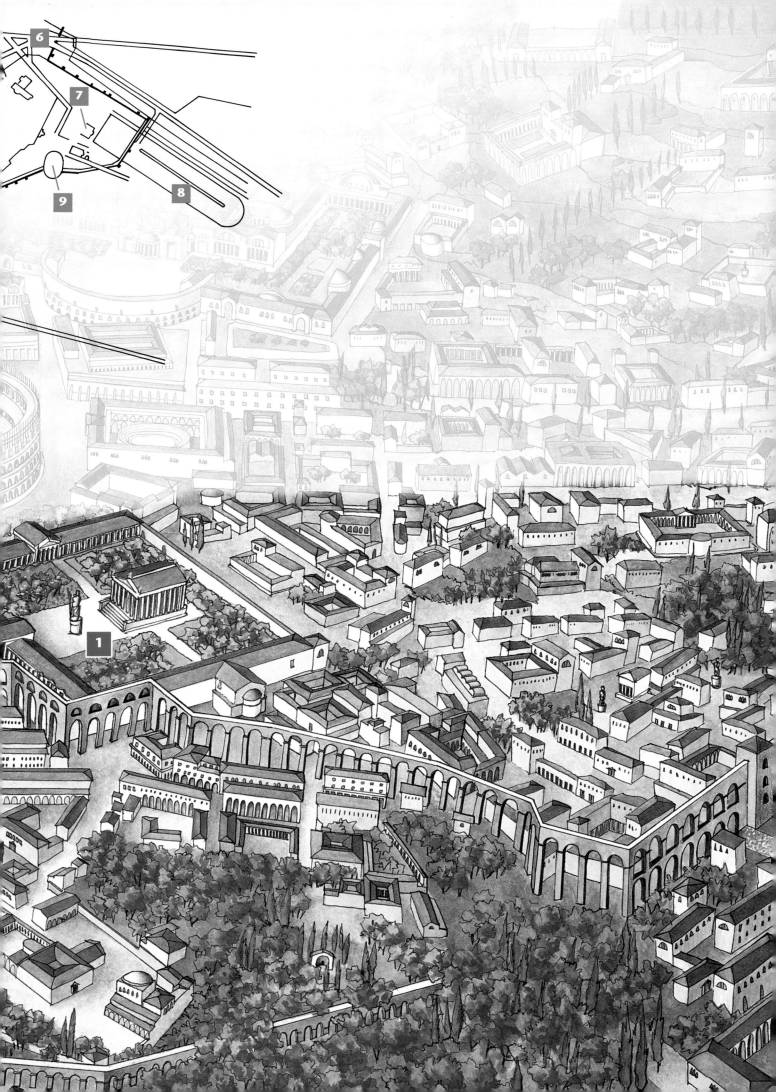

## THE TEMPLE OF DIVUS CLAUDIUS AND THE CLIVUS SCAURI

Across from the Palatine, remains can still be seen of a temple dedicated to Claudius by his wife Agrippina in 54 AD. Nero demolished part of it to build a large monumental nymphaeum. When Nero died, Vespasian rebuilt the temple (the visible remains, near the monastery of SS. Giovanni e Paolo are from this reconstruction). The building stood on a large rectangular foundation 180x200 meters in size, surrounded by a series of rooms on two levels. In the center of the west side was the stairway to the Temple. The style was typical of the time of Claudius, and was known as "rustic" due to the rough, apparently unfinished appearance of the masonry. To the north was a large cascading fountain. In the center of the foundation was the prostyle hexastyle temple building, surrounded by a green area.

The *Nero Nymphaeum*, visible on Via Claudia, is especially well preserved. It consists of a long wall of bricks with a large room in the center and a series of niches on the sides, that were probably intended to create a sort of scenic background to the gardens of his Domus Aurea.

The road that runs between S. Gregorio and SS. Giovanni e Paolo takes its name from the original name of the street, *Clivus Scauri* (probably named after Aemilius Scaurus, a censor in 109 BC). It included a series of imperial-age dwellings, a *cryptoporticus*, and a *basilica hall* with an apse. The latter, behind the S. Andrea Oratory, has been connected to the famous library of Pope Agapitus I (535 AD). A group of buildings from the 3rd century AD was also found on Piazza SS. Giovanni e Paolo; they were probably *tabernae* used as shops. To the north, the basilica of SS. Giovanni e Paolo stands on imperial-age edifices: two large dwellings with a number of levels, small private thermal baths and another dwelling, under the nave, of which the

façade along the *Clivus Scauri* survives — visible on the left side of the church. The latter edifice was originally a large multi-story *insula* divided into numerous apartments that was later transformed into a luxurious home. Particularly interesting is the *"confession"* visible halfway up the courtyard stairs: a niche with frescoes from the 4th century AD, depicting a history of Christian martyrs, who may be Crispin, Crispinian and Benedetta during the time of Julian the Apostate.

## THE ARCH OF DOLABELLA

"P. Cornelius Dolabella, son of Publius, and Gaius Junius Silanus, son of Gaius, Flamin of Mars, consuls, by decree of the Senate, contracted (the arch) and inspected it."
*P. Cornelius P.f. Dolabella C. Iunius C.f. Silanus flamen Martial(is) co(n)s(ules) ex s(enatus) c(onsulto) faciundum curaverunt idemque probaver(unt)*

Near Piazza SS. Giovanni e Paolo, on Via di San Paolo della Croce, there is a travertine arch known as the *Arch of Dolabella*. It was the support for the archway of a Nero-era aqueduct, from 10 AD according to the inscription. The arch has been identified as the *Porta Caelimontana* that originally opened into the Servian Walls, and was reconstructed during the Augustan period.

## THE MILITARY HOSPITAL AREA

Within the Military Hospital, between Piazza Celimontana and Via Santo Stefano Rotondo, there have been a number of recent excavations that have revealed a complex and interesting history of settlement. Of particular interest is the discovery of an enormous house, the *Vectilianae aedes*. It may have been the residence of the emperor Commodus, in which he was strangled late in 192 AD. The two-story complex stood on the top of the Caelian, on an area about 8000 square meters in size. It included winter and summer quarters, courtyards, state rooms, thermal baths and service buildings, and its decorations indicate that it was one of the richest residences in the area. It was built in the late Antonine

The Lateran occupied a small part of the Caelian Hill. In this area, a series of excavations have revealed a large number of edifices. Below the S. Giovanni Hospital (Sala Mazzoni), for example, is the *Villa of Domitia Lucilia*, mother of the emperor Marcus Aurelius.

Nearby, 10 meters down on Via Amba Aradam, below the INPS building, is a series of edifices built on terraces, traceable to the Julian-Claudian era. They were later joined into a single residential complex that has been identified as the *Domus of Fausta*, the sister of Maxentius and wife of Constantine.

The most important complex in the area is nevertheless the one below the Basilica of St. John Lateran. Below the apse is a trapezoidal-shaped dwelling from the 3rd century AD; below the nave are the remains of a rich house from the first century AD, built on a terrace and featuring rich fourth-style decoration. It was probably one of the houses of the Laterans, whose property Nero confiscated in 65 AD. The emperor's horse guard barracks, the *Castra Nova Equitum Singularium*, were built on the same area at the end of the 2nd century AD, but were demolished in the 4th century to erect the Basilica.

The *Basilica of St. John* originally had a nave and four aisles with an apse and two rooms in the back to form the transept. Dating back to 318 AD, it is the oldest Christian basilica in Rome.

period using Republican era structures, and was remodeled in the 4th century, probably becoming the residence of Q. Aurelianus Symmacus.

The area has also revealed the remains of a *domus*, which probably belonged to Gaudentius, a young senator and errand boy for Symmacus in the 4th century AD.

Farther east is the so-called *Basilica Hilariana*, built by *Publicius Hilarus*, a pearl merchant, follower of Cybele and member of the guild of *Dendrophori* (carriers of the sacred pine). The most recent excavations show that it was not really a basilica, as it does not have a nave and aisles, but an edifice used for meetings of the religious guild. Despite the fact

that excavations have not been able to fully investigate the area — for example, the typical ditch for the *taurobolius*, the ritual sacrifice to which the new adept was subjected, has not been found — beautiful mosaic floors have been preserved, including one showing a pierced eye that probably functioned as a magical charm.

*106 Next to the church of SS. Giovanni e Paolo, we can see some remains of the Temple of Divus Claudius, which the emperor built in 54 AD, in memory of his wife Agrippina. It was* destroyed by Nero, who transformed it into a great monumental nymphaeum to embellish his palace.

*106-107 Clivo di Scauro, near the churches of S. Gregorio* and SS. Giovanni e Paolo, preserves the name of the primitive Roman road, Clivus Scauri, which was named after a member of the Aemilii Scaurii family. The appearance of the *imperial-age road is essentially the same, with the façades of tall dwellings on the sides, connected by seven brick arcades (those visible, however, are from a medieval reconstruction).*

# THE PORTA MAGGIORE AREA

The Porta Maggiore area, which probably took its name from the fact that it led to the church of Santa Maria Maggiore, is 43 meters above sea level and is thus an ideal point of convergence for many aqueducts, such as the *Anio Vetus*, the oldest, the *Aqua Marcia*, the *Aqua Tepula* and the *Aqua Iulia*. A portion of the archway is still visible on Piazzale Labicano, with three superimposed aqueducts.

The present-day Porta Maggiore was originally a monument created from the archways of Claudius' aqueducts, the *Aqua Claudia* and the *Anio Novus*, where they crossed Via Prenestina and Via Labicana. It was

*108 left  Many aqueducts converged near the present-day Piazza di Porta Maggiore, as this was the highest ground in the city. What we now know as Porta Maggiore, which was added to the Aurelian Walls, was originally the monument created by two superimposed aqueducts, the Aqua Claudia and the Anio Novus, whose conduits can still be seen in cross section. Windows with a tympanum and*

1. PORTA MAGGIORE
2. TOMB OF THE BAKER EURYSACES
3. UNDERGROUND BASILICA OF PORTA MAGGIORE

transformed into a true gate only when it was added to the Aurelian Walls. It consists of two travertine fornices with pylons at the sides, in which were fashioned windows with tympana and Corinthian semicolumns. Above was a high attic divided by listels into three sections, with inscriptions by Claudius and Vespasian (who restored it in 71 AD), where the aqueduct channels are located. The complex was created using the so-called "unfinished" technique common during the time of Claudius, in which many of the travertine architectural elements remained in rough form. The northernmost fornix was oblique because it followed the route of the ancient Via Prenestina, which ran by one level higher.

*Corinthian engaged columns are set into the piers of the gate. The elements in travertine were left rough, appearing almost unfinished, according to a technique common in Claudius' time.*

*108 right  Outside Porta Maggiore is the tomb of Eurysaces, a baker from ancient Rome. The tomb's special structure is related to the deceased's profession; the hollow cylindrical elements are in fact perfect replicas of the containers in which flour was kneaded into dough.*

*109 top left  Near Porta Maggiore, under the railroad tracks, is an underground building from the Tiberian era, built by digging directly into the tuff. It has a rather irregular structure consisting of an atrium and a large area divided into a nave and two aisles by large pillars, ending in an apse to the east.*

*109 bottom left  The interior of the underground complex known as the Basilica of Porta Maggiore, whose precise function is unknown, is completely plastered and decorated with excellent stucco work. Especially well preserved is the decoration on the vault, with a small square in the middle depicting the abduction of Ganymede by a winged Genius.*

## THE TOMB OF THE BAKER EURYSACES

Still visible right outside the gate are the remains of the Tomb of the Baker Eurysaces, which have survived because they were included in the tower between Porta Maggiore and Porta Labicana. The structure, originally over seven meters high, stands on a travertine podium with four smooth pillars at the corners. It has five sections. Pairs of vertical cylinders can be seen among the pillars, with a horizontal fascia above that contains the following dedicatory inscription:

*"Est hoc monimentum Marcei Vergilei Eurysacis pistoris* (baker),
*redemptoris* (contractor), *apparet* (subordinate, i.e. of a magistrate)".

Above the inscription, in the center of the monument, was a series of hollow, horizontal cylindrical elements that clearly depict containers in which dough was mixed; Eurysaces was in fact a baker, and his profession was further explained in the frieze showing various phases of bread making. Even the urn, now at the Museo delle Terme, that holds the ashes of his wife Atistia, is shaped like a kneading trough (*panarium*) for bread dough. The cella must have been rather small, with an east entrance, now lost. On this side there was also the life-size relief of the couple, now at the Museo dei Conservatori in Campidoglio.

## THE UNDERGROUND BASILICA OF PORTA MAGGIORE

Near Porta Maggiore, below the train tracks (Via Prenestina access), an extraordinarily well-preserved but extremely difficult to interpret basilica has been found. The edifice, from the Tiberian period, was constructed quite oddly. In fact, trenches for walls and pillars were dug into the tufa, and then cement with flakes of flint was thrown into them. Then the vault was built,

cast on the same ground; only later was the earth removed to make room for the hall and atrium. The structure thus built was then plastered and decorated. It includes a basilica hall with a nave and two aisles, preceded by a vestibule and ending with an apse. The irregularity of the plan is, of course, the result of the way it was built. Various theories have

been advanced on the function of the edifice, which may have been a tomb or a funeral basilica. The wall decoration makes it even more difficult to interpret, as no clear unifying motif has been found. For the most part, decorations are in the third style, with mythical and realistic scenes such as Sappho leaping from the cliff of Leucade, masks, and other decorative elements.

## THE SESSORIUM

In the area between Porta Maggiore and the Lateran, there are remains of a series of antique edifices that can be considered part of a single large complex, known as the *Sessorium* or Palace of Helena. It is an imperial palace that must have been started by Septimius Severus and then completed by Heliogabalus. The complex included the *Helena Baths*, the *Castrense Amphitheater*, the *Circus Varianus* and the remains on which the basilica of Santa Croce in Gerusalemme stands. The Aurelian Walls, completed later, on one hand obliterated some of the buildings they crossed, but on the other were designed to create a broad circuit that included the Palace within them.

Traces of the *Helena Baths*, including a cistern with a series of parallel concamerations, were discovered in the Piazza di Porta Maggiore area. It was a thermal facility from the Severian era that was then remodeled by Helena, the mother of Constantine.

The so-called *Castrense Amphitheater* was located between the present-day basilica of Santa Croce in Gerusalemme and the Aurelian Walls. As the term *castrum* did not mean so much "camp" as "imperial dwelling" in the late epoch, it was probably part of the complex. The slightly elliptical amphitheater was surrounded by steps that rose to the third floor (today, only remains from the first and part of the second floor survive). The building was made entirely of brick, and the outside had a series of fornices supported by pillars framed by Corinthian semicolumns, while the third floor was closed. Here, as in the Colosseum, the awning was attached.

An open corridor fully 300 meters long ran through here, and passing along a large hall, at the point where the Santa Croce Church was later built, led to the so-called *Circus Varianus*. The name comes from *Varius*, the family name of Heliogabalus. It must have been more than 500 meters long and over 100 meters wide. In the center was the long *spina* that held the obelisk taken from the tomb of Antinous, Hadrian's favorite. The present-day basilica of *Santa Croce di Gerusalemme* stands on much older structures. In fact, it reuses a rectangular space that was transformed into a Christian basilica during the time of Constantine. At that time, the various entrances to the hall were closed and an apse was added to the east side.

*109 bottom right Between S. Croce and the Aurelian Walls, we can see the remains of a complex known as the Amphitheatrum Castrense. It is a performance center built entirely of brick, and is* *part of the Sessorium, the imperial palace begun by Septimius Severus and completed by Heliogabalus. The outside arcades, framed by Corinthian engaged columns, are still visible.*

1. CIRCUS VARIANUS
2. HALL WITH APSE
3. SESSORIUM
4. S. CROCE IN GERUSALEMME
5. AMPHITHEATRUM CASTRENSE

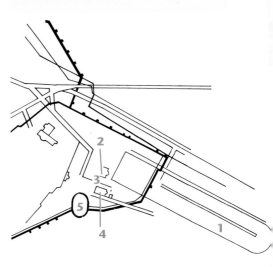

*S O U T H - E A S T   S E C T O R*

*110 Caracalla's Baths had a broad enclosure, in which there were a series of areas used for various activities intended to exercise not only the body, but also the mind, and a central structure that held the actual baths.*

The Lesser Aventine area, between present-day Viale Aventino and Viale delle Terme di Caracalla, lay partially within the Servian Walls. As early as the 3rd century BC, this area contained a large pool known as the *Piscina Publica*, which must have been a public pool. When Caracalla's Baths were completed in the 3rd century AD, to some extent they must have replaced this *Piscina*, or swimming pool. There were several sanctuaries dedicated to antique cults here, such as the well-known *Temple of Bona Dea* and the *Temple of Isis*. Important residents of this area included Cornificius, a prefect and powerful friend of Septimius Severus; Caracalla; Macrinus; Fabius Cilo; and Hadrian, before he became emperor.

The Antonine Baths, the original name for Caracalla's Baths, are the best surviving example of a thermal facility from the imperial age. Caracalla began work in 212 AD, and diverted a branch of the *Aqua Marcia* (the *Aqua Antoniniana Iovia*) here, to resolve the problem of water supply. The structure took about five years to complete. Overall, the baths included a large enclosure, over 400 meters wide at the apses, and a central structure in which the baths themselves were located. All around was a vast garden.

On the north side was a portico preceded by a series of rooms on two levels, probably shops, which also acted as a structural support for the hill at that point. On the opposite side was a "half *stadium*," equipped with stairs for spectators that also served to hide the enormous cisterns behind them. These tanks could hold up to 80,000 cubic meters of water. Placed symmetrically to the stadium, two other rooms probably served as libraries.

On the east and west sides were two large *exedrae* with an area with an apse in the center, preceded by a colonnade, and two smaller rooms at the sides, one octagonal in shape with a cupola roof.

In the center of the complex, the rooms were arranged symmetrically around a central axis, according to the typical model of the imperial era. There were two entrances that led to the *apodyteria*, or dressing rooms, which had a central corridor opening onto two rooms on each side, with barrel vaults. The floor was decorated with mosaics. From here, patrons could go to the *palaestra* and test their mettle with physical exercise either indoors or outside; the area was, in fact, a large roofless courtyard surrounded on three sides by a portico with giallo antico columns, with a vaulted roof and polychrome "herringbone" mosaic floors. On one side was a large semicircle. The mosaic floor, of which some very large fragments are still

*110-111 The Antonian Baths may be the most extraordinary example of Roman thermal baths in existence. Built in the 3rd century AD by Caracalla, but completed only by Heliogabalus and Septimius Severus, who completed the outer enclosure, they cover an almost square surface area 337 by 328 meters in size.*

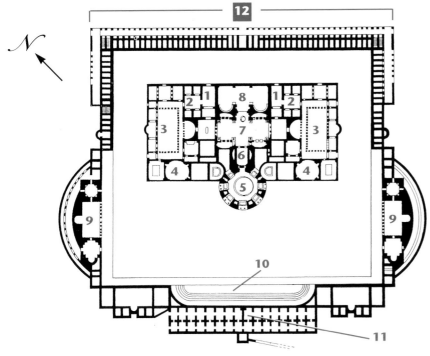

*111 top The marble decoration of the masonry structures visible has not survived, but it certainly embellished the areas, making them especially pleasant to visit. All that remain are a few remnants of friezes, capitals and marble columns.*

CARACALLA'S BATHS

1. ENTRANCES
2. DRESSING ROOMS (APODYTERIA)
3. PALAESTRAE
4. HEATED ROOMS
5. CALIDARIUM
6. TEPIDARIUM
7. BASILICA
8. NATATIO
9. LATERAL EXEDRAE
10. STADIUM
11. CISTERN
12. PORTICO AND SHOPS

intact, was particularly beautiful, and includes the famous *mosaic with athletes*, now at the Vatican Museums. At this point, patrons could proceed to the actual baths, which were shared by both sexes. The *calidarium* had an enormous circular hall with a cupola roof, of which two imposing supporting pillars remain. This room was positioned within the complex so that it would receive sunlight all day long through a group of large windows. From the *calidarium*, one proceeded to the *tepidarium*, in which there were originally two large tubs at the sides. In the center of the complex was the basilica, which was once covered by three large cross vaults, supported by imposing pillars, with granite columns at the front. Two large granite tubs were placed on the short sides and can now be seen in the Piazza Farnese. The *natatio* was the last room to the east, on an axis with the *calidarium*. It was an uncovered swimming pool that had one wall, opposite the outer façade, with a series of niches for statues. The decorative aspect was quite pronounced: In addition to mosaics, the baths were embellished by valuable works of art, some of them enormous, like the works *Hercules at Rest* and the *Farnesian Bull*.

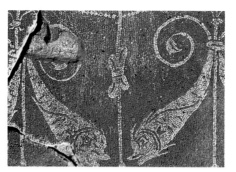

The underground sections of the complex are particularly interesting, but unfortunately not easily accessible. In addition to service areas, one of the largest *mithrea* of Rome was discovered here. It was a room with a cross-vault ceiling supported by pillars, with two large benches at the sides for the faithful. One entered through a vestibule and another hall, perhaps the stall for the bull to be sacrificed for the initiation of new followers.

112-113 To resolve the serious problem of water supply, Caracalla diverted a branch of the Aqua Marcia here; this branch then took the name of Aqua Antoniniana Iovia. We know that the emperor succeeded in completing the complex, at least the central portion, in five years.

113 top The mosaic decoration was very beautiful, although scenes with figures were not found anywhere. There were also floors with simple geometric motifs of white and black tesserae, which covered the surfaces of unimportant areas.

113 right The photograph shows the passage that led from the western palaestra to the great basilica, right in the center of the complex. Here, behind a row of columns in giallo antico, there was originally a large semicircular area covered by a half dome.

112 top and bottom The thermal complexes were often decorated with rich mosaic floors. In fact, because part of the imperial political program was implemented through public largesse, it is clear that the more establishments were provided with all the comforts and made pleasant, and the more they acted as a true public service, free to anyone, the more effective the propaganda would be. There was a large variety of mosaic subjects: Plant motifs, to the above left, floral and geometric motifs, to the above right, figures, with marine scenes, below left, athletes, etc., fit in perfectly with the different rooms. Mosaics were arranged like carpets in almost all areas, sometimes even on the bottom of swimming pools, with figures of fish that seemed to be alive and darting underwater.

The first public baths were built in Rome between the end of the 3rd and the beginning of the 2nd century BC. Before that, in wealthier homes, baths were located in special areas called *lavatrina* and were used for reasons of personal hygiene. When everyone was given the opportunity to use a well-equipped area, not only for simple daily bathing, but for more complete body care, which included physical exercise and immersion in hot water, baths ended up becoming a daily need in the imperial age. Majestic complexes were built, richly furnished and equipped with every comfort, and were regularly frequented by an impressive crowd of every age, sex and social station. The rich came with their retinues and often conducted part of their political activities here, receiving clients and making alliances. In the larger buildings, women had a section to themselves, while in smaller facilities they could come at special times, generally in the morning. There was a group of non-bath areas within the enclosures where one could walk, listen to music, watch shows, play, eat, read and admire works of art.

The manner of taking a bath actually became an art codified by medical science. Galen, one of the most famous physicians of the imperial era, prescribed a system that included four steps. First, one had to gradually raise body temperature, thus opening the pores of the skin, through physical exercise in the palestra and by sitting in well-heated rooms. The *laconicum* was used for this purpose: It was generally a circular room with apses and a cupola roof that provided drafts of warm air. Then one proceeded with a hot bath in the *calidarium*. This was generally a rather quiet room with numerous curved elements; it was preferably circular, with a tub in the center,

*114 top* Visitors to the palaestra could test their mettle through various exercises both outdoors and inside. There was an open area in the center and an arcade with columns in giallo antico, with a vaulted roof and mosaic floor; on one side there was a large semicircular area.

*114 center* The remains of the baths' basilica are right in the center of the complex. It has a rectangular plan, which was once covered with cross vaults supported by imposing pillars, with granite columns on the front. The two large granite basins on the short sides can now be seen on the Piazza Farnese.

115 top left While the
bath ritual was more or
less rigidly established,
the physical exercises
that preceded it and took
place within the
palaestra were not, and
were left to the
individual visitor,
who could test his or
her mettle in wrestling,
boxing, weightlifting,
running or fencing.
Women devoted
themselves primarily
to games with the
ball and hoop,
although some
preferred more
"masculine" exercises
such as weightlifting.

covered by a high cupola in which there were numerous windows that used the sun as a further source of heat. Then came a cold bath to reactivate the circulation. In baths that did not have a special *frigidarium* for this, tubs of cold water were placed in the exedrae of the *basilica hall*. The basilica was in the center of the complex, and thus also acted as a link, reception area and meeting place, and also resolved the difficult problem of practicability of the facilities, which could be frequented by as many as 3000 people at a time, as were the Diocletian Baths. The itinerary ended with a bath in the *natatio*, the swimming pool, and massages and body oils that protected the body from the change in outside temperature.

It was a real problem to heat and supply the enormous quantity of water needed for the myriad thermal facilities in Rome (it has been estimated that there were about 1000 of them in the 4th century AD). Until the first century BC, an outside furnace and stoves for the inside were the most common solution.

In 89 BC, a new, quite practical system was developed, known as the *Hypocaust*. It consisted of parallel rows of brick pillars arranged in checkerboard fashion, resting on an underpavement of tiles or large bricks, tilted toward the source of heat (an expedient that served to obtain a better diffusion of heat). Above, there were large, so-called "two-footed" bricks, on which rested a layer of cocciopesto; the floor itself followed. For the side walls, hollow spaces were inserted with *tegulae mammatae* followed by rectangular, hollow bricks, which connected to the loose stone foundation below.

115 top right and center
The great social and
political role played by
thermal baths, which
could be termed true
"people's villas," fully
justifies the great efforts
of engineers and
architects to find
increasingly innovative
technical solutions that
were grandiose but at the
same time practical (such
as, for example, the use of
adequate materials).

115 bottom The
system for heating the
thermal areas included
the use of
suspensurae, air
spaces located below
the pavement,
supported by small
pillars (often behind
the walls as well,
through small tubes),
which helped diffuse
warm air from the
boiler, the
prefurnius.

114 bottom The rich
decoration inside
Caracalla's Baths that
must have made this
complex especially
pleasant for visitors,
unfortunately has not
survived. The few remains
of sculptures have been
transferred to the large
national museums, as have
the mosaics. Only
architectural elements
remain in situ, such as
marble capitals and parts of
columns, providing a pale
reflection of the sumptuous
original decoration.

# THE VIA APPIA

The *Via Appia* began at the *Circus Maximus*, near the present-day Piazza di Porta Capena, ran past Caracalla's Baths and crossed the *Via Latina*. As the law forbade burying the dead within the city walls, as the centuries passed, the roads that branched off from the center gradually assumed a strong funerary nature, due to the succession of monuments in various sizes and shapes. Large funeral processions left for the cremation pyre built outside the walls. If the deceased was a patrician, not only did surviving relatives participate in these processions, but so did the ancestors (played by actors wearing masks that resembled the ancestors). Following were men carrying images of what the deceased had done in his lifetime, and finally the Dead himself, his face uncovered, carried in a litter. Not only was it a sacred obligation to bury the dead, but there was also a strong need to keep the memory of the deceased alive by building grandiose

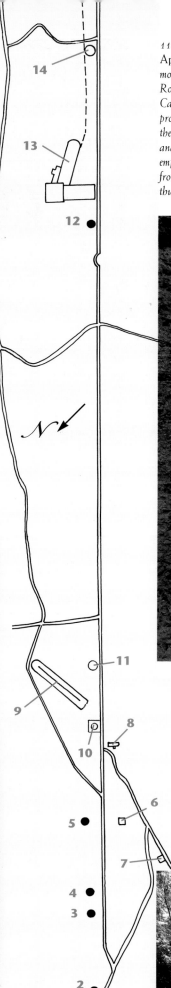

*116 left The Via Appia was one of the most important roads in Rome. From Porta Capena, Roman proconsuls departed for their assigned provinces, and magistrates and emperors left and returned from here. The road was thus equipped with official structures related to this function, such as the building where the Senate conferred with generals on their return from the provinces, the Mutatorium Caesaris, where the emperor changed his clothing, and the Temple of the God Rediculus.*

### VIA APPIA

1. PORTA APPIA (PORTA S. SEBASTIANO)
2. SO-CALLED TOMB OF GETA
3. COLOMBARIUM OF AUGUSTUS' FREEDMEN
4. COLOMBARIUM OF LIVIA'S FREEDMEN
5. TOMB OF THE VOLUSII'S FREEDMEN
6. CATACOMBS OF ST. CALLISTO
7. CATACOMBS OF DOMITILLA
8. CATACOMBS OF ST. SEBASTIAN AND CHURCH OF ST. SEBASTIAN
9. VILLA AND CIRCUS OF MAXENTIUS
10. MAUSOLEUM OF MAXENTIUS
11. MAUSOLEUM OF CAECILIA METELLA
12. MAUSOLEUM WITH PYRAMID
13. VILLA OF THE QUINTILII
14. CASAL ROTONDO

*116 bottom right There were various types of tombs located along the Via Appia; some looked like houses, with painted decorations, some like tumuli, pyramids, little temples or shrines. Marble relief work decorated the monuments, often with portraits of the deceased.*

116-117 *Beyond the Porta di San Sebastiano in the Aurelian Walls, the suburban portion of the Via Appia began. We know that in ancient times it was rather monumental in* *appearance, due to the succession of tombs of various sizes and shapes. According to law, in fact, except in special cases, the dead could only be buried outside the city walls.*

structures where a large number of people could see them: along the roads. The family tombs, like that of the *Scipii*, in the Republican era, sometimes looked like actual houses with painted decorations. But they could also take on a different form, like a *tumulus* or a *pyramid*. Even the less well-to-do, while still alive, could ensure themselves a place in a large collective tomb, within whose walls were carved countless niches to hold urns, thus giving them the name of *colombarii* (dovecotes).

*117 top Yesterday as today, there was a strong need to keep the memory of the dead alive, including through architectural works that held their remains, adorned with* *relief work and statues placed where a large number of people could see them – along the roads.*

*117 center The Tomb of Annia Regilla, also known as the Temple of* *the God Rediculus, is actually a two-story patrician tomb from the early 2nd century. The burial chamber was on the lower level, while the upper portion was used for religious purposes.*

*117 bottom The so-called Casal Rotondo, near the great Villa of the Quintilii, is the* *largest circular tomb on the Via Appia, and is similar to the Tomb of Caecilia Metella.*

# THE TOMB OF THE SCIPII

The *Tomb of the Scipii* is located a little past Caracalla's Baths, on the left side of the *Via Appia* and before *Porta San Sebastiano*. The monument was built by Lucius Cornelius Barbatus in the early 3rd century BC and was remodeled in the 2nd century by Scipio Aemilianus. It consists of two hypogea, the smaller one added later, between 150 and 135 BC. Outside, the high rough foundation in tufa, in which the entrances to the tomb were carved, was completely decorated with frescoes. An analysis of the remains has shown various paintings, one over the other: The oldest are probably military scenes, while the most recent have

simple, stylized wavy red decorations. The façade, which unfortunately has been almost completely lost, looked like a theater wing; it faced northwest and had a surface dotted with tufa semipillars, with an Attic base, and niches used for the statues of Scipio Africanus, Scipio Asiaticus and Ennius. The style clearly showed the taste for Hellenistic architecture common in the 2nd century BC. The largest room is rectangular, with four central pillars. The tufa tombs, reproductions of which can be seen here in their original positions (the originals are at the Vatican Museums), are located along the side walls around the central pillars. In the back, on an axis with the main entrance, were the oldest tombs, those of L.Cornelius Scipio Barbatus and his son L. Cornelius Scipio. These tombs are an older, monolithic type, unlike the later ones, which consist of large slabs placed side by side.

The *Tomb of Scipio Barbatus*, from 280 BC and based on models from Greek Sicily, is the only one decorated. It has a ceiling with dosserets with volutes in the corners and a molded Doric frieze above with an inscription in Saturnian verses on one side.

"Lucius Cornelius Scipio Barbatus, son of Gneus, a strong and wise man, whose appearance was fully equal to his valor, was consul, censor, and aedile with you. He took Taurasia and Cisauna in Samnium, subjected all of Lucania and took hostages from there." On the right, resting against a pillar, is the *tomb of his son Lucius*, consul in 259 BC. Following are the tombs of other family members buried here (there must have been about 30), except for that of Scipio Africanus, who is buried in his villa in Literno.

The second hypogeum, a side corridor built at a later time, contains tombs that can be dated to a period between the mid-second and first century BC. In the 3rd century AD, a multi-level *domus* was built over the tomb, evidence that the memory and importance of the monument had been completely forgotten by this time.

118 left *The* Tomb
of the Scipii *is a little
beyond Caracalla's
Baths, on the left side of
the* Via Appia. *The
monument, consisting of*
*two underground
chambers, was begun
in the 3rd century BC
and held the remains of
many members of the
Scipii family.*

## THE COLUMBARIUM OF POMPONIUS HYLAS

Not far from the *Tomb of the Scipii*,
near Via Latina, is the *Columbarium of
Pomponius Hylas*, a structure in *opus
caementicium* faced with green brick, from
the early imperial era. The tomb,
partially carved out of the rock, is richly
decorated in stucco and has a series of
niches all around it. The niches are
placed on a podium and framed by
small columns supporting a tympanum.
Many freedmen of the imperial family
(Julian-Claudian era) were buried here.
The first owners of the tomb, however,
were a couple, who are depicted on the
sides of a niche: Granius Nestor and
Vinileia Hedone.

## THE ARCH OF DRUSUS

Proceeding down the street, we
come to the so-called *Arch of Drusus*, a
monument constructed from one of the
archways of the *Aqua Antoniniana*, the
aqueduct built by Caracalla to supply
his baths. In the 5th century AD,
Honorius incorporated it into the Porta
Appia (Porta San Sebastiano), to form a
sort of inner gate.

119 top *Near the*
Tomb of the Scipii
*is a columbarium
that belonged to a
certain Pomponius
Hylas, according to
the inscription on a
mosaic found here. It
is a relatively
important imperial-era
structure, as the
freedmen of the Julia-
Claudia imperial
family were buried here.*

119 bottom *On the*
Via Appia, *at the
walls Aurelian used to
enclose the city of Rome
in the 3rd century, we
can see the remains of
the Arch of Drusus,
which was a monument
created from one of the
arcades of the branch of
the Aqua Marcia that
supplied water to
Caracalla's Baths, the
Aqua Antoniniana.*

118-119 *Even the less
wealthy could ensure
themselves a tomb,
albeit not a great
monument, by being
buried in a more or less
expensive collective
tomb known as a*
columbarium. *One
of these is the*
Columbarium of
Pomponius Hylas,
*which has a series of
small niches on two
levels that were used to
hold the remains of the
decreased, and stucco
decoration.*

Proceeding up the *Via Appia*, to the third kilometer, on the left is a large tract of land that belonged to the emperor Maxentius in the 4th century. The remains of a *residential palace* stand on a small rise, connected by a long corridor to a large *circus* for chariot races. The circus was a little over 500 meters long and had 12 *carceres*, or starting stalls, on the short side to the west, between two tall towers that must have contained the

**5**

**1**

**3**

*N*

**4**

**2**

**6**

VILLA AND CIRCUS OF MAXENTIUS

1. VILLA OF MAXENTIUS
2. MAUSOLEUM OF MAXENTIUS
3. CIRCUS OF MAXENTIUS
4. CRYPTOPORTICUS
5. IMPERIAL BOX
6. CARCERES (STARTING GATES)

mechanisms for raising the gates. The complex was not exactly elliptical, but had been designed to be slightly wider at the start and where the chariots completed their first lap. As in the *Circus Maximus*, here as well, the *spina* probably contained the eggs and dolphins used to count the laps completed, as well as an obelisk and a number of statues. All around were the bleachers, supported by vaults made using a special construction technique that utilized globular fragments of terra-cotta pots drowned in mortar, which had the effect of making the structure lighter. The *pulvinar*, the emperor's platform, was on the long side to the north, in a position that provided an excellent view of the most important moments of the race.

To the west, right on the *Via Appia*, are the remains of a circular mausoleum, originally located within a large square enclosure. The

*120 bottom* Typical circus elements, such as the eggs and dolphins used to count the number of laps, an Egyptian obelisk, now in the Piazza Navona, and a large number of statues, must have been located in the center of the track at the Circus of Maxentius, on the spina. The emperor and his entourage sat in the box seats on the long side to the north.

*120-121 Between the church of St. Sebastian and the tomb of Caecilia Metella, on the left side of the Via Appia, is the large Villa of Maxentius*

*complex next to the emperor's residential palace and the circus connected to it, where we can still see the remains of his mausoleum. This is a*

*circular edifice preceded by a pronaos based on the model of the Parthenon, surrounded by a wide square enclosure.*

*121 bottom The two towers of the long circus, which originally connected to the villa through a corridor, are still quite visible on the short*

*side to the west. The towers flanked the 12 starting gates, the carceres. The mechanisms that raised the gates must have been located here.*

structure was reminiscent of the Pantheon, with a pronaos that led to the circular cella. The interior had a vaulted roof supported by a large central pillar. A series of niches, alternatively semicircular and rectangular, used for the tombs, dotted the inner wall.

Probably the complex as a whole was used for funeral games in honor of Romulus or Maximian, who died in 309 and 310 AD, respectively.

The best known monument on the *Via Appia* is certainly the enormous *Mausoleum of Caecilia Metella*, which dominates the landscape. The tomb, from the late first century BC, has a cylindrical drum almost 30 meters in diameter and 11 meters high, built on a square base. On the outside, around the drum, is a decorative frieze sculpted of blocks of Pentelic marble, with bucranes and garlands. The side facing the road still has a large panel with a relief of military trophies and a dedicatory inscription above it (*"Caecilia Metella, sister of Quintus Caecilius Metellus Creticus, wife of Crassus"*), which clearly indicates the woman's high social status. One entered the tomb through a narrow passageway that led to a high vertical channel with a vaulted roof. At the base of it was the entrance to the actual burial chamber.

In the 12th century, the monument was transformed into the tower of a large fortress, which ensured its survival but also changed it in some ways, such as the battlements added to the upper portion.

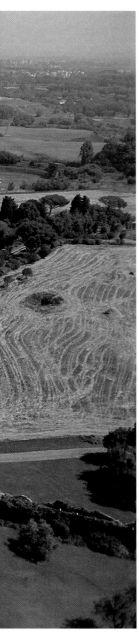

122 top  When leaving Rome, the Tomb of Caecilia Metella *dominates the landscape on the* Via Appia *just beyond the Villa of Maxentius. The monument has been preserved due to its transformation into a fortress in the 12th century.*

122-123  *This tomb, built in the late first century BC, held the remains of a woman of illustrious lineage, Caecilia Metella. The structure has a square base with a cylindrical drum on it, ending in a vaulted roof. Only a few traces remain of the original marble covering of blocks of travertine with simple, smooth ashlar work.*

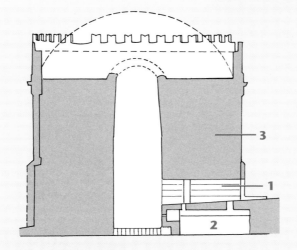

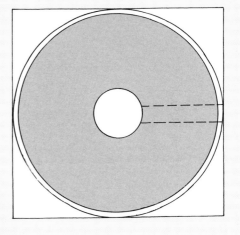

1. ENTRY CORRIDOR
2. BURIAL CHAMBER
3. DRUM

123 top  *The interior of the* Tomb of Caecilia Metella *was accessible through a narrow passageway that led to the burial chamber, located below the entry corridor. It was certainly modeled after Greek tombs, an indication of the family's high social and cultural status.*

123 bottom  *On the side of the* Tomb of Caecilia Metella *facing the street, we can see, inserted in the wall, relief work depicting military monuments and two standing statues. Above is the dedicatory inscription of the tomb to Caecilia, sister of Q.C. Metellus and wife of Crassus.*

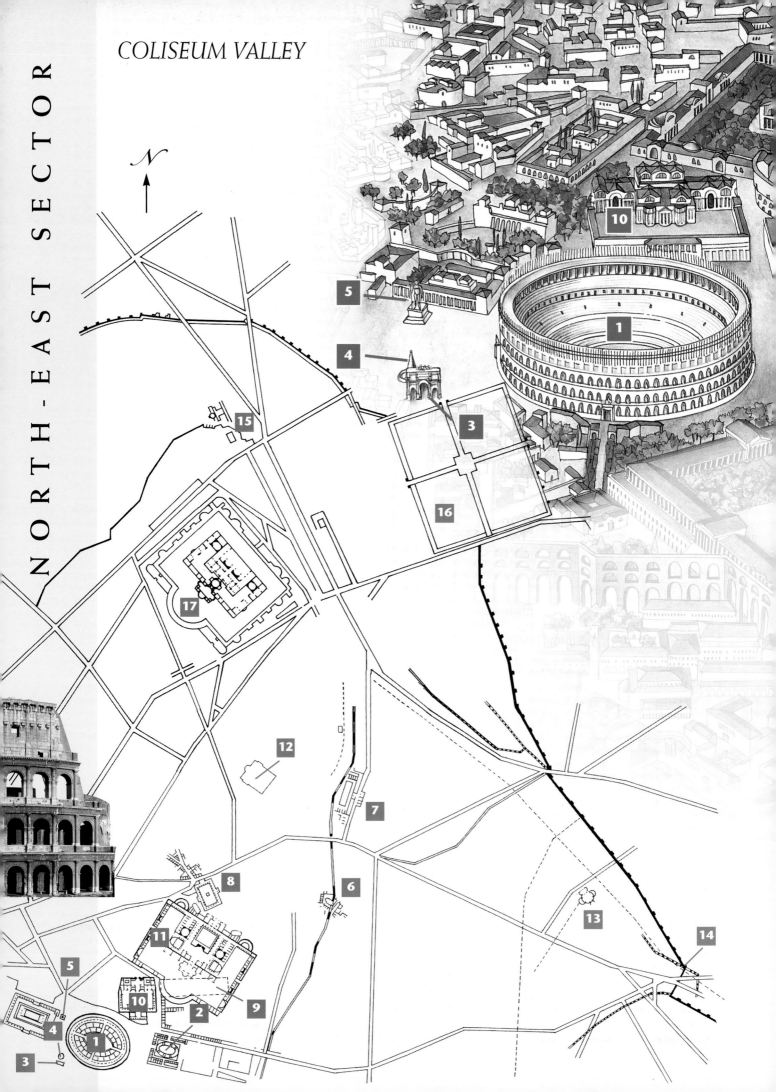

COLISEUM VALLEY

1. COLISEUM
2. LUDUS MAGNUS
3. ARCH OF CONSTANTINE
4. META SUDANS
5. NERO'S COLOSSUS
6. HORTI OF MAECENAS
7. MACELLUM OF LIVIA
8. PORTICUS OF LIVIA
9. DOMUS AUREA
10. BATHS OF TITUS
11. TRAJAN'S BATHS
12. BASILICA OF JUNIUS BASSUS
13. TEMPLE OF MINERVA MEDICA
14. PORTA MAGGIORE
15. HORTI SALLUSTIANI
16. CASTRA PRAETORIA
17. DIOCLETIAN'S BATHS

124 bottom MAP OF THE ESQUILINE AREA showing the most important monuments.

125 top Hypothetical reconstruction of the Coliseum Valley.

125 bottom We know that the original name of what we call the Coliseum was actually the Flavian Amphitheater. Only in the 11th century did it begin to be called the Coliseum, due to its vicinity to Nero's Colossus, the enormous statue that adorned the entrance to the emperor's dwelling.

The *Coliseum Valley*, located between the Palatine, the Velia, the Oppian and the Caelian, was traditionally one of the points of the "square city" founded by Romulus. It was part of the so-called *Septimontium*, one of the oldest urban organizations arising around the original nucleus. In the 6th century BC, the valley was drained and the area settled. Many buildings, primarily public ones, were constructed here during the imperial era.

After being appropriated for Nero's *Domus Aurea*, the Flavians returned the area to the people. The *Flavian Amphitheater* was built here, along with a series of related edifices such as the gladiator barracks, hospitals and storehouses. The new *Imperial Mint* complex, the *Moneta*, which had been transferred here from the Capitol (some remains have been found below the basilica of San Clemente) was also located a short distance away. In fact, we know that when the ancient State Treasury, located at the foot of the Capitol quite close to the first *Moneta*, burned during the great fire of 80 AD, it was never rebuilt, and the Mint was transferred to another part of the city.

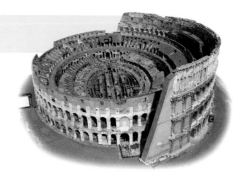

The *Coliseum* is the name by which the *Flavian Amphitheater* has been known since the 11th century, and comes from the Nero-era colossus that was located just a short distance away. It was built in only five years during the reign of Vespasian (75 AD) and was completed and opened by Titus in 80 AD. We know from Latin writers that the celebrations lasted 100 straight days and included the sacrifice of over 5000 animals.

The last spectacle held in the Coliseum was during the reign of Theodoric in 523 AD. Actually, Honorius and Valentinian had already opposed spectacles, until they were finally abolished. After the 6th century, numerous dwellings were set up in the empty aisles of the Coliseum, and it also began to be used as a quarry for materials that could be reused. In the 12th century, the edifice was incorporated into the fortress of the Frangipanis. Pope Benedict XIV consecrated the Coliseum to the passion of Jesus Christ and placed 14 stations of the Via Crucis within it, thus beginning a tradition that still continues to this day.

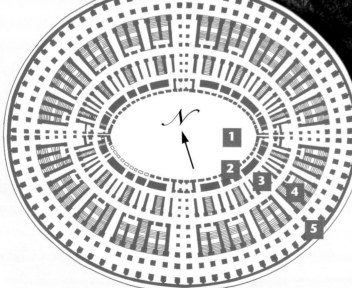

1. Arena
2. Seats for the senators
3. Moenianum primum
4. Moenianum secundum
5. Moenianum summum

126 top *Beginning in the 11th century, the name* Coliseum *was popularly adopted to indicate the amphitheater. It comes from Nero's Colossus, which stood a short distance away. Begun by Vespasian, it was completed by Titus in 80 AD. Games of various types were held here, such as hunts and gladiator combat.*

126-127 *The Coliseum has an oval design; the various orders of bleachers are supported by a complex series of superimposed walls. On the outside, we can still see four superimposed architectural orders on the north side, done in* opus quadratum *in travertine, with the arcades framed by Tuscan, Ionic and Corinthian engaged columns. Shields and windows alternate on the fourth order.*

THE EXTERIOR. The amphitheater is oval in form, 188 meters long at its longest point and 156 meters at its shortest. Total height is 52 meters, divided into four stories of architectural orders, in travertine *opus quadratum*. The full elevation of the outside ring has survived only on the northern side. The first three orders had 80 arches framed by Tuscan engaged columns on the first order, Ionic columns on the second, and Corinthian columns on the third; the fourth order was formed by 80 panels dotted with Corinthian pilasters, with alternating windows and *clipea* (round copper shields); there were three brackets in each square, corresponding to an equal number of openings in the cornice above, used to hold the wooden beams to which the *velarium* was attached. The *velarium* was a large linen awning used to protect spectators from the sun and rain; it was maneuvered by a special corps of sailors from the fleet of Misenum.

Entrances were marked by numbers carved over the arches, which corresponded to numbers marked on the tickets. In fact, despite the fact that these public spectacles were free, to attend, one had to have a token indicating an assigned seat and the way to get there.

127 bottom *The Amphitheater of Statilius Taurus originally stood in the valley between the Esquiline and the Velia. This edifice was destroyed in a fire, and Nero built a small lake in its place. Only during the time of Flavius did Rome finally receive an amphitheater worthy of the capital of such a large empire: the Flavian Amphitheater.*

128-129 The amphitheater's cavea was impressively large. The four sectors that seated the populace, from richest to poorest, depending on class, were located here in horizontal succession. To protect the spectators from the sun and rain, the velarium was unfolded above them. Its mechanism was set into brackets on the outer façade.

128 bottom The Coliseum's bleachers were divided into four sectors, where the populace was seated according to social station. Seating was rigidly preestablished.

129 top left On the last ring of the cavea were the wooden beams to which the velarium was attached. This was a large cover made of linen that protected spectators from summer heat and rain. A special corps of sailors from the fleet of Misenum was in charge of maneuvering the velarium.

129 top right Two underground corridors divided the Coliseum arena into four sections. The central corridor, which followed the major axis, continued below the steps at the east entry to reach the

nearby Ludus Magnus. The 80 arcades on the ground floor led to the stairs and cavea. Behind the entrance, there were five concentric corridors, covered by a barrel vault and resting on enormous travertine pillars, on which the first floor of the cavea rests. Of the four main entrances, the one to the north, which is still preserved, was perhaps the most important, and was used by the emperor and his entourage.

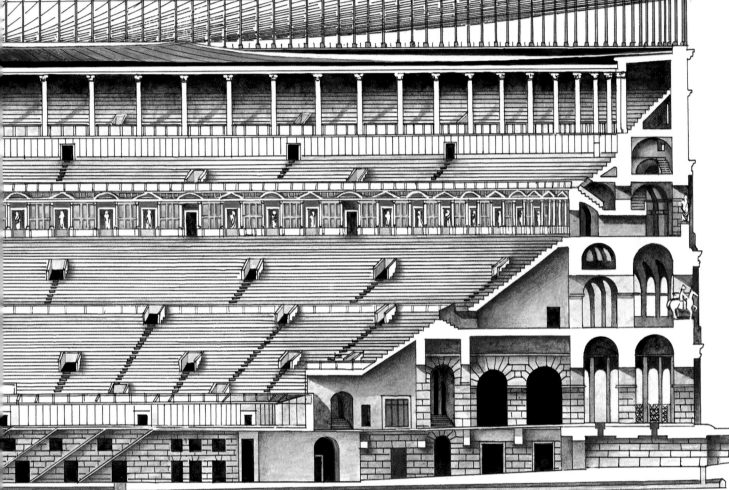

Seats were distributed in a rigidly established manner. There were four main entrances: Two on the shorter axis, preceded by a small portico with two columns, led to the galleries and were reserved for political authorities. The entrances on the longer axis were for the gladiators. It has been calculated that the Coliseum could hold up to 73,000 spectators. All around it was an open area, paved in travertine and surrounded by a two-story portico.

THE INTERIOR. Entering the amphitheater today, what is immediately striking is the enormous maze of corridors, which originally were not visible. These were in fact *underground*, below the arena, covered with wood flooring and used to perform the services necessary to hold the games. Equipment and animals were kept here, and here were the hoists that used a complex system of counterweights to lift wild beasts and heavy stage equipment into the arena. The central corridor continued below the entrance corridors east to the *Ludus Magnus*, the gladiators' barracks. The bleachers consisted of steps faced with marble and divided into a number of sectors, where the spectators were seated based on their social class. The *first sector* had wide bleachers with seats set up for the senators. Their names were carved into the bleachers themselves or on the crush barrier built along the edge of the podium to protect the authorities, who would otherwise be exposed to risks created by their proximity to the arena. The carved names were gradually rubbed away and replaced with names of the subsequent ruling class (those that survive refer to senators from the 5th century AD). Below the podium was an open corridor, perhaps a latrine, used by service personnel. The second sector, known as the *moenianum primum*, was reserved for mounted soldiers and consisted of eight rows of marble bleachers that were narrower than the previous ones. They could be entered through the third ring corridor, while other identical stairs led to the third sector. This was divided into two sections: the *moenianum secundum imum* and *summum*. Above was the fourth sector,

the *moeniaum summum ligneis*, surrounded by a large portico and with seats on wooden structures. From the galleries, one could exit rapidly through the perfect system of small stairways uniformly distributed among the 80 arches on the ground floor and the top of the edifice.

THE GAMES. In the Republican era, before the amphitheater was built, games were held in the Roman Forum or in the Forum Boarium, and later in the Campus Martius, in which Nero built a special temporary wooden structure. The Coliseum was used for two types of shows: gladiator combat, known as *munera*, and battles against or between wild animals, the *venationes*. At least initially, gladiator battles were

the loser was permitted to ask for mercy (*missio*). Actually, given the enormous costs of these games, organizers had every reason to spare their lives, and allowing all the losers to be killed was considered a sign of special generosity on the part of the sponsors. The *venationes*, which came into fashion after the conquest of the Mediterranean, were especially popular with spectators, who could watch battles among strange and exotic animals. There is also evidence of the practice of feeding deserters to wild beasts as early as the 2nd century BC, beginning with Scipio Minor, who seems to have started this type of "show," known as the *damnatio ad bestia*. Thereafter, it became extremely popular.

## LUDUS MAGNUS

Behind the *Coliseum*, between *Via Labicana* and *Via San Giovanni in Laterano*, remains can still be seen of a large Roman gladiator school, the *Ludus Magnus*. There were also other schools in the area, where gladiators from all over lodged and trained in various specialties: the *Ludus Matutinus*, the *Ludus Dacicus* and the *Gallicus*. Here, athletes lived essentially as prisoners and were subjected to steely discipline based on harsh daily training. Built in the Domitian era, the complex had an elliptical arena surrounded by steps (part of its semicircular shape can still be seen) and a group of lodgings around it. On the shorter axis, there were platforms for the authorities, who from here could watch the training and decide the fate of the combatants.

Around the *Ludus Magnus* there were other Coliseum structures, like the *saniarium* for the wounded, the *spoliarium* for dead bodies, the *armamantarium*, the *Castra Misenantium* and the *Summum Choragium* for stage equipment.

*130 top Taking the road that led from the Coliseum to the Esquiline and the gardens of Trajan's Baths, to the right we can see the remains of the semicircular Ludus Magnus, the great school where gladiators practiced and were trained.*

considered a sort of collective ritual in which the strength of the noble class was expressed. Over the centuries, the *munera* continued to be important offerings to the community, for reasons that included their use as political propaganda. Gladiators were selected from those condemned to death, prisoners of war and slaves, but could also be free men; the combatants fought until one of them was killed, although

*130 center Observing from above the amphitheater's bleachers as they appear today, what is most amazing is the incredible maze of corridors that ran below the floor, which is now gone.*

*130 bottom The authorities sat in the sector closest to the arena, protected by a transenna. The names of the senators were inscribed in the marble-covered bleachers, and were gradually canceled and replaced by those of the next generation.*

*131 top As in modern stadiums, spectators who entered the amphitheater to watch the games had to have a ticket that indicated the appropriate entrance and sector, which was reached through the ring corridors and then the flights of stairs.*

131 center  The holes still visible in the floor of the underground corridors have made it possible to reconstruct the complex system that was used to lift large machinery and wild animals into the arena. The winches used to hold the counterweights must have been set into the holes.

131 bottom left  Machinery, various types of objects, and hoists were kept in areas below the bleachers as well as below the arena. Animals were held here.

131 bottom right  Service areas related to the games opened up off the long, now roofless corridors in the underground levels of the Coliseum. What is now visible comes from the restoration work performed over the years.

In Rome, games were originally shows that were not so much for the benefit of human beings as for the gods, according to a strictly set ritual. The most ancient games were horse races, which took place in the *Circus Maximum*. At first, the religious nature of the event was marked by the ceremony that took place at the end of the races, when the winner's horse was sacrificed.

The actual games began with the preparation of teams, known as *factiones*, which were identified by different colors. Many people were involved in organizing the races, such as those responsible for checking the riders and animals and maintaining the chariots. A tribunal of judges, whose platform was located halfway down one of the long sides of the circus, guaranteed that the races would be conducted properly, and enforced the rules. Before the start, while the spectators chatted and consumed beverages and doughnuts sold in the bleachers, the teams stayed hidden from the curious crowds, in an isolation that was also aimed at avoiding the risk of possible harm. The show

began with a procession that included the athletes, the magistrates who had sponsored the games, priests, and musicians, jesters and acrobats. The spectators then began to place bets and the teams to draw lots. The race, which was from 4 to 6 km long, began from the starting stalls or *carceres*. After completing the first lap, when passing was forbidden and the chariots were given an opportunity to adjust, the competition began, and the seven laps began to be counted (by lowering one by one the seven eggs placed in the center of the circus on the *spina*). The chariots had a sort of horizontally pivoted brake that when intentionally pressed as the charioteer shifted his weight, compressed the hub of the outer wheel, allowing him to turn around the first meta more adroitly. Along the return stretch, which descended slightly, the horses were spurred on to take advantage of the slope and gain some distance. The race ended when the finish line in front of the judges' stand had been crossed seven times: The first team that reached

*132 top This mosaic from the 4th century AD shows a battle among three gladiators. These athletes were trained in special schools, the most famous of which was known as the Ludus Magnus.*

*132-133 In addition to battles, the Roman amphitheater also featured wild animal hunts, the venationes.*

the finish line was announced by the blare of trumpets and the enthusiastic roar of the crowd.

Theater performances must also have originated as large processions in honor of the gods. Only in the 3rd century BC did these processions transform into *ludi scaenici*, from simple pantomimes to tragedies and comedies. Greek influence must have been particularly strong, although more specifically Italic and Latin characteristics continued. At the end of the Republican era, Rome still did not have permanent buildings for shows, and used simple, temporary structures built of wood instead. The first theater was built by Pompey in 55 BC, and despite a bad reception by older Romans, who tended to consider it a sign of softness and

decadence, in the end it must have been accepted as a simple facsimile of a temple.

Other kinds of games were celebrated for funeral ceremonies, including *gladiatorial combat*, which was introduced around 264 BC. This type of combat became so popular with the public that in 105 BC it was added to public spectacles. It spread rapidly, and as time passed, gladiator games lost their original funeral significance and became simple shows. They were honest fights between gladiators, who were recruited from men condemned to death, escaped slaves, or volunteers. These fights, known as *munera*, perfectly represented the traditional concept of virility that permeated Roman society. Growing interest in the *munera* resulted in the development of a large

organization governed by the *leges gladiatoriae*. The magistrates responsible for organizing the games were at first *aediles* and *praetorians*, then curatores appointed by the emperor himself. The *lanista* handled training and room and board for the gladiators, housing them in the *ludus* (the largest was the *Ludus Magnus*, behind the Coliseum), a school/barracks in which steely discipline was enforced. Beginning in the 2nd century BC, battles between wild beasts, known as *venationes*, also became frequent. The populace especially loved this type of exotic, bloody spectacle. The emperor Constantine abolished the *munera*, although they continued in Rome until the mid-5th century AD, when they were permanently abolished by Honorius.

*132 bottom During Etruscan times, gladiator combat had an almost religious significance, and was in fact organized during the funerals of illustrious men to offer a blood tribute to the gods. During Roman times, these battles became public shows for their own sake.*

*133 bottom left The little terra-cotta statues show two gladiators armed with swords. These athletes were often criminals or slaves guilty of serious crimes. Nevertheless, there were also numerous freedmen drawn by the good pay, who masterfully showed off their skills.*

*133 bottom right This bas-relief portrays a show with ferocious animals. The venationes, or wild animal hunts, often included scenery that recreated the animals' original habitats.*

# THE ARCH OF CONSTANTINE

"Imp(eratori) Caes(ari) Fl(avio) Constantino Maximo / P(io) F(elici) Augusto s(enatus) p(opulus)q(ue) R(omanus) / Quod instinctu divinitatis mentis / Magnitudine cum exercitu suo / Tam de tyranno quam de omni eius / Factione uno tempore iustis / Rem publicam ultus est armis / Arcum triumphis insignem dicavit"

The Senate and the people of Rome dedicate this great triumphal arch to the emperor Caesar Flavius Constantine, the Greatest, Pius, Felix, Augustus, because through divine inspiration and a magnanimous spirit, with his army he avenged the state both against a tyrant and his faction, by the just force of arms.

AGE OF TRAJAN
(98-117)
AGE OF HADRIAN
(117-138)
AGE OF MARCUS AURELIUS
(161-180)
AGE OF CONSTANTINE
(312-337)

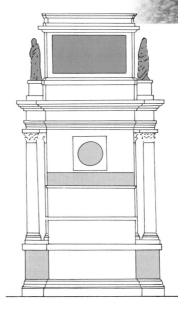

134 center  The Arch of Constantine was built in 315 AD in honor of Constantine, to commemorate his victory over Maxentius at the battle of Milvius Bridge. An older monument probably already existed, which was simply modified and decorated with marble relief work, during the period of Constantine.

The arch was built in 315 AD in honor of Constantine, along the ancient Triumphal Road. It was to commemorate the emperor's victory over Maxentius after the battle of the Milvius Bridge; it was also a way of celebrating Constantine himself for the *decennalia*, the festivals honoring his tenth year of rule. The arch has three fornices, a larger one in the middle and two smaller ones at the sides, ending in

deliver. The various images in fact followed a clear guideline, in which Constantine is the center of the empire's history, one who both continues and innovates the policies of his predecessors, the *optimi principes*, with his policy of restoration. The arch, an extremely traditional monument, was thus chosen to celebrate his victories and to guarantee and legitimate that authority for him, that only a past of

wars, triumphs, glory and consensus could ensure.

We know where all these sculptures came from: The four Trajan panels (two in the main passage and two on the shorter sides) were part of a single continuous relief from the *Basilica Ulpia*, in the Forum of Trajan, as were the statues of Dacian prisoners; the eight Aurelian panels (two on each longer side) came from an arch that celebrated

134-135 *The Arch of Constantine, surmounted by a high attic, had a large central fornix and two smaller ones on the sides. It is decorated with relief work that for the most part came from other monuments. Relief work from the time of Trajan, Hadrian and Aurelius was thus added along with the Constantinian sculptures.*

135 top right
*The Hadrian-era medallions may have been from a temple dedicated to the cult of Antinous, the emperor's young disciple, who died prematurely. The image shows a medallion depicting a sacrifice to the goddess Diana.*

135 bottom *There were four panels from the Trajan era, two on the short sides and two within the central fornix, which originally may have decorated the Basilica Ulpia in Trajan's Forum. Here we see a battle scene.*

an attic at the top. Perhaps the most beautiful and complex element is the marble relief decoration covering the entire monument. To complete the project, which was finished during Constantine's reign according to a very precise, single plan, most of the material used was pillaged from other monuments. Next to the reliefs of Constantine, sculptures from the era of Trajan, Hadrian and Marcus Aurelius were added, with the resulting combination of different styles and time frames in a single monument. This action seems rather clear if one considers the message it was meant to

the victories of Marcus Aurelius over German populations and probably stood on the slopes of the Capitol, the *Arcus Pani Aurei*. In all these reliefs, the faces of the emperors were changed and remodeled to resemble Constantine. The figures of Victories, river and seasonal deities, the medallions on the two shorter sides, and the great historic frieze that runs halfway up on the lateral fornices and the sides of the arch, depicting his departure from Milan, the siege of Verona, the battle of the Milvius Bridge and his entry into Rome, are all from the time of Constantine.

The overall organization is based on blending harmonious themes, in a complex system of symmetries and references. The south side, facing out from the city, includes episodes of war; the north side, toward the Coliseum and thus facing inward, contains episodes of peace and public life.

In the 12th century, the arch and the Coliseum were included in the fortress of the Frangipanis. Studies and restoration began in the 15th century, with additional work continuing to the present.

136 top *Two Constantine-era medallions are located on the short sides, one on each end. On the east side, shown in the photo, is a scene of the god Apollo in the form of Sol, emerging from the sea driving a quadriga.*

136 center *In the middle of the Arch of Constantine, above the smaller fornices, we can see eight medallions from the time of Hadrian, four on each side, which depict hunting and sacrificial scenes. From the left, we can see a scene showing a departure for the hunt, and a sacrifice to the god Silvanus.*

In the area between the *Arch of Constantine* and the *Coliseum*, there was a large monumental fountain whose raised remains remained clearly visible until they were destroyed in the 1930s, when work was begun on the Via dei Trionfi and the Via dell'Impero. The fountain was built in the Flavian era in an especially important zone — the point of arrival of numerous roads that ran together here, and the point of convergence for four or perhaps five Augustan regions. It consisted of a cone 17 meters high and 7 meters in diameter, crowned above with a floral element, and a large circular basin. The foundation contained numerous niches. Overall, the monument closely resembled the form of a *betilo*, the aniconic symbol of the god Apollo, and also symbolically evoked the birthplace of the emperor Augustus.

The eight Hadrian-era medallions (on the two main sides), which were once thought to belong to an arch leading to a sanctuary dedicated to Hadrian's favorite, the young Antinous, are worth a separate discussion. The most recent analyses of the monument have revealed that the arch itself was not built from scratch. A series of discoveries have in fact shown that Constantine reused an already existing monument. It has been theorized that the arch, which originally had just one fornix, was from the Flavian era (perhaps an arch in honor of Domitian), and was only later modified and transformed into a structure with three fornices. Perhaps the most significant element is that, from a study of the reused slabs, it was noted that the *medallions* inserted into the two longer sides were not actually reused, but belong to the monument itself, the second phase of which could thus be placed in the Hadrian era. Constantine would thus have used this arch as a starting point to make all changes and later additions. The story was different for the Trajan friezes, for example, which were removed from another monument and added to the structure.

*136 bottom Next to the inscription on the high attic that tops the monument, is a decoration of eight panels from the time of Marcus Aurelius (four on each side), framed by statues of Dacian prisoners. On the north side, in the photo, are two panels (from the right) depicting the emperor's clemency for a barbarian leader, and the distribution of gifts to the populace.*

*137 top Above the vaults of the smaller fornices are four long relief works, which continue onto the short sides as well, and should be read as a single long Constantinian frieze, depicting important episodes in the emperor's victory over Maxentius. On the short side to the west is the first of a series of relief works, showing the army's departure from Milan; to the south is the siege of Verona and the actual battle of Milvius Bridge; on the east side, in the photo, is the triumphal return to Rome; and to the north, we see Constantine's speech to the crowd and a scene of liberalitas.*

*137 bottom left On the south side of the Arch of Constantine, above the left fornix, are two medallions from the time of Hadrian. In the photograph, we can see the medallion depicting a bear hunt.*

*137 right The Meta Sudans was a monumental fountain in the form of a cone with a large circular basin, thus called because it resembled the metae found in circuses. It was exactly at the point where the five Augustan regions converged.*

## THE STATUE OF NERO

The colossus that Nero built in front of the vestibule of his *Domus Aurea* was commissioned to a Greek sculptor, Zenodoros, and was inspired by the famous Colossus of Rhodes. Its enormous dimensions were reconstructed using pictures, original sources and a study of the proportions of the foundation, which remained essentially intact until 1933, when it was completely destroyed. The statue was about 35 meters tall, so that when Hadrian wanted to move it to continue work on building his *Temple of Venus and Rome*, he had to use a wagon pulled by 24 elephants. After Nero's death, the statue was not destroyed, but was gradually transformed by various emperors into a *simulacrum of Helios* and subsequently of Hercules.

# THE ESQUILINE AND OPPIAN HILLS

## THE DOMUS AUREA

The Esquiline was one of the most populous quarters of ancient Rome. Its history reaches far back in time, as according to tradition, Servius Tullius included the hill within the city and also fortified the more vulnerable east side, erecting a protective *agger*. Working-class dwellings were concentrated primarily at the foot of the hill, which must have been much more unhealthy than the summit.

The most well-known and poorest working-class quarter is certainly the *Subura*, near which were also paper storehouses and many book shops. On the top of the Esquiline were the richest dwellings of Roman nobility. During the Republican period, illustrious persons like Pompey and Quintus, Cicero's brother, built their homes in the area toward the Velia, while Caesar preferred to reside in a modest house right in the

the end of the Republican era, and at his death willed it to Augustus. Tiberius himself lived there after his return from Rhodes in 2 AD.

The structure, almost 25 meters long, is known as the *Auditorium of Maecenas*. It consists of an entry stairway, a rectangular vestibule, a large hall ending in an exedra with steps (which are actually ill-adapted for spectators in a possible *auditorium*) and a vaulted roof. It must have been a semi-underground area even in antique times, as seems confirmed by the beautiful Augustan-era third-style painted decorations visible in the niches in the walls. The pictures of gardens, as in this case, are elements found in rooms that had no view of a green area. It has thus been theorized that the hall could have been a *nymphaeum* or a *cenatio*, a summer dining room.

Like other *Horti*, in the imperial era

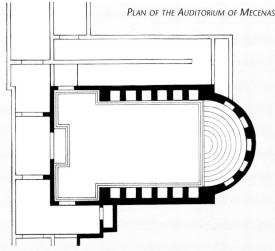

PLAN OF THE AUDITORIUM OF MECENAS

rooms of the palace, the damnatio memoriae that burned after Nero's death and the demonization of the emperor led to the nearly total destruction of the complex. Nevertheless, the Octagonal Room still remains as testimony to its once great architectural worth. The Octagonal Room was the fulcrum of the western sector of the Domus Aurea, from which the rooms radiated out. The walls of the room with its cupola roof are almost non-existent, due to the numerous wide openings within them.

138-139 *Little remains of the great villa that Maecenas built on the Esquiline. There is, however, an underground structure known as the Auditorium that* belonged to the complex. Actually, due to the plan and the painted decorations with plant motifs, it was probably a summer cenatium with a nymphaeum.

139 top *The Domus Aurea occupied a vast area that ran from the Palatine and the Velia to the Caelian. Although sources describe the sumptuous*

*Subura.* There were vast necropolises on the eastern side, which were gradually replaced by villas and gardens, starting at the end of the Republican era. Splendid villas with enormous gardens were built on the Oppian Hill, like the *Horti Liciniani*, the *Horti Tauriani* and the *Villa of Maecenas*. Some remains of the *Villa of Maecenas* have been found on Largo Leopardi, near Piazza Vittorio Emanuele. It must have been immense, although only a fraction of it remains today. Maecenas built the villa around

this villa passed into imperial hands and became part of a vast green area, one immense park that included the Esquiline and the Quirinal to the Pincian. The great Nero-era structure, the *Domus Aurea*, encompassed part of these possessions, connecting them with imperial property on the Palatine.

There were not many temples or public buildings on the Esquiline. Some of the few that exist include the *Macellum Liviae*, and of course, the *Titus Baths* and the *Trajan Baths*.

"A colossal statue, 120 feet high, in Nero's image, could enter the vestibule of the house; it was so vast that it included three porticos a mile long and a lake, indeed almost a sea, surrounded by edifices as large as cities. Behind it were villas with fields, vineyards and pastures, and woods full of every kind of domestic and wild animal. In the other sections, everything was covered with gold, decorated with jewels and shells. The dining rooms had ceilings covered with movable sheets of ivory, with holes so that flowers and perfumes

could fall through. The largest dining room was circular and rotated continuously like the earth, day and night. The baths were supplied with sea and sulfur water. When Nero opened the house, ..., he said that finally he would begin to live in a house worthy of a man." (Suetonius, Nero, 31, 1).

In 64 AD, a large fire destroyed the *Domus Transitoria* on the Palatine. Nero then had another, even larger one built, the *Domus Aurea*, which covered all earlier structures. In addition to the Palatine, it extended along the valley between the Caelian, the Palatine and the Oppian. The architects in charge of the work were Celer and Severus, while *Fabullus* was in charge of the painted decorations. The complex included a

*PLAN OF THE DOMUS AUREA*

A. EASTERN SECTOR: RESIDENCE OF THE IMPERIAL COUPLE
B. WESTERN SECTOR
1. PORTICOED FRONT
2. ROOM WITH "OWL VAULT"
3. ROOM OF "YELLOW VAULTS"
4. ROOM WITH THE "BLACK VAULT"
5. PERISTYLE
6. NYMPHAEUM
7. CRYPTOPORTICUS
8. OCTAGONAL ROOM
9. NYMPHAEUM WITH APSE

*139 bottom Most of the areas still visible below Trajan's Baths, which belong to the eastern side of the Domus Aurea, have style IV decorative paintings, with fantastic architectural perspectives on a white background and small squares with figures. These frescoes inspired the so-called "grotesques" of Renaissance painting.*

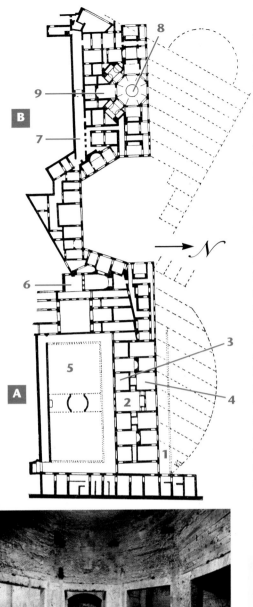

monumental *vestibule*, preceded by a colossal *statue* depicting the emperor, an artificial *lake* surrounded by a series of *porticoes*, and a group of gardens. The *Temple of Divus Claudius* on the Caelian was transformed into a monumental *nymphaeum* that must also have served as a scenic façade for the gardens. Of course, great care was taken in building the palace itself, the residence of Nero and his wife. Despite destruction by the Flavians after the emperor's death, aimed at returning this whole area to public use, a sector was conserved by being included in the foundation of the Trajan Baths. It is a long portion with two different sides, east and west, done in two completely different architectural styles. The west side may have been

part of the first structure Nero built, the *Domus Transitoria*, which Titus continued to use even after Nero's death, while the eastern section, part of the *Domus Aurea* itself, was from a later period.

The western section, which is entered through a stairway near the exedra of the Trajan Baths, had a rather traditional architecture, with rooms organized around a large courtyard. To the south, a series of richly decorated rooms looked out onto a portico, and were symmetrically located to the right and left of a central chamber. Probably they were *cubicula*, the imperial couple's bedrooms. These rooms must have been extremely luminous due to the light from the opposite portico; they must also have had a beautiful view of the

valley, with its gardens and lake. The courtyard was surrounded by a portico on three sides, with a cryptoporticus on the fourth side. On the east side of the courtyard, one could glimpse, with a dreamlike sense of distance, a series of successive rooms that ended in a rich *nymphaeum*. It was a small vaulted hall with side windows opening onto lateral courtyards and a cascading fountain. Inside an octagon, in the center of the vault, is the figure of Polyphemus receiving a cup of wine from Ulysses.

A series of rooms decorated with fourth-style pictures of fantastic architecture, marks the passage to the east section. This had richer, more varied architecture, with rooms radiating out around a pentagonal courtyard. Particularly beautiful was the decoration of one of these rooms, located on an axis with the courtyard and characterized by a showy "gilded vault." Farther to the east were other rooms whose focal point was an octagonal hall with a cupola roof. The walls had so many openings onto the surrounding rooms that they were almost non-existent.

### THE DOMUS AUREA FRESCO

An enormous fresco recently discovered near the Domus Aurea has elicited great interest. During several excavations in a cryptoporticus in the Trajan Baths, a wall with two arches of a portico was discovered, with an enormous fresco depicting a "bird's eye" view of a city that has not yet been positively identified. The realism of the painting has led experts to suspect that it is not an imaginary city, but a real place, which is certainly not Rome. The whole arcade was probably painted with a series of similar views.

# TITUS AND TRAJAN BATHS

There are few remains of the *Titus Baths*, although their plan can be reconstructed based on several designs by Palladio. We know that Titus built them very quickly in 80 AD, which leads experts to believe that he was simply remodeling thermal facilities from Nero's *Domus Aurea*, which also has the same orientation.

The *Trajan Baths* face a completely different direction, and thus the solution used was based on finding a better position in the sun. The same solution was used in the *Caracalla*, *Diocletian* and *Decius Baths*. The complex (about 315 x 330 meters in

VISIBLE REMAINS. The Oppian Hill park still contains some of the enclosure with a *nymphaeum*, a hall with two apses and a library, while the central building is part of one of the two gymnasiums.

SEVEN ROOMS. The cistern that supplied the baths, of which a few remains can be seen across from Via delle Terme di Traiano, is known as "Seven Rooms." It consisted of nine long rooms that connected to each other and a monumental façade with niches that were alternately curved and straight. In the fourth century, the upper portion was occupied by a *domus*.

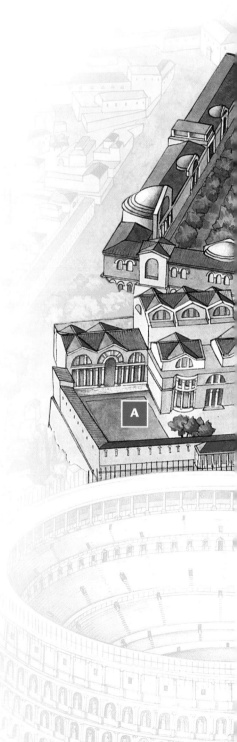

size) had a large enclosure with numerous apses, including a large exedra. Inside was a central building with rooms arranged symmetrically around an axis. The route began from a propylaeum that led to the vestibule and from here to the *natatio* and gym, to continue along the central axis constituted by a *calidarium*, *tepidarium*, and *basilica*, leading out to the exit again through the swimming pool.

140 *Trajan's architect, Apollodorus of Damascus, built a large thermal complex on the site of the Domus Aurea. The central building, with its rooms arranged symmetrically around an axis, was surrounded by a vast enclosure, which was* interrupted at the back by a large exedra, which is still visible.

140-141 top *The large exedra in the enclosure of the Trajan Baths, originally covered with a vault decorated with caissons, has a series of niches on two levels.*

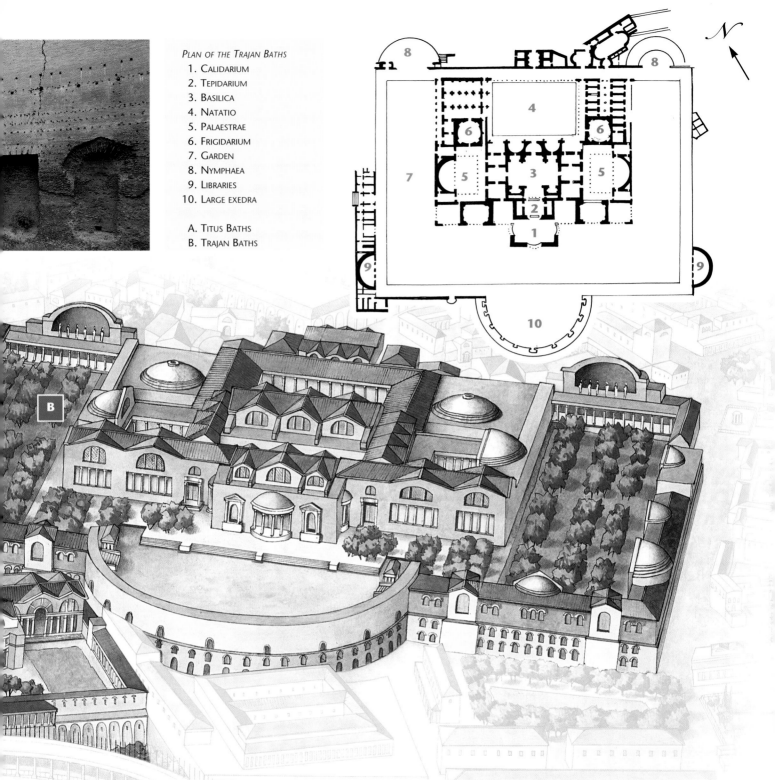

PLAN OF THE TRAJAN BATHS
1. CALIDARIUM
2. TEPIDARIUM
3. BASILICA
4. NATATIO
5. PALAESTRAE
6. FRIGIDARIUM
7. GARDEN
8. NYMPHAEA
9. LIBRARIES
10. LARGE EXEDRA

A. TITUS BATHS
B. TRAJAN BATHS

141 *The Trajan Baths are the first example of a thermal complex built according to a plan that would become typical of all imperial thermal facilities. Space was organized with the central rooms arranged in an axial, symmetrical fashion. Around it, a large enclosure helped isolate and create a vast park area.*

*142 left On Via San Vito, we can still see one of the three fornices of the* Arch of Gallienus. *It was originally the Esquiline Gate of the Servian Walls, completely rebuilt by Augustus and then rededicated by Marcus Aurelius Victor in the 3rd century AD, in honor of Gallienus.*

The remains of the *Arch of Gallienus,* incorporated within the Servian Walls, can be seen on Via S. Vito, near Santa Maria Maggiore. The arch has been identified as one of the entry gates in the first walls of Rome, the antique-era *Porta Esquilina.* It was a gate with three entries, with the largest one in the center, and angular Corinthian pillars. The arch was completely rebuilt by Augustus.

*142-143 The so-called Temple of Minerva stands majestically on Via Giolitti. It is actually a magnificent nymphaeum that was part of the imperial villa of the Licinii, the Horti Licianiani. It was built in the 4th century in* opus caementicium.

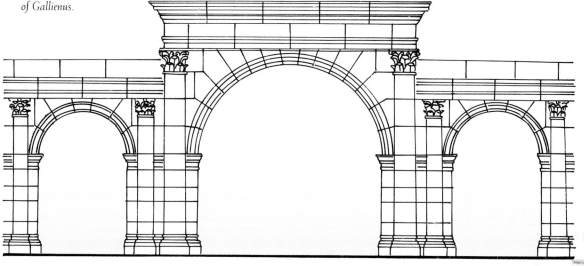

## THE BASILICA OF JUNIUS BASSUS

## THE TROPHIES OF MARIUS

Near the church of Santa Maria Maggiore, on Via Napoleone III 3, are the remains of a large aristocratic residence from the late antique period that probably belonged to Junius Bassus, who was consul in 331 BC. A state hall with an apse can be identified, preceded by a forked atrium, with a splendid *opus sextile* decoration (a decorative technique that used colored marble, ivory and vitreous paste intarsia), now on display at the Palazzo Massimo alle Terme. Two panels depicting the kidnapping of Hylas by nymphs, and a high-ranking person on a *quadriga,* probably Junius Brutus himself, are particularly beautiful. These mosaics clearly show how aristocratic Roman society, not yet converted to Christianity, used symbols to express ideological meanings, still keeping Pagan beliefs alive in the 4th century.

On the north side of Piazza Vittorio Emanuele, a green brick structure can be seen that has been known as the *Trophies of Marius* ever since Renaissance times. It was a monumental public fountain, probably supplied by a branch of the *Aqua Claudia* or the *Anio Novus.* The *nymphaeum,* completely covered in marble, was built by the emperor Alexandrus Severus (it is in fact known as the *Nymphaeum Alexandri*) before 226 AD. It has a trapezoidal plan on three floors decorated with numerous sculptures. Below, a large basin collected water that ran down from the upper level, and above was the monumental façade with an apse in the center and two arches at the sides. The marble trophies that were originally placed here were two reliefs from the Domitian era that were reused in the monument and later removed (they can now be admired on the balustrade of the Capitol).

*143 right The nymphaeum has a decagonal plan that is actually quite close to a circle, with nine deep niches placed all around it, except for the side with the entrance. There are nine large windows, above which was the circular cupola.*

On Via Giolitti, where it intersects Via Micca, is a large structure known as the *Temple of Minerva Medica*. The edifice belonged to the *Horti Liciniani*, which dates from the 4th century AD. It had a decagonal plan (25 m in diameter) with semicircular niches on all sides but the entrance. It had a cupola roof that gradually passed from the decagonal base to the hemisphere on top. A series of side rooms and pillars strengthened the slender structure.

On Via Luzzatti (no. 2) are the remains of a large funeral complex known as the *Hypogeum of the Aurelii*. It can be dated to the middle of the 3rd century AD, and has a series of underground rooms on a number of levels. One of the most significant is the *cubiculum* to the north. This small, irregularly-shaped room is decorated with a series of paintings that cover the walls completely. Even the vault is decorated with polychrome panels that frame individual persons or small scenes. The pictures often address the theme of Christ the good shepherd, triumph after death, judgment and the assumption to celestial Jerusalem.

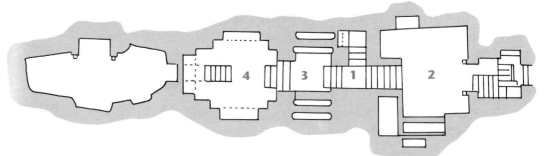

PLAN OF THE HYPOGEUM OF THE AURELII

1. LANDING
2. CUBICULUM WITH BARREL VAULT AND MOSAIC DEDICATED TO AURELIUS FELIXISSIMUS
3. VESTIBULE
4. ROOM WITH GRAVE AND PAINTED FIGURES

# THE QUIRINAL AND THE VIMINAL

The Quirinal and Viminal hills were in ancient times two spurs called *colles*, unlike the others, which were known as *montes*. Today the situation has changed radically, as the valleys to the side have silted up, and the original slope from the eastern plain can no longer be seen. In fact, in ancient times the level was almost 17 meters lower at some points. According to legend, the first inhabitants of the Quirinal were the Sabines of Titus Tatius who were then incorporated in the Latin city. The hill had sanctuaries dedicated to antique cults: Remains of the *Temple of Quirinus* have been found near Palazzo Barberini;

and the *Temple of Salus*, built in the 4th century BC after the Second Samnite War, once stood where the Palazzo del Quirinale stands today; the ancient temple was decorated with paintings of the famous Fabius Pictor. This was also the site of the *Auguraculum*, an area used by augers connected to *comitia* activities in the *Saepta* of the *Campus Martius*.

In the Republican era, the Viminal was primarily a residential district, with no important sanctuaries or public monuments. The *Castra Praetoria*, or praetorian barracks, were built outside the Servian Walls during the reign of Tiberius. During the imperial era,

numerous sanctuaries were built, including that of the *Gens Flavia* (near the church of St. Cecilia), built by Domitian as a family tomb, near the *Domus Flavia*, the family home where the emperor himself was born; the *Temple of Serapis*, near the Piazza del Quirinale; and the so-called *Barberini Mithraeum*, discovered between Via Quattro Fontane and Via S.Nicola.

The *Mithraeum* was built in the 3rd century AD on the remains of an earlier edifice from the 2nd century AD. The architecture of the rooms was typical of this type of building, with a vaulted hall and side benches for adepts. What makes it unique, however, is the rich painted decorations, which in addition to the usual scenes of the god Mithras killing a bull in the presence of torch-bearers, has a series of little panels portraying the sacred story of the god.

Important people lived in this area, including Pomponius Atticus, Cicero's friend, Vespasian and his brother Flavius Sabinus, and the poet Martial, who lived in an apartment near the Piazza del Quirinale. The northern area, near the Pincian, had a vast green zone. Here was a garden that belonged to Caesar and was later bought by Sallust.

Remains of these *Horti Sallustiani*, considered to be some of the most beautiful in the city, were found under the present-day Piazza Sallustio. Fourteen meters down is a building consisting of an irregularly-shaped area and a series of rooms radiating out from a circular hall with a double cupola roof, with alternating flat and concave segments. This part of the villa was at the top of the hill, in a position that dominated the entire valley. It was

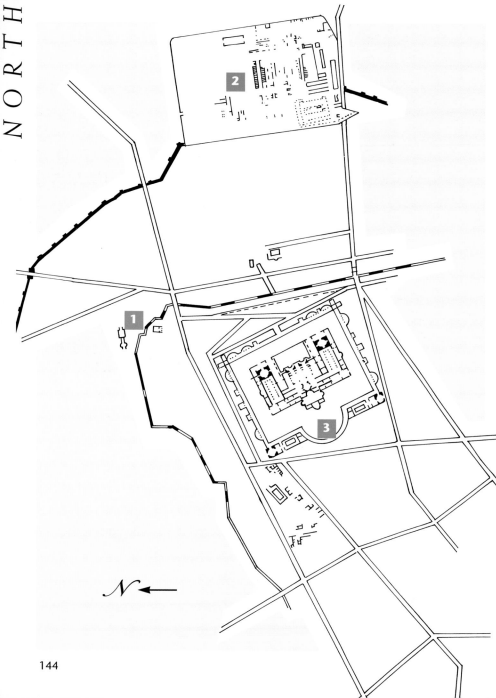

1. HORTI SALLUSTIANI
2. CASTRA PRAETORIA
3. DIOCLETIAN'S BATHS

probably a summer *cenatio* where banquets were held in the circular hall. The complex dates back to the reign of Hadrian.

Two large thermal facilities were built at the end of the imperial period. To the east are the *Diocletian Baths*, and to the west the *Constantine Baths*. Little remains of the Constantine Baths, which stood in the area between present-day Via XX Settembre and Via Nazionale. We know that it was a small, rather elegant complex, whose plan has survived through Renaissance era drawings. The baths were built by Maxentius on a large artificial terrace that obliterated many earlier dwellings.

## THE CASTRA PRAETORIA

At the advice of Sejanus, between 21 and 23 AD, Tiberius built a large camp for the praetorian guard, the emperor's bodyguard established by Augustus, which until that time had been stationed in various parts of the city. The great camp stood outside the Servian Walls, between present-day Via Nomentana and Via Tiburtina. A portion is still clearly visible to the right on Viale del Policlinico, incorporated within the Aurelian Walls. The camp had a large rectangular enclosure 440 x 380 meters in size, in green brick, a little less than 5 meters high and adorned with battlements at the top. There were four gates in the middle of each side (the entries to the east and north are still visible along the Aurelian Walls); as in city installations, two roads crossing at a right angle ran from here. There was a group of rooms with barrel vaults against the enclosure, with a parapet walk on top. To the sides of the main internal roads were the praetorian lodgings, which used a rational arrangement of structures that stretched out lengthwise and sideways. In the center was also a group of

various buildings, such as command headquarters (*praetorium*), the treasury (*aerarium*), the armory (*armamentarium*), and the storehouses (*horrea*). Beginning with the era of Silla, only special units could be stationed in Italy, such as the praetorian guard itself; thus, the *Castra Praetoria* is the only example of *castrum* still visible in Italy, with features typical of every Roman military camp; moreover, it is the only one where the height of the perimeter walls has been so well preserved.

*145 Between Via Veneto, the Aurelian Walls, Via XX Settembre and Via Piave are the imposing remains of the villa of the writer Caius Crispus*

*Sallust, which once belonged to Caesar. The villa was extensively remodeled, especially by Hadrian, and was then destroyed in 410 AD during the invasion of Alaric.*

The Diocletian Baths are the largest thermal facilities ever built in Rome. They covered a vast area between the Quirinal, the Viminal and the Esquiline, in one of the most populous quarters of the city. The complex was built in *opus latericium* between 298 and 306 AD, by Maximinian and Diocletian. It included an immense artificial platform that covered an area 11 hectares in size and had a succession of fountains, pavilions, exedrae, conference rooms and lecture halls (*auditoria*), within a large enclosure. Inside were the actual baths, built in the by-now customary fashion, with a central axis and symmetrically placed rooms to the sides. The water was supplied by a branch of the *Aqua Marcia* ending in a large cistern below the present-day Piazza dei Cinquecento. It has been estimated that 3000 people could use the baths at a time.

VISIBLE REMAINS. The baths were partially destroyed by the modern city, and partially conserved by being added to Rome's urban structure in a number of ways. Remains of the central complex can be found on one side of Piazza della Repubblica; one of the apses makes up the entrance to the church of Santa Maria degli Angeli, which was built right in the central hall of the baths; another group of rooms is included in the nearby Museo delle Terme. One of the two circular halls in the outside enclosure was transformed into the church of S. Bernardo alle Terme, while the other is still partially visible between Via Viminale and Piazza dei Cinquecento.

*146 left  A large number of rooms from the Diocletian Baths are at the Roman National Museum. The entry to the museum itself is through what* was once the eastern palaestra, *and proceeds through two large halls, one of which may have been* an apodyterium, *or dressing room.*

*146 top  A splendid example of reusing an ancient monument by one of our greatest sculptors, Michelangelo, is the church of Santa Maria degli Angeli. The façade is the back wall* of the calidarium of the Diocletian Baths. The interior stands on the tepidarium *and the basilica hall, conserving eight of the gigantic pink granite columns that supported the roof.*

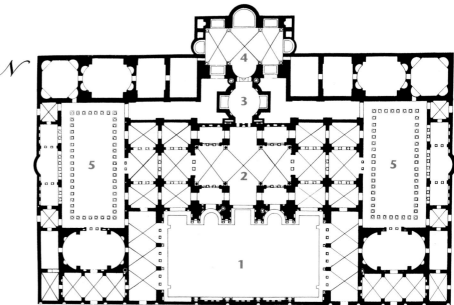

146-147 *Diocletian's Baths originally occupied a vast area between the Viminal, the Quirinal and the Esquiline. Maximianus built the complex in 298 AD, on behalf of Diocletian, in* opus latericium. *It covered* an area 11 hectares in size, delimited by a large enclosure in which the various rooms were located. The imprint of the large western exedra can be seen in the buildings that stand on the Piazza della Repubblica.*

1. NATATIO
2. FRIGIDARIUM
3. TEPIDARIUM
4. CALIDARIUM
5. PALAESTRAE

*147 bottom The baths' central complex, part of which is conserved at the Roman National Museum, was arranged in the by-now customary structure, with a central axis and rooms arranged symmetrically on the sides. The water that* supplied the baths came from the Aqua Iovia, a branch of the Aqua Marcia, and was collected in a cistern, which was destroyed when the Termini train station was built (the name itself comes from a corruption of the word terme, or baths).*

*147 top While little remains of what was the largest thermal complex ever built in Rome, because it was damaged in various ways by the modern city, much of it is now recognizable* within the city's urban structure: Santa Maria degli Angeli, the Roman National Museum, the Department of Education, and the church of St. Bernard are some of the clearest examples.*

# HADRIAN'S VILLA

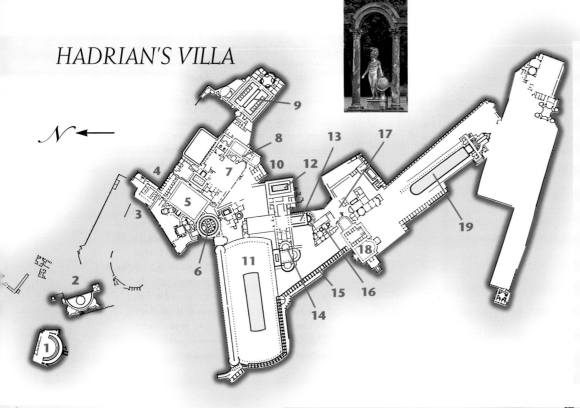

1. GREEK THEATER
2. NYMPHAEUM
3. IMPERIAL TRICLINIUM
4. PAVILION OF TEMPE
5. COURT OF THE LIBRARIES
6. MARITIME THEATER
7. IMPERIAL PALACE
8. DORIC ATRIUM
9. PIAZZA D'ORO
10. FIREFIGHTERS' BARRACKS
11. POECILE
12. QUADRIPORTICUS WITH FISH MARKET
13. NYMPHAEUM
14. EDIFICE WITH THREE EXEDRAE
15. 100CHAMBERS AND CRYPTOPORTICUS
16. SMALL BATHS
17. LARGE BATHS
18. VESTIBULE
19. CANOPUS

*Hadrian's Villa* is perhaps one of the most remarkable examples of a suburban Roman villa. It is built on various levels on more than 120 hectares of land, on the slopes of the Tiburtine hills southwest of Tivoli. It is a perfect blend of architecture and nature, with monumental buildings that wind harmoniously through the landscape. The architectural solutions used here reach new heights, utilizing devices that are classical yet innovative, in such a variety that they even begin to anticipate future developments in architecture.

According to sources, the emperor began building the complex on the remains of an earlier late Republican era edifice after he returned from his first voyage to the eastern provinces. It was completed in two stages, between 118 and 125 AD and between 125 and 133 AD. It seems that Hadrian was so impressed by the places he had visited that he wanted to preserve their memory by building monuments that evoked, for example, Athenian or Egyptian buildings. Like a single organism, the villa is arranged in a succession of spectacular perspectives, in private and state structures connected to splendid porticoes and peristyles, pools and fountains, while the servants' routes wind through underground cryptoporticoes hidden to the eyes of guests.

The villa, inhabited first by Hadrian and then by his successors, became an

example of the union between leisure and business: It was not only a retreat for the emperor in his later years, but was also used during times of executive and administrative decentralization, which became increasingly necessary as the imperial age advanced.

The complex was gradually pilfered of its works of art (even Constantine began to carry off many of them to embellish Byzantium) until the Middle Ages, when it became a quarry for the inhabitants of Tivoli.

VISITORS' ITINERARY

After we enter, our visit can begin from the *Poecile*. The name comes from the supposed connection with the famous portico adorned with paintings, the *Stoà Poikile*, of ancient Athens, beneath which philosophers walked and debated. It is an extremely vast area (232 x 97 meters) with short, curved lines, surrounded by a *quadriporticus* with pillars and a roof, with a garden and pool in the center, to be used for walks at any time of the year. To create this vast area,

148-149 *The villa of the emperor Hadrian stood not far from the ancient Via Tiburtina, four kilometers from Tivoli and about 19 Roman miles (28 kilometers) from Rome, about a three-hour trip on horseback. The residential complex consisted of alternate rectangular and circular forms. A clear example is the so-called Maritime Theater, a residence within a residence, villa within a villa, with its colonnaded portico, circular canal and a small island in the center.*

149 top *The portrait of Hadrian that sources describe, and what has been passed down from the impressive architectural works that have survived, is certainly that of an extremely intelligent, absolute monarch with an unflagging meditative curiosity and great interest in philosophy and art, although somewhat dimmed by a certain cynicism.*

149 center *This aerial view allows us to admire the complex structures of Hadrian's villa. The emperor probably*

149 *specially chose this place for his dwelling based on the ambitious architectural plans he was developing, as well as because for the first few years the earlier Republican villa could still offer adequate hospitality.*

149 bottom *The figure of the emperor Hadrian still has its ambiguities, such as his passion for the young and handsome Antinous, who died young and is depicted in works of art of every kind throughout the empire, and is venerated as a god.*

the earth was leveled and given a substructure to the southwest, toward the valley, with a series of rooms on three or four levels, the so-called 100 Chambers, which were utilized as warehouses or lodgings.

On the other side is the Philosophers' Hall, a rectangular hall with apses that has seven niches in the walls, too shallow to hold the statues of the Philosophers, as was initially thought, but large enough to hold bookshelves for a library, which seems more likely. From here, we go directly to the Maritime Theater, one of the loveliest structures, and perhaps Hadrian's retreat when he retired into solitude. It is a sort of miniature villa with a circular design, with a peristyle in the center and nine rooms around it, on a little island surrounded by a canal, accessible only through two small drawbridges. All around, the area is enclosed by a wall and portico with Ionic columns.

Going back, crossing a thermal bath complex known as the *Heliocaminus*, known for its vast circular shape with vaulted roof, with a basin in the center (originally thought to be a "sand bath" when heated), we come to the Stadium. It was probably a large *nymphaeum* that included a porticoed garden embellished with fountains and canals. Halfway down its long sides, to the east, we come to a *quadriporticus* with a fishpond in the center, and to the west a building with three exedrae that is thought to have been a *cenatium*, a room for official banquets. Proceeding to the south, we come to the *Small and Large Baths*: two large thermal complexes in which, through a route that wound through square and circular rooms, one could enjoy traditional hot and cold baths. There appears to be no basis to the common interpretation that the smaller baths were for women and the larger ones were for men. The architectural solutions used for some of these areas are particularly bold, like the octagonal room in the Small Baths, with its alternately convex and concave sides, or the *palaestra* and the vestibule of the Large Baths.

Near the end of the Villa, to the southeast, the view suddenly opens up into a narrow man-made valley traversed by a canal, the so-called *Canopus*. The name comes from the canal and famous city that stood near Alexandria in Egypt, a well-known retreat and pleasure grounds, and the site of the Temple of Serapis, the venerated destination of many pilgrims. In the center of the valley was the canal, a sort of long pool embellished with colonnades, with architraves that were alternately curved and rectangular, and statues that reflected in its waters. To the west, we can still admire six caryatids that

replaced the columns here. At the end was a large semicircular exedra, the *Serapeum*, a temple-*nymphaeum* that, with water fountains and Egyptian-like sculptures, was used as a *cenatium* for summer banquets.

To the southwest is the Tower of Roccabruna, in an especially panoramic position on the hill that overlooks the Canopus Valley. It is an isolated edifice built of bricks and blocks of tufa, including a circular room with niches and, on the upper level, a room that is octagonal on the outside, but circular on the interior, with a cupola roof.

Returning toward the Baths, we can

*150 top  The Small Baths used very innovative solutions. We can see a variety of different plans in just one small area.*

*150 center left  On the southeast side of the vast colonnaded peristyle, known as the Piazza d'Oro, is a series of rooms in an array of different styles, facing an octagonal hall with alternately concave and convex sides. This hall must originally have been covered by a segmented cupola resting not on a continuous wall, but on columns and pillars that constituted the basic structure.*

150 bottom *The Large Baths were designed at the same time as the Small Baths, as a single complex. The biggest difference between them, apart from size, is that the Large Baths use primarily square, more classical structures.*

*150-151 This aerial view shows the remains of the Poecile, with its double arcade, originally covered, and the adjacent buildings. In the foreground, east of the stadium, in an area that has been identified as a winter residence, we can see a large quadriporticus with a central basin, ending in a wall with a series of niches, still visible, where statues once stood.*

*151 top To construct the Poecile, the hill was cut off on one side, while the earth had to be supported on the west side by a powerful substructure. In the foreground, we can see the completed masonry work, the so-called One Hundred Chambers, which encompassed a number of rooms, probably lodgings and service areas.*

visit the northern part of the complex. Crossing the so-called *Praetorium*, which in reality must have housed warehouses in a series of rather narrow rooms on a number of levels, and proceeding east, we come to the Piazza d'Oro. This is almost a structure unto itself, and can be interpreted as a summer *triclinium* or state complex. It takes its name (which means "Golden Square") from the richness of its decoration and the ingenious architectural solutions employed. Through an octagonal vestibule, covered by a cupola with gores supported by arches resting on brackets, with alternately rectangular and circular niches, we enter an enormous peristyle, with a basin in the center. The courtyard was originally surrounded by a portico with two aisles, with 60 columns of alternating granite and cipolin. At the end, there were several rooms arranged around a unique hall with an octagonal design, with the sides alternatively concave and convex, each supported by two columns.

Turning back and proceeding north, we can visit the so-called *Palace Nymphaeum*, and farther west, the Hall of Doric Pillars, a true basilica. This takes its name from the central area, which may have had a pavilion vault, surrounded by a portico with pillars, probably on two levels, with Doric bases and capitals. From here, through a hall with two columns between the *antae*, one entered what must have been one of the most important areas of the villa: the Throne Room. The solemnity of the

152 top
One entered the Piazza d'Oro through a vestibule with an original roof; it has been suggested that the structure of its cupola, with segments terminating in a large central eye, is a forerunner of Byzantine architecture.

152 center  The edifice with three exedrae, north of the villa, was originally a cenatium, or official banquet hall. At first, it was simply a rectangular, roofed area ending with a porticoed apse, to which two more exedrae were later added. The marble facing of the hall was especially luxurious and shows the importance of the area.

152 bottom  The great courtyard called the Piazza d'Oro was surrounded by a portico with two covered naves, which originally must have framed a garden with a central basin. Outside the portico, to the east and west, were two service corridors covered with cross vaults (cryptoporticoes).

place must have been further emphasized by not only its position in the heart of the palace, but also by the rich materials used (the finest marble in the entire complex). It is a rectangular room with an apse in the back wall, where the emperor probably sat, removed from common mortals. The same structure is also found in the Royal Hall of the *Domus Flavia* on the Palatine.

Continuing on, past a peristyle, we come to the Courtyard of Libraries. This is the oldest area of the Palace, where its original, Republican-era center was located. It has a vast peristyle surrounded by a portico and embellished by a *nymphaeum* midway along the north wall. Behind it are two rooms with cross vaults, which were initially interpreted as two libraries, Greek and Latin. They are now thought to be multilevel summer *triclinia* (given their position facing north), connected by a trapezoidal portico and surrounded by smaller rooms.

To the north is the Pavilion of Tempe, with a long terrace that overlooked the vale of Tempe, so called after the place of the same name in Thessaly. The three-level structure consists of a large open hall, a belvedere, with rooms to the sides that may have been used for the Praetorian guards. This is one of the reasons it is believed that

*152-153 What we know as the Maritime Theater was actually a sort of miniature villa, the emperor's favorite refuge when he wanted to be alone. It had a circular edifice surrounded by a canal and a porticoed ring covered by a barrel vault and separated from the rest of the villa by a high wall. Because of its central position, it acted as a sort of link between the eastern and western sides of the villa.*

154 top *The famous Canopus complex occupied a narrow depression that was supported by a series of buttresses and substructures. In the center is a long canal, while in the back is a temple-nymphaeum known as the Serapeum that had a semicircular exedra and was used as a cenatium.*

*Hadrian's Villa*

155 center *The canal, 119 meters long and 18 meters wide, ends to the north with a curved side (in the photograph) and has a colonnade with a mixtilinear architrave.*

*Two colonnades run along the long sides of the Canopus. The eastern one was double, while the western one was simple. Statues were located around the canal. Still remaining*

*is the one depicting the Nile and a crocodile, reflecting the Egyptian theme of the entire complex. Within the basin were the bases that supported the Scylla groups, of which fragments have been found.*

155 top left *Statues of mythological characters, mirrored in the waters of the canal, stood between the columns that surrounded the Canopus. The only ones surviving are those of Ares, Athena, Hermes and two Amazons.*

155 top right *Along the west side of the Canopus, the columns are replaced by statues of six caryatids, two of whom depict Silenus, while the other four are replicas of those of the Erectheum at the Acropolis in Athens.*

154 bottom and 155 bottom right *The villa was richly decorated. Polychrome mosaics embellished the state rooms, often with emblems in the center that had an almost pictorial chiaroscuro effect, due to the use of very small tesserae. The works of art also included statues by famous artists done in precious marble, such as the Drunken Faun in red pavonazzetto marble, now at the Palazzo dei Conservatori.*

the villa's main vestibule may have been here. Crossing over to the end of the terrace, we come to the Temple of Venus. This is a small, circular temple within a large semicircular exedra, with Doric columns. The model for the edifice came directly from the temple of Cnidus, where ancient writers tell us the famous statue of Aphrodite by Praxiteles was located; a copy is found here. Beyond the road are the remains of the small Greek Theater, which must have been used for performances for the court (it held only 500 spectators). A portion of the cavea remains, up against the slope, from which one could see the stage along with the lovely background of hills.

# OSTIA

While sources agree that primitive Ostia was founded in the age of Ancus Marcius in the 7th century BC, when Rome was expanding to the Tyrrhennian coast, archaeological excavations have never been able to confirm this information, and it has been proposed that a city from the time of the kings may have existed a bit farther up the Tiber. Investigations deep below the city of Ostia, however, clearly show that the city originated in the 4th century BC, after the conquest of Veii by Rome and its subsequent consolidation of control over the entire coast.

Ostia has always played a very important role in defense, and probably one of its first and most important duties was military control of the salt marshes that since ancient times had been located at the mouth of the Tiber (the name itself connects it to the river: *ostium* means mouth or outlet), where the waters became marshy and evaporated, leaving salt deposits. In ancient times, salt was a precious resource, both for conserving food and for tanning hides. Control of the salt marshes also meant control of the roads leading into this area, and the first settlement rose right at the intersection of these paths. It was a

*castrum*, with a town structure that closely followed that of a Roman military camp, with two main perpendicular roads, the *Decumanus* and the *Cardus Maximus*. It remained a *castrum* until the 3rd-2nd century BC, by which time it had outgrown its exclusively military functions. It became not only a naval base defending the capital, but also a port suburb, and changed its economic and political structure. Enclosures then became walls, the gates became architecture and the Forum was built at the intersection of the Cardus and Decumanus, a main square that became a meeting place for the diverse population that sources identify as the first Roman colony. While at first there were only

300 colonists, as time passed, the population of the town climbed as high as 50,000. Between the end of the 2nd and the beginning of the first century BC, new city walls were built that included a territory 30 times larger than that of the primitive *castrum* (although, according to normal town planning schemes, a great deal of green space was left between the actual town and the walls). Beginning in the early imperial age, a number of different facilities were gradually built in the city: the theater; the Piazzale delle Corporazioni, or the Guild Square; the aqueduct and the thermal baths. One of the greatest problems that had to be faced was bringing the port up to standard. The

1. NECROPOLIS OF PORTA ROMANA
2. FIREFIGHTERS' BARRACKS
3. NEPTUNE BATHS
4. HORREA OF HORTENSIUS
5. THEATRE
6. FORUM OF GUILDS
7. GREAT HORREA
8. DOMUS OF FORTUNA ANNONARIA
9. HOUSE OF DIANA
10. FORUM BATHS
11. FORUM
12. CAPITOLIUM
13. TEMPLE OF ROME AND AUGUSTUS
14. CURIA
15. BASILICA
16. HORREA EPAGATIANA
17. ROUND TEMPLE
18. MACELLUM
19. SCHOLA OF TRAJAN
20. BATHS OF MITRA
21. HOUSE OF THE SERAPIS
22. SEVEN WISE MEN BATHS
23. GARDEN HOUSES

*157 top right*
*The Decumanus Maximus was the ancient road to Ostia that ran in a straight line, then turned toward Porta Marina. The first stretch of the road had a series of arcades, which along with the public edifices, gave it a monumental appearance. The rest of the road appeared more commercial.*

*157 center right*
*The great hexagonal port Trajan desired to expand Claudius' port, which had become inadequate for the city's needs, is still visible near the Fiumicino international airport.*

river port had become increasingly unfit for use, due to the quantities of detritus that had gradually deposited at the mouth, blocking ships from supplying grain to the capital. Claudius then built a port right above the mouth of the river and placed a tall lighthouse on the coast, resting on the concrete-filled hull of the ship Caligula had used to bring the Vatican obelisk to Rome. It was an unfortunate choice of location, as the area was subject to rapid silting. Trajan then took steps to solve the problem by building an octagonal port in a more inland basin and connecting it to the Tiber by means of a canal, the Trajan Ditch. The birth of the new port complex, which appropriately enough

*156 The necropolis of Porta Romana stood along the stretch of Via Ostiense outside the city, with numerous graves and cremation tombs.*

*156-157 The archaeological excavations of Ostia have revealed a surface area about 50 hectares in size: The plan of the city still recalls its primitive structure as a* castrum, *with two right-angle roads that intersected in the center, dividing it into four quadrants.*

*157 bottom right The statue of Minerva was found in the Piazzale della Vittoria. The statue is from the Domitian era, and stood next to a spring where travelers stopped to drink and water their horses.*

158 *The theater did not rest against a slope, as most other theaters did. A series of arcades completely supported the cavea, creating a circular arcade that looked out over the* Decumanus Maximus, *with shops located below. The bleachers visible today have been extensively restored, as the theater is still used for summer performances.*

# Ostia

thousand years of continuous habitation, Ostia is a precious treasure documenting the development of housing. It contains a variety of *domus* types that date from the Republican era all the way to the late Imperial Age, although most dwellings are from the 4th century AD.

Around the mid-3rd century AD, trade became slower and slower, until it stopped altogether, leading to the inevitable death of the city as well. Until the 5th century, a number of neighborhoods were still inhabited, but the slow silting up of the ports and the aqueduct led to a gradual exodus toward the nearby church of St. Andrew, the new center of the medieval town. It was then that Ostia began to be used as a quarry, especially for marble.

A visit to Ostia Antica could begin at the necropolises that were located outside the city walls, as required by law. Along the Via della Tombe, which runs parallel to the Via Ostiense, and located at different levels, are various types of tombs, depending on social class, period (the most ancient ones date back to the

*158-159 Built in the Augustan era, the Theater of Ostia was designed to hold 3000 spectators. Commodus rebuilt it in the 2nd century AD, increasing the seating capacity.*

*159 top In the back of the barracks' central courtyard was an area used for the imperial cult, the caesareum, before which we can still admire a mosaic floor depicting a sacrificial scene.*

became known as *Portus*, gave Ostia a new lease on life; it now had both a seaport and a river port. A clear sign of this is that the city level rose by about a meter. In addition, more monuments appeared on the Forum, and numerous public buildings were constructed, like the basilica, the curia, and the headquarters of various guilds. New living quarters rose over the primitive dwellings, which were demolished to make room for more rental lodgings.

Ostia has dwellings of every type and historical development. While Pompei has excellent examples of *domus* that are nevertheless frozen in a very brief historical period, 79AD, and while in Rome the remains of ancient houses are almost totally obliterated by a

2nd century BC) and type of funeral practice — cremation or burial. One of the most frequent types, beginning in the late Augustan age, is the *columbarium*, characterized by a series of niches in which funeral urns were placed.

Proceeding along the road, we enter the city through the ancient Porta Romana, built in the Republican era in *opus quadratum* tufa and rebuilt in the Domitian era at a higher level, with marble architectural decoration. Right beyond the entry, after the Piazzale della Vittoria, named after the statue of Minerva Victoria found here, is the beginning of the *Decumanus Maximus*, the main road that crossed the city horizontally.

Turning right onto the Via dei

Vigili, we come to the Firefighters' Barracks. This is a rather large structure from the Hadrianic era, which played an important role in housing 400 firefighters who had to be always ready to act in a city continuously at risk due to the enormous quantities of merchandise packed into it and the large number of wooden structures. The building stands around a central porticoed courtyard, in back of which was the *caesareum*, a space used for the imperial cult. The barracks lodgings were on two floors and faced the courtyard. Outside were three small inns, which can be identified by the mosaics depicting cups of wine, where the firefighters could linger on their days off.

*159 bottom left* The theater played an important role in the city's social life. Done in opus reticulatum and rebuilt in brick by Commodus, the façade facing the street had 21 arcades. Only a few theater masks from the 2nd century AD remain, and are now located in the center of the edifice.

*159 bottom right* The firefighters' barracks in Ostia played a very important role, given the constant risk of fire due to widespread use of wooden dwellings and the many warehouses loaded with merchandise. It was built during the urban development Hadrian completed in the 2nd century AD.

On the *Decumanus Maximus*, we can see the remains of the shops that lined the way. One of the best known is the *Caupona of Fortunatus*, a large inn that has given us the name of its owner and its function through the inscription found on the mosaic floor, below the figure of a crater.

Proceeding along the road, immediately to the right, is a semicircular portico that supported the steps to the theater. Various shops were once located below the portico. It is possible to climb to the top of the cavea to view the scene in all its beauty, with the Guild Square in the back and the countryside running toward the river. Built in the Augustan era, it was a small theater that at first could hold only 3000 spectators. It was expanded and modified until, in the 4th century AD, it could even host water shows.

The Guild Square was also built in the Augustan era. It was probably a structure connected to the theater through the four-sided portico, which spectators used for shelter in case of rain. The offices of various guilds were located under its porticoes, especially ship owners and merchants. The floor mosaics found document the wealth and diversity of commercial activities that revolved around the city, from rope merchants to tanners. Frequent motifs are images of various kinds of ships, amphorae, unloading operations, and a tower with steps that portrays the lighthouse of Claudius' port, the symbol of Ostia. In the center of the square was the Temple of Ceres, *in antis* on a high podium.

In front of the theater was one of the numerous Ostia storehouse complexes, the *Horrea of Hortensius*, although the largest was undoubtedly the great *Horrea*

160-161 *The Piazzale delle Corporazioni, a large area 125 meters long and 80 wide, was probably created for the purpose of accommodating theater spectators, who lingered here before and after performances. The double covered arcade that surrounded the square could also protect them during bad weather.*

160 bottom *As the mosaic shows, importers and animal sellers also plied their trade on the Piazzale delle Corporazioni.*

161 top right The various offices on the Piazza delle Corporazioni included the navicularii, shipwrights from various parts of the Roman empire, as well as maritime agencies from Carthage, Cagliari, Syllectum in Africa, and so forth.

behind the *Decumanus Maximus*, on the right, accessible from the Via dei Molini. The original front, however, must have directly faced the Tiber, to facilitate transshipment. Around a vast central courtyard were large areas used to store merchandise. They were windowless and had thick walls that provided some insulation, just as the empty spaces left below the floor protected the goods from humidity.

Going down the Via di Diana, on the right we see the House of Diana, distinguished by the balcony that runs around the edge of the building. The

*Ostia*

161 top left The offices of the various guilds were located around the square, below the porticoes. The rich series of mosaics that decorated the 60 posts testify to the wide variety of commercial activities that took place in Ostia at that time. There are frequent representations of various kinds of boats and the tower with stairs ascending to the top, as the famous lighthouse of Claudius' port was depicted.

161 center left and 161 bottom The mosaics before the 64 offices of the Piazzale delle Corporazioni acted as shop signs, and provide important information about the type of activity the merchants engaged in. Some refer to businesses related to ship traffic. There are frequent references to the sea, such as seahorses, fish and dolphins. Others, for example, depict trade in wild animals for the popular games that took place in the amphitheaters.

161 center right On the long side to the right, in the fourteenth position, we can see a mosaic depicting an elephant and an inscription that advertises pachyderms and ivory from Sabrata, Libya.

162 center *South of the Forum is the Temple of Rome and Augustus, across from the Republican-era Capitolium. Today we can see fragments of the back face of the temple, remounted on a modern wall. A statue of the goddess Rome dressed as an Amazon or a Victory, from the first century AD, has been placed before it. The statue may have acted as an acroter.*

162 bottom *On the eastern side of the Forum square were the Forum Baths, the largest in the city. Built in 160 AD and restored in the 4th and 5th centuries, they have rich architecture with alternating curved and straight lines, according to the taste typical of the Antonine age, embellished with columns in cipollino, mosaics, and statues of Hygeia and Aesclepius.*

162-163 *In the center of the Piazzale delle Corporazioni are the remains of the stairway and high podium (in the photo) with two of the Corinthian columns from a Domitian-era temple, which may have been dedicated to the goddess Ceres.*

162 top *North of the Forum, we can still see the remains of the Capitolium, the main temple, built during the time of Hadrian on an earlier edifice and dedicated to the Capitoline triad, Jupiter, Juno and Minerva. The brick structures, originally covered with sheets of marble, still remain.*

house with its block of flats originally had four floors. The ground floor was used for shops, and the street level also included what was probably a caretaker's lodge and a public bathroom. Inside the square central courtyard was a cistern. On the left wall a clay tablet was found representing Diana the Hunter.

Continuing along the road, we come to the famous *Thermopolium* of Via di Diana, a sort of cafeteria that still has a marble-covered counter for pouring wine, shelves, a cooking stove, a large half-buried *dolium*, benches for patrons and a sign depicting the fruit and food that was served at the place.

At the end of the main road, at the intersection of the *Cardus Maximus*, an area was cleared for the Forum, the center of the city and the site of the most important political, economic, religious and commercial activities. The current arrangement, which dates to the Hadrianic era (2nd century AD), has a square flanked by porticos on the long

*163 top right  On the western side of the Decumanus Maximus is a beautiful marble "oil lamp" fountain with a cover supported by four small columns and a*

*transenna that protected the basin from the street side. The basin has a small pillar in the center, ending in a spout in the form of an oil lamp with seven burners.*

*163 bottom left  The House of Cupid and Psyche is a typical example of a patrician single-family dwelling from the 4th century AD. It has two floors and sumptuous interior decoration, with splendid floors in opus sextile (colored marble inlays).*

*163 bottom right The domus was built around a courtyard embellished with a large colonnaded nymphaeum, adorned with a beautiful group of marble statues depicting Cupid and Psyche embracing, now at the Ostia Museum.*

thermal baths in the city. They were built in 160 AD and restored in the 4th century, with a series of rooms expertly graduated in size to take best advantage of exposure to sunlight. The rooms face a large open-air gymnasium enclosed by porticoes.

Taking the *Via degli Horrea Hepagathiana*, we reach this large masonry storehouse with its beautiful gate and tympanum supported by engaged columns with a Corinthian capital, whose architraves still bear the names of the two owners, Hepagathius and Hepaphroditus. These storehouses also had a series of rooms on two levels, arranged around a central courtyard.

Turning right on the Via delle Foce,

sides. On a high podium on one of the ends is the Capitolium, a building dedicated to Jupiter, Juno and Minerva, like the more famous one in the capital. All that remains of it are the structures in opus latericium and the large niches on the sides. On the other end is the Temple of Rome and Augustus, with the statue of the goddess Rome dressed as an Amazon. Beyond the porticoes were very important public buildings, including the Curia, a square area that hosted assemblies of people's representatives, and the judicial Basilica, with a great colonnaded hall. In the center stands the circular sacellum of the Lares Augusti, the deities who protected the emperor.

Beyond the Via della Forica, which takes its name from a public bathroom, were the Forum Baths, the largest

behind a sacred area where some of the oldest edifices of the cult of Ostia are located, including the Temple of Hercules, is the *Domus of Cupid and Psyche*. This is a beautiful example of a luxury *domus*, perhaps a summer residence, from the late era (4th century AD), with rooms arranged around a sort of atrium. Among them, an inner garden included a colonnaded front and a *nymphaeum* in back, with five niches. The group of marble statues that gave the house its name was found here.

Continuing up the Via delle Foce and turning left, behind the *Insula of Serapis*, a

typical example of multilevel apartment houses of the 2nd century AD, with apartments facing a porticoed courtyard, we come to the Seven Wise Men Baths. These were thermal baths used by residents of the two nearby apartment houses. One of the rooms still contains figures of three of the seven wise men who gave the building its name: Solon of Athens, Thales of Miletus, and Chilon of Sparta.

Continuing south along the Via delle Volte Dipinte, we can visit the Garden Houses complex, which stood isolated and far from the noisy streets and shops. It was a residential building that probably belonged to people in the middle class. It had two parallel blocks of luxury apartments that shared a large private garden embellished with six fountains. The state rooms were located toward the outside, while the private rooms were within.

Going back to the *Decumanus Maximus*, we come to the Porta Marina, which opens into the Silla-era walls. Beyond it are the Marciana Baths, built in the 2nd century AD, of which only vestiges remain.

*164 top Little is now visible of the Marciana Baths, the complex built to the west in the 2nd century AD, along the Via della Foce.*

*164 bottom left Standing on the right side of Via di Diana is one of the best preserved rental dwellings*

*of the city. It is a domus from the 2nd century AD characterized by a large central courtyard that illuminates the rooms facing it, and a series of shops facing the street. The name comes from a shrine found here dedicated to the cult of the goddess.*

*164 bottom right These warehouses, the* Horrea Hepagathiana, *were some of the largest in the city. An*

*inscription on the monumental gate tells us that the two freedmen who owned them were Hepagathius and Hepaphroditus.*

*164-165 The House of Bacchus and Ariadne is at the northwest end of the Via della Foce. Multi-level rental apartment buildings*

*like this were rather common in Ostia. Unlike typical apartment houses, private homes were generally owned by more well-to-do families.*

*165 top left Shown is the* Caupona of Fortunatus. *The great popularity of bars and taverns, as we might translate the Latin term today, as*

*well as shops, inns, and thermal baths, was also due to the city's constant stream of people from different cultures and with different habits.*

165 bottom Another very interesting thermal complex is the so-called Seven Wise Men Baths. The laconinum (sauna), calidarium, frigidarium, remains of frescoes, heating system, as well as beautiful black and white floor mosaics, still survive. In one of the apodyteria, or dressing rooms, we can still admire part of a fresco depicting the Seven Wise Men giving counsel on intestinal functions.

165 top right At the intersection of Via della Fontana and the Decumanus Maximus is the tavern of Fortunatus, which had various entrances. The edifice is fairly well-preserved, with the marble-covered masonry bar still inside, where drinks were served. The characteristic element of this type of establishment is the vaulted basin that was found in the lower section. It was probably used to wash plates, as it was often directly connected to the aqueduct pipes.

165 center right The photograph shows a detail of a floor mosaic from the House of Bacchus and Ariadne. Many dwellings in Ostia take their name from mosaics rather than architectural details, statues or artifacts found in them.

# GLOSSARY

**ACROTER** Decorative element in the form of a vase, palmette or other shape, that crowned corners of the pediment or the top of the roof of temples or other buildings.

**AMPHITHEATER** Oval-shaped building used for shows, with steps supported by arches and an arena in the center.

**APODYTERIUM** A room for disrobing in an ancient bathhouse.

**APSE** A semicircular structure with a vaulted roof, placed at the end or on the sides of a room.

**ARA** Altar generally used for sacrificial offerings.

**ARCHITRAVE** Horizontal architectural element that connects columns or pillars. Its primary function was to relieve the weight of overlying structures.

**ARENA** An open, uncovered area in the center of stadiums, circuses and amphitheaters, where shows were held.

**ASHLAR** Architectural structure made of rows of blocks with rounded faces.

**ATRIUM** Room in a Roman domus (house), with an opening generally in the center of the ceiling, around which other rooms were arranged.

**ATTIC** Raised portion at the top of a building, above the cornice, which often acted as a simple ornamental crowning touch.

**BASILICA** Public edifice characterized by a large hall divided into aisles by a series of columns, used for meetings and tribunal sessions.

**BASOLO PAVING** Street paving that used basoli, large, irregularly shaped rocks with a smoothed surface.

**BRACKET** Architectural element jutting out from a wall, that supported structures such as beams and cornices.

**CAISSON** Decoration on vaults or ceilings, characterized by series of hollow, decorated compartments.

**CALIDARIUM** Heated room in Roman bathhouses, with swimming pools used for hot baths; it generally had a cupola roof.

**CARYATID** A statue, usually of a woman, that replaced columns or pillars in supporting the trabeation of an edifice.

**CAVEA** The steps of theaters, amphitheaters and stadiums.

**CLIVUS** An uphill urban street.

**CREPIDINE** Foundation or platform.

**CRYPTOPORTICUS** Underground portico illuminated by small openings.

**CUBICULUM** A room, generally a bedroom, in a Roman house.

**EXEDRA** Semicircular or rectangular room or portion of room.

**FACE** Outside surfaces of wall.

**FICTILE** Molded, baked clay object.

**FORNIX** Empty space in a door or arch between one pillar and another.

**FRIEZE** Horizontal element with elongated trabeation, decorated with triglyphs and metopes, either figurative or plain.

**FRIGIDARIUM** Room in Roman bathhouses used for cold baths.

**GRIFFIN** Fantastic creature with the body of a wild animal and the head of a bird of prey.

**GROTESQUE** Wall decoration with delicate plant motifs and figures.

**HEXASTYLE** Edifice characterized by six columns on the front.

**HORREUM** Edifice used to store goods, generally two stories high, with numerous rooms arranged around a large courtyard.

**HYPOCAUSTUM** Heating system characterized by the passage of warm air into an air space below the floor.

**HYPOGEUM** Underground room.

**LARARIUM** Small altar for the cult of the *Lari*.

**META** Small, often conical structure, located at the end of the *spina* of the circus.

**MITHRAEUM** Sanctuary dedicated to the cult of the god Mithras.

**NATATIUM** Room in bathhouse that contained a swimming pool.

**NAUMACHIA** Show featuring battles between ships, held in the amphitheater or a special building.

**NYMPHAEUM** Large, showy structure with apses, embellished with statues, niches and fountains.

**ODEON** Small roofed theater used for music and public readings.

**PEDIMENT** Terminal element of an edifice (but also of doors, niches and windows) with a triangular, double-pitched form.

**PELTA** Small, crescent-shaped Amazon shield. In the Roman world, it was used by gladiators.

**PERIPTERY** Edifice surrounded on all sides by a row of columns.

**PERISTYLE** Inner courtyard surrounded by a portico with columns.

**PRONAOS** Roofed area, generally porticoed, across from the temple's cella.

**PROPYLAEUM** Monumental entrance to an edifice.

**PROSTYLE** Edifice with columns on the front side.

**QUOIN** Block of square stone.

**ROSTRUM** Iron or bronze ram placed on the prow of ships, to be used in battle.

**SACELLUM** Small religious edifice.

**SUBSTRUCTURE** Masonry structure acting as a support.

**SUSPENSORS** Small brick pillars that supported the floor of a number of bathhouse rooms, creating an air space in which warm air circulated.

**TABLINUM** Main room of the house, on an axis with the entrance.

**TEPIDARIUM** A moderately heated room in a bathhouse.

**TETRASTYLE** Edifice with four columns at the front.

**TRABEATION** Group of architectural elements consisting of the architrave, the frieze and the cornice.

**TRICLINIUM** Banquet hall in Greek and Roman homes, with three beds for the guests, arranged in a horseshoe shape.

**USTRINUM** Fenced place used to cremate bodies.

**VELARIUM** Large tarpaulin drawn over the top of theaters and amphitheaters, used to protect spectators from the sun and rain.

# BIBLIOGRAPHY

Various Authors *Dizionario di mitologia*, Zanichelli, BO 1969

Various Authors *Roma*, in the "Dizionario dell'Arte Antica," pp. 784-996

Various Authors (edited by the National Research Center), *Archeologia Laziale*, XII, I, pp. 13-193, 1995

Abbondanza Letizia *La Valle del Colosseo*, edited by Soprintendenza Archeologica di Roma, Rome 1998

Balbi De Caro S., *La banca a Roma*, in "Vita e costumi dei Romani antichi," no. 8, Museo della Civiltà Romana, Rome, 1989

Bell, R.E. *Dictionary of Classical Mythology*, Oxford 1984

Benevolo L. and Scoppola F. *Roma. L'area archeologica centrale e la città moderna*, in Various Authors, "Lavori e Studi di Archeologia" (edited by the Soprintendenza Archeologica di Roma), no. 10, 1988.

Bianchi Bandinelli R., *Roma. L'arte romana al centro del potere*.

Bianchi Bandinelli R., Torelli M., *Etruria Roma*, UTET, Turin 1986.

Chini Paolo *La religione*, in "Vita e costumi dei Romani antichi" no. 9 Museo della Civiltà Romana, Rome, 1990.

Cinti D. *Dizionario Mitologico*, Sonzogno 1989

Claridge Amanda *Rome*, Oxford Archaeological Guides, Oxford University Press 1998.

Coarelli F. *Roma*, Guide Archeologiche Laterza, Laterza 1997

Coarelli F. *Guida archeologica di Roma*, Mondadori 1974

Coarelli F. *Il Foro romano. Il Periodo archaico. Il Periodo repubblicano e augustano*, Rome 1985

Coarelli F. *I santuari, il fiume, gli empori*, in Storia di Roma, Vol. II pp. 127-151

Grimal P. *Vita quotidiana nell'antica Roma*, San Casciano Val di Pesca (FI), 1998

Gross P. *L'organizzazione dello spazio pubblico e privato*, in Storia di Roma Vol. I

Gross, Torelli *Storia dell'Urbanistica. Il mondo romano*.

Guidobaldi Paola *Il Foro Romano*, edited by the Soprintendenza Archeologica di Roma, Rome 1998

Insolera I, *La città nella Storia d'Italia. Roma*. Laterza 1980

Lugli C. *Monumenti Antichi di Roma*, Bardi Ed., Rome 1938

Mancioli Danila *Giochi e Spettacoli*, edited by the Museo della Civiltà Romana, Rome 1987

Moreselli C and Tortorici E.

*Curia Forum Iultum – Forum Transitorium*,

In Various Authors, "Lavori e Studi di Archeologia" (edited by the Soprintendenza Archeologica di Roma), no. 14, 1989.

Pensabene P. *Il Tempio di Saturno*, in Various Authors, Lavori e Studi di Archeologia"

(edited by the Soprintendenza Archeologica di Roma), no. 5, 1994

Picozzi V. *La monetazione romana imperiale*, P&P Santamaria, Rome 1966

Quilici L. *Le strade. Viabilità tra Roma e Lazio*, in "Vita e costumi dei Romani antichi," no. 12, Museo della Civiltà Romana, Rome, 1990

Ribichini S. *Il Dio degli inizi*, in Archeo, Oct. 98, pp. 106-108

Rosati, F. P. *La moneta romana*, in Archeo, no. 42, 1988, p. 46

Rosati, F. P. *La moneta di Roma Repubblicana*, University Press, Bologna 1986

Sapelli Marina *Museo Nazionale Romano. Palazzo Massimo alle terme*, edited by the Soprintendenza Archeologica di Roma, Rome 1998

P. Scurati-Manzoni, *L'architettura romana dalle origini a Giustiniano*, MI 1991

Coarelli, *I dintorni di Roma*, (I need to find the exact reference)

Giuliani, *tecniche edilizie…*

Staccioli Romolo A. *Guida di Roma Antica*, BUR, III ed. 1996

Stambaugh John E. *The Ancient Roman City*, The Johns Hopkins University Press, III Ed. 1990

Tomei Maria Antonietta *Il Palatino*, edited by the Soprintendenza Archeologica di Roma, Rome 1998

Zaccaria Ruggiu *Spazio Privato e spazio pubblico nella città romana*, CEFR 210, Rome 1995.

# PHOTOGRAPHIC CREDITS

*Top*  The *Decumanus Maximus* ran in a straight line through the
entire city of Ostia, then turned toward *Porta Matina*.

*Bottom* photograph brings out the composite beauty of the mosaics
that embellished the offices on the *Piazzale delle Corporazioni in
Ostia Antica*.